*Creative
and
Mental
Growth*

FIFTH
EDITION

Viktor Lowenfeld
W. Lambert Brittain
Fifth Edition

The Macmillan Company
Collier-Macmillan Limited, London

Creative and Mental Growth

The Macmillan Company
866 Third Avenue, New York, New York 10022

Collier-Macmillan Canada, Ltd., Toronto, Ontario

Library of Congress catalog card number: 79–89928

PRINTING   8910   YEAR   456789

Preface

THIS BOOK IS designed for parents, teachers, and others who have an interest in children and in their art. This fifth edition incorporates many changes brought about because of recent research findings and the development of theory both in and outside the area of art education. This edition also continues the basic premises upon which the last four editions have been based: that the child is society's most precious good and that creative activities become meaningful only when the dynamic interdependence among growth, development, and creation is understood.

Viktor Lowenfeld had tremendous impact upon education, and to a great extent it is because of him that art education has become recognized as an important part of the curriculum in the public schools. This was not only because of his interest in and influence on art, which was considerable, but also because of his concern and involvement with children, their interests, their growth, and most of all, with themselves as children.

My colleagues are many and I owe each of them many thanks. To a great extent I looked upon pertinent experiments that have been done over the past years as having been done especially for me, so that the preparation of this edition could build upon these investigations. I have no doubt that the increased interest in children's art will continue to find support in psychological and educational research programs, not only in our colleges and universities but also within the school systems where new teaching methods and rearrangement of priorities can most easily be tested.

There are many who have helped in the preparation of this edition. It is my pleasure to acknowledge their contribution. These include my graduate students, past and present, who have constantly kept me on my toes, my undergraduate classes who have insisted upon the practical and relevant, and particularly the children who have been willing subjects and who have provided the drawings and illustrations for this volume. It is the children who have been the true test of the theories upon which this book is based.

I also wish gratefully to acknowledge the following for their help in securing the illustrations for this volume: Albright-Knox Art Gallery, Buffalo, New York, Gift of Seymour H. Knox, Plate 16; Andrew Dickson White Museum of Art, Cornell University, Figures 153, 155, 159, and 161; Barrett Gallagher, photographer, Figures 2, 37, 47, 50, 51, 146, 150, and 156; Marlene Ginsburg, art teacher, Figure 32; Cornell Research Program in Early Childhood Education, Figure 3; Jack Grant, photographer, Figures 34, 110, 123, 144, and 145; Jean Holland, Duke of York School, Plates 4 and 10; Lynn Haussler, photographer, Figures 41, 42, and 43; Indiana University of Pennsylvania, Plate 5; Herman Miller, Inc., Figure 162; Museum of Modern Art, New York, Figures 154 and 160; Gordon Myer, Art Department, Ithaca High School, Ithaca, New York, Figures 144 and 145; New York State College of Agriculture, Cornell University, Figures 6, 100, 101 and 157; New York State College of Human Ecology, Cornell University, Figures 3, 52, and 158; Photo Science Studios, Cornell University, Figures 25, 29, 69, and 105; Irene Russell, *Research Bulletin*, The Eastern Arts Association, Vol. 3, No. 1, 1952, Figure 22; and Jean Warren, photographer, Figure 72, and for her valuable technical assistance.

I wish to express my particular appreciation to Professor Herbert

Ginsburg of Cornell University for his careful and critical reading of the manuscript and to the loyal staff at Cornell for their time and concern. A special note of appreciation goes to Mrs. Viktor Lowenfeld and to Dr. John Lowenfeld for their continued interest and support.

W. L. B.
Department of Human Development and Family Studies
Cornell University, Ithaca, New York

Contents

3

Art in the Elementary Classroom 53

4

The Beginnings of Self-expression: The Scribbling Stage, 2–4 Years 89

5

**First Repre-
sentational
Attempts: The
Preschematic
Stage, 4–7 Years
117**

6

**The Achieve-
ment of a Form
Concept: The
Schematic
Stage, 7–9
Years
145**

7

The Dawning Realism: The Gang Age, 9–12 Years 189

8

The Importance of Art in the Secondary School 223

9

The Age of Reasoning: The Pseudo-Naturalistic Stage, 12–14 Years
255

10

The Period of Decision: Adolescent Art in the High School, 14–17 Years
287

11

The Development of Aesthetic Awareness 315

12

Summary 343

Bibliography 347

Index 361

Color Plates

The Meaning of Art
for Education

1

ART HAS a potentially vital role in the education of our children. The process of drawing, painting, or constructing is a complex one in which the child brings together diverse elements of his experience to make a new and meaningful whole. In the process of selecting, interpreting, and reforming these elements, he has given us more than a picture or a sculpture; he has given us a part of himself: how he thinks, how he feels, and how he sees. For the child, art is a dynamic and unifying activity.

Formal education takes on a tremendously important role when we realize that our children—from the age of five or six to sixteen, eighteen, or beyond—are forced by law and job requirements to spend ten, twelve, sixteen, or even twenty years behind school doors. That is a stiff sentence just for being born a child. Yet the serving of this sentence is supposed to

1

Figure 1. *For the child, art is an engrossing activity, which brings together into a new form the youngster's thinking, feeling, and perceiving.*

qualify a youngster to take his place as a contributing and well-adjusted member of society. From some points of view education has done its task; looking around us today, we can see great material gains. But serious questions can be raised about how much we have been able to educate beyond the making and consuming of objects. Have we in our educational system really put emphasis upon human values? Or have we been so blinded by the material rewards that we have failed to recognize that the real values of a democracy lie in its most precious good, the individual?

In our present educational system most emphasis has been put upon the learning of factual information. To a great extent the passing or failing of an examination or of a course, or the passing on to the next grade, or even the remaining in school depends upon the mastery or memorization of certain bits of information that are already known to the instructor. The function of the school system, then, would seem to be that of producing people who can file away bits of information and can then repeat these at a given signal. Once the student has achieved a certain competency at producing the proper bits of information at the correct time, he is considered ripe for graduating from school. What is most disturbing is that the skill in repeating bits of information may have very little relationship to the "contributing, well-adjusted member of society" we thought we were producing.

We do not want to give the impression that mankind is saved by merely developing a good creative art program in the public schools; but the values that are meaningful in an art program are those which may be basic to the development of a new image, a new philosophy, even a totally new structure for our educational system. More and more people are recognizing that the ability to learn differs from age to age and from individual to individual and that this ability to learn involves not only intellectual capacity but also social, emotional, perceptual, physical, and psychological factors. The process of learning is very complex and there may, therefore, be no single best teaching method. Our tendency to concentrate on developing the capacity to regurgitate bits of information may be putting undue emphasis on only one factor in human development, the one that is measured by intelligence tests. Intelligence as we now test it does not encompass the wide range of thinking abilities that are necessary for the survival of mankind. The abilities to question, to seek answers, to find form and order, to rethink and restructure and find new relationships, are qualities that are not generally taught; in fact, they seem to be frowned upon in our present educational system.

It may be that one of the basic abilities that should be taught in our public schools is the ability to discover and to search for answers, instead of passively waiting for answers and directions from the teacher. The experiences central to an art activity embody this very factor. This is equally true of a nursery-school child putting together a construction called "Spring" from straws, colored paper, and bottle caps, or of a college student painting a picture that necessitates the mixing of colors and the invention of new forms.

Very young children have a freedom to act without regard for the amount of knowledge mankind has already amassed about such an action. Children learn to walk without an intellectual understanding of the motor control involved. What a person knows or does not know may bear no relationship to creative action. One sometimes hears that there are definite steps to the creative process and that preparation is a first and most important step. However, it can be seen that children create with the aid of whatever knowledge they happen to have at the time. The very act of creating can provide new insights and new knowledge for further action. Probably the best preparation for creating is the act of creation itself. Waiting to act until a good factual preparation can be obtained, or stopping children from creating until they know enough about the subject to act intelligently, may inhibit action rather than promote it. Giving the child opportunities to create constantly with the knowledge he currently has is the best preparation for future creative action.

One of the basic ingredients of a creative art experience is the relationship between the artist and his environment. Painting, drawing, or constructing is a constant process of assimilation and projection: taking in through the senses a vast amount of information, mixing it up with the psychological self, and putting into a new form the elements that seem to suit the aesthetic needs of the artist at the time. If we look at formal education, we realize that the basis for the development of learning rests upon 26 letters and 10 numerals. These 36 abstract figures are manipulated and reshuffled from kindergarten through college. The development of mental growth, then, tends to become an abstract function as these figures take on different and more complicated meanings. However, it is not the knowledge of these figures or the ability to rearrange them that make for mental growth, but rather understanding what these figures mean. Being able to assemble letters in proper sequence to spell *rabbit* does not constitute an understanding of a rabbit. To really know a rabbit a child must actually touch him, feel his fur, watch his nose twitch, feed him, and learn his habits (see Figure 2). It is the interaction between the symbols, the self, and the environment that provides the material for abstract intellectual processes. Therefore, mental growth depends upon a rich and varied relationship between a child and his environment; such a relationship is a basic ingredient of a creative art experience.

Man learns through his senses. The ability to see, feel, hear, smell, and taste provides the means by which an interaction between man and his environment takes place. But the process of educating children can some-

times be confused with developing certain limited predetermined responses, and the curriculum in public schools tends to be little concerned with the simple fact that man, and the child too, learns through these five senses. The development of perceptual sensitivity, then, should become a most important part of the educative process. Yet in most areas other than the arts the senses are apt to be ignored. The greater the opportunity to develop an increased sensitivity and the greater the awareness of all the senses, the greater will be the opportunity for learning.

We know too well that factual learning and retention, unless exercised by a free and flexible mind, will benefit neither the individual nor society. Education has often neglected those attributes of growth that are responsible for the development of the individual's sensibilities, for his spiritual well-being, as well as for his ability to live cooperatively in a society. The growing number of emotional and mental illnesses in this nation, coupled with our frightening inability to accept human beings as human beings regardless of nationality, religion, race, creed, or color, are vivid reminders that education so far has failed in one of its most significant aims. While our high achievements in specialized fields, particularly in the sciences, have improved our material standards of living, they have diverted us from those values that are responsible for our emotional and spiritual needs. They have introduced a false set of values, which neglect the innermost needs of an individual. Art education, as an essential part of the educative process, may well mean the difference between a flexible, creative human being and one who will not be able to apply his learning, who will lack inner resources, and who will have difficulty relating to his environment. In a well-balanced educational system, in which the development of the total being is stressed, each individual's thinking, feeling, and perceiving must be equally developed in order that his potential creative abilities can unfold.

The Meaning of Art for Children

Art is not the same for a child as it is for an adult. Although it may be difficult to say just what art means for any particular adult, usually the term "art" has very definite connotations. Among them are museums, pictures hanging on walls, painters with beards, full color reproductions, attics with northern exposure, models posing in the nude, a cultural elite, and generally a feeling of an activity that is a little removed from the real world of making a living and bringing up a family. Somehow art is supposed to be "a good thing," and books on art or "good" pictures for the walls of one's home ought to bring some kind of elevating spirit into life. But for the common man art may be like taking a dose of medicine. Art for the adult, at any rate, is usually concerned with the area of aesthetics or external beauty.

Art for the child is something quite different. For a child art is primarily a means of expression. No two children are alike, and, in fact, each child differs even from his earlier self as he constantly grows, perceives, understands, and interprets his environment. A child is a dynamic being; art becomes for him a language of thought. A child sees the world differently from the way he represents it, and as he grows his expression changes.

Sometimes teachers, intrigued by the beauty of children's drawings and paintings, will save these paintings and admire them as examples of true spontaneous art. Occasionally they go a step further and suggest the proper colors or correct forms. The enthusiasm of some teachers for the intuitive manner in which children paint leads them to impose their own color schemes, proportions, and manner of painting upon children. From this discrepancy between the adult taste and the way in which a child expresses himself arise most of the difficulties that prevent children from using art as a true means of self-expression.

Figure 3. *These are four drawings of a man done by Rachel, a kindergarten child, over a short period of time. Part **a** shows a five year old's concept of a man. Note the lack of arms; but Rachel does include a head, body, and legs with toes. In **b** Rachel has drawn much more, and her concept of a man now includes arms with hands and fingers. The toes are now attached to a foot and buttons have appeared. In **c** the single line used for legs and arms is now double, as if the arms had volume. Note the hat that does not rest on the head but floats above it. The final drawing **d** shows a rather complex and complete drawing, much more typical of a six year old.*

7

If it were possible for children to develop without any interference from the outside world, no special stimulation for their creative work would be necessary. Every child would use his deeply rooted creative impulses without inhibition, confident in his own means of expression. Whenever we hear children say, "I can't draw," we can be sure that some kind of interference has occurred in their lives. This loss of self-confidence in one's own means of expression may be an indication of a withdrawal into one's self. Often the mistake is made of evaluating children's creative work by how the product looks, its colors and shapes, its design qualities, and so forth. This is unjust not only to the product itself but even more to the child. Growth cannot be measured by the tastes or standards of beauty that may be important to an adult. However, art has been traditionally interpreted as relating mainly to aesthetics, and this concept has in some cases limited the opportunity for art to be used in its fullest sense. In art education the final product is subordinated to the creative process. It is the child's process—his thinking, his feelings, his perceiving, in fact, his reactions to his environment—that is important.

Occasionally we hear of a child who is outstanding in art. This may often be a girl who performs in ways that are neat and proper, who satisfies the artistic likes of her teacher. Sometimes a child who is frustrated in school subjects such as reading, writing, or arithmetic may turn to art for a release from his frustrations, because in art there is no right or wrong answer. Both of these children may get a great deal of satisfaction from drawing, and if they are rewarded for their efforts, they will certainly continue to try to gain recognition. However, it may be the youngster who is silent and withdrawn who most needs the opportunity for art expression. It may be a difficult thing for a teacher who has certain tastes and artistic standards of his own to understand that his standards are irrelevant for the self-expression of youngsters.

Every child, regardless of where he stands in his development, should first of all be considered as an individual. Expression grows out of, and is a reflection of, the total child. A child expresses his thoughts, feelings, and interests in his drawings and paintings and shows his knowledge of his environment in his creative expressions. A ten year old who is concerned with the mechanical operation of parts, gears, levers, and pulleys will work through these relationships in his drawings. Note the intense concentration shown in Figure 4. Much thought and planning have gone into the details of the operation of the airplane that the boy is drawing. In Figure 5 the wings and the joining of the various struts have been thought through in detail. Notice the lever for adjusting the rudder. That this looks little like an adult concept of a plane has little relevance here. Each child reveals his interests, capabilities, and involvement in art, although these may in some cases bear little relationship to "beauty."

Figure 4. *The concentration of this ten year old boy is typical of a child who is confident of his own creative ability.*

Usually when we think of children gifted in art, we mean children who show some ability to draw and paint. In the professional world of art, however, we find very few adult artists who actually make a living by drawing and painting. A much larger number become architects, textile designers, art historians, ceramists, teachers, interior designers, sculptors, advertising designers, and so forth. There are certainly large differences in these fields, and a child who enjoys working with objects or working out mechanical details, as in the illustration above, may be just as gifted as the child who is able to draw well. In fact, it might be well to consider every child as being potentially talented in art.

Figure 5. *This plan for a working model of an airplane, drawn by a ten year old boy, may not be aesthetically pleasing to an adult, but the boy's thinking-through of the functions of the various parts shows an inventive awareness of mechanical details.*

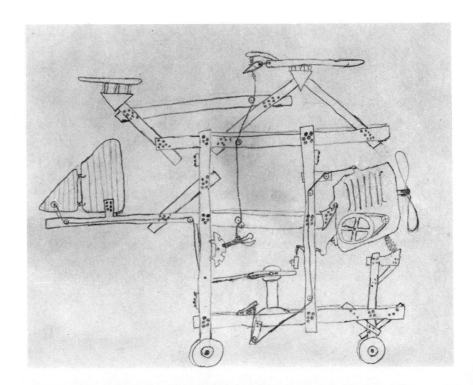

Although the artistic standards of the teacher must be subordinated to the needs of children in art education, this does not mean that the paintings or drawings of children cannot have great beauty in themselves. Rather, it is through the process of art that art itself unfolds. If we were to focus on the art product, we would be concerned primarily with the making of beautiful objects rather than with the effects that making has upon children. Art education, therefore, is primarily concerned with the effect that the process has on the individual, whereas the so-called fine arts are more concerned with the resulting products.

Every school, not only in the kindergarten and elementary classrooms but also in the secondary school, should try to encourage each youngster to identify with his own experiences and help him to go as far as he can in developing concepts that express his feelings and emotions, and his own aesthetic sensitivities. We should never be satisfied with the stereotyped response, the unfeeling or automatic drawing. The child may be insensitive to his own feelings, and it is more important that a relationship between the youngster and his own environment be stimulated and made meaningful than that an adult concept of what is important or beautiful be imposed upon him.

The essential ingredient is the child, a child who has feelings, emotions, love, and hate, and who has no need for the stick figure that may be taught in first grade, or the abstract design that is taught in the junior high school. His individual expression is just as important to him as the artist's creation is to the adult. The teacher should recognize that his own learning experiences will avail children nothing, for it is the children's learning that becomes important in the educational process. It is not the adult's answer but the child's striving toward his own answer that is crucial.

The Senses As Basic to Learning

It is only through the senses that learning can take place. This may sound like an obvious statement; however, its implications seem to be lost in our educational system. It may be that education merely reflects the changes in our society, for man seems to be relying less and less on actual sensory contact with his environment. He is becoming a passive viewer of his culture rather than an active maker of it. Football games are to be watched, not played. Music has become a soothing background syrup in the shopping center rather than a means of actual involvement. The television has become a mass means of distraction in which the viewer's only involvement is that of turning the *on* or *off* switch. Even groceries come packed in their own sterile plastic containers, removed not only from touch but also from smell.

Schools have done little to educate these senses that are our only avenue to learning. Although a number of activities are included at the nursery-school level that involve manipulation and movement, most of these activities are taught as ends in themselves. The purpose seems to be to develop particular skills so that these can be checked off as having been taught, rather than utilizing them as a means to expression. The first-grade teacher is satisfied when children learn how to manipulate scissors, but the possibilities of using scissors creatively are limited. The farther up the educational ladder we go, the farther removed children become from relying on their own senses, until a good deal of learning becomes not only vicarious, but also abstract in nature.

Our forefathers were in daily contact with their environment. Not only did they build their own homes and grow their own food, but they also made their own music and art. Even in the last fifty years there have been dramatic changes. The local hardware store has lost its bin of nails, sacks of grain and seed are no longer available to run one's fingers through, the grocery store no longer smells of freshly ground coffee or oranges that have gotten a little too old. The smell of freshly baked bread or the taste of one's own homemade rootbeer are sensory experiences that have almost disappeared. Possibly today's increased interest in camping is a reflection of the urge to experience the senses more fully.

There is little opportunity today for youngsters to dam up a stream, dig a tunnel to China, or build a tree house. The complete involvement of oneself in a project of a purely physical, sensory nature is rapidly disappearing. Paint-by-the-number kits and preplanned, precut projects for the homemaker have made art sterile. A woman is now more concerned about selecting the proper decorator for her living room than with the expression of her own likes and dislikes, or with seeing her home as a reflection of her own family's interests.

Touching, seeing, hearing, smelling, and tasting involve the active participation of the individual. There is evidence that even the young child needs to be truly involved in these experiences. The disadvantaged child may never have been encouraged to see, touch, or become involved in his environment. The deprived youngster may be isolated from any external stimulation. It is not just a question of the presence of sounds, or of having things available to touch and see; it is the stimulation of the interaction between the youngster and his environment through the senses that makes the difference between the child who is eager to explore and investigate his environment and the one who retreats from it. Obviously, deprived youngsters can come from what might be called

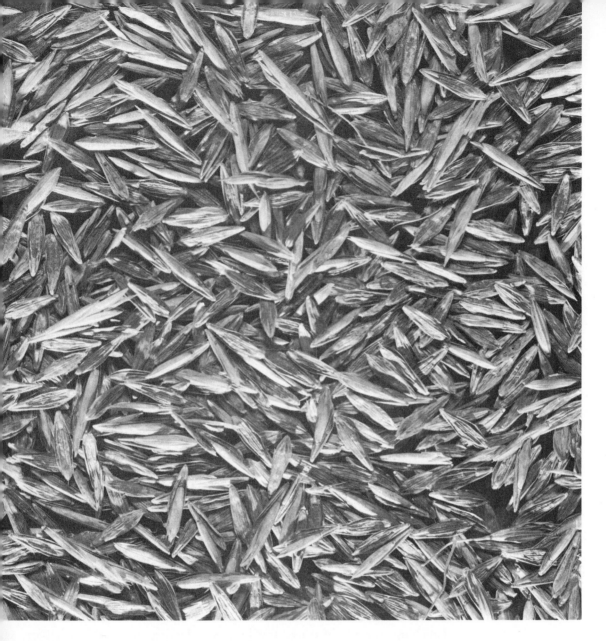

Figure 6. *Prepackaged merchandise, each item in its own sterile plastic pack, has removed the senses of touch and smell from many of the goods we buy. Here, grass seed in an open bin makes an interesting visual pattern.*

affluent surroundings. Even if a child's basic physical needs are met he may nevertheless be seriously deprived in other areas of development. One observational study of young deprived children reported that these youngsters were not alert to, or even responsive to, the teacher's spoken directions, or to a display of colored paper, scissors, and paste set out for them. Although the children were constantly scanning the environment these objects failed to attract their attention, because their vision was used primarily to protect themselves (Malone, 1967).* It is obvious that for young children the senses are extremely important, but in later years too the development of refined sensory experiences should be a continuing process, with education playing a major role in this development. Art education is the only subject-matter area that truly concentrates on developing the sensory experiences. Art is filled with the riches of textures, the excitement of shapes and forms, the wealth of color, and youngster and adult alike should be able to receive pleasure and joy from these experiences.

Auditory sensitivity means detailed listening, not just hearing; visual sensitivity means an awareness of differences and details, not just recognition; the same is true for touching, and for all sensory experiences. We are living in a time in which mass production, mass education, and mass seeing and experiencing have suppressed the sensitive relationships of the individual. Art education has the special mission of developing within the individual those creative sensitivities that make life satisfying and meaningful.

The Importance of Self-identification and Self-expression

People today have to a great extent lost their ability to identify with what they do. Few of us can point to our own contribution to society. The assembly line has made man a machine. He is not a part of the planning or design of the product but performs a function that requires no special skill. In some cases the man on the production line may not even realize what he is making. The questions "Who am I? Where am I going? What do I stand for?" become a serious dilemma. It is not only youth who are searching for identity. Although no one is happy to become a number, we are all rapidly becoming merely a series of numbers for the purposes of tax deductions, bank collections, vehicle identifications, insurance payments, licensing skills, and even hospitalization. In a democratic society it is essential that the individual be able to know what he thinks, say what he feels, and help remake the world around

* References in parentheses refer the reader to the Bibliography at the end of the book.

him. The need for self-identification should be a vital concern of our educational system.

When a job becomes nothing more than a means of making money, it is very difficult to identify with one's work. It is rare today to find someone who enjoys a job for itself. Work becomes merely a means of making money to survive, and the rewards and satisfactions of life are sought in entertainment or diversions.

Our educational system has done little to change the increasing loss of identity with oneself. Rewards are given for neat papers, for correct answers, for recalling the proper information at the right time. Little is done to stimulate the child to find the rewards from within the learning process: to find satisfaction in solving his own problems, to take pleasure in developing greater knowledge and understanding for its own sake, or to measure success or failure in areas of importance to the self.

To a great extent our educational system is geared toward one phase of growth: intellectual growth. Here learning can be measured easily, but this is defining learning in a very narrow sense. Learning does not merely mean the accumulation of knowledge; it also implies an understanding of how this knowledge can be utilized. We must be able to use our senses freely and creatively and develop positive attitudes toward ourselves and our neighbors for this learning to become effective. Children rarely have the opportunity to share ideas and develop attitudes about themselves and others. Although from the outside the school may look like a center of learning, this learning takes place in isolated cells, with fifth graders rarely seeing a kindergarten child except when passing in the halls. Adults are excluded, and except for the teachers many children see no adults for hours at a time. For a fifth grader, the world is largely made up of other fifth graders.

No art expression is possible without self-identification with the experience expressed as well as with the art material by which it is expressed. This is one of the basic factors of any creative expression: it is the true expression of the self. The art materials are controlled and manipulated by one individual, and the completed project is his. This is as true at a very young age as it is for the adult artist. It is the individual who uses his art materials and his form of expression according to his own personal experiences. Because these experiences change with growth, self-identification embraces the social, intellectual, emotional, and psychological changes within the child.

There is also the need for the ability to identify with others. To be able to identify with those we fear, those we do not understand, or those who appear strange to us, is essential for a peaceful society that combines humans of different creeds, colors, and heritages. Scientifically we have made great gains, but socially we no longer know our immediate neigh-

Figure 7. *An artist of any age manipulates and changes his art material to make a product that is his own expression.*

bors, and are unable to communicate with them peacefully. It is only through self-identification that we can begin to identify with others. As a child identifies himself with his own work, as he learns to appreciate and understand his environment by becoming involved in it, he develops the spirit that helps him understand the needs of his neighbor. The process of creation involves incorporating the self into the activity; the very act of creation provides understanding of the process that others go through in facing their own experiences. To live cooperatively as well-adjusted human beings and to contribute creatively to such a society become most important objectives for education.

The term "self-expression" has often been misunderstood. Self-expression is giving vent in constructive forms to the feelings, emotions, and thoughts of an individual at his own level of development. What matters is the mode of expression, not the content. It is important to mention this, because one of the greatest mistakes that can be made in the use of the term "self-expression" is to think of it in terms of an unstructured or uncontrolled emotion, or, on the other hand, to consider it as mere imitation.

The very young child expresses himself freely through babbling or crying. This may be a truer means of self-expression than a higher form of art, if that work of art is dependent on others or upon imitations of a scene or content that is not relevant to the person producing it. Technical perfection bears little relationship to self-expression, and the production of technically excellent art products may be far removed from the real expressive needs of the producer.

There is great satisfaction in expressing one's own feelings and emotions in art. Even the very young child who knows nothing about the technical difficulties in pencil rendering, or the various gradations of graphite hardness, can get great satisfaction from making a scribble with a soft pencil. He is expressing his own importance through his own means, and the satisfaction he derives from his achievement is self-evident. The self-confidence that can develop from this type of expression provides the basis for more advanced levels of art.

The child who expresses himself according to his own level becomes encouraged in his own independent thinking and expresses his own thoughts and ideas by his own means. The child who imitates can become dependent in his thinking and rely for his thoughts and expression upon others. Because the imitative child cannot give expression to his own thoughts, his dependency upon others can lead to frustration. The inhibited and restricted child, accustomed to imitation rather than self-expression, leans on parents, teachers, or peers for direction. Art through self-expression can develop the self as the important ingredient in experience. Since nearly every emotional or mental disturbance is connected with a lack of self-confidence, it is easy to see how the proper stimulation of the child's creative abilities can provide a safeguard against such disturbances. Autistic children have no capacity for self-identification, and in some cases seem unwilling to admit even their own existence. One method of therapy for them builds up self-respect, supports confidence, and gives a feeling of worth in their own actions (Bettelheim, 1950).

This area of discussion is closely related to the development of self-concept. The individual's own expression is of prime importance, and art probably contributes as much to this area of development as to any other. It has been recognized that young children need to see themselves as being worthy to deal with the complex environment in which they find themselves. This is also true of older children, although the self-concept of ability and attitudes toward achievement are much harder to change as the child grows older. One study that attempted to change the self-concept of ninth grade youngsters discovered that this change was accompanied by a corresponding change in academic performance (Brookover, 1967). Art may have a role in the development of the self, particularly with young children, that is so important as to demand its inclusion in the curriculum, if for no other reason.

Figure 8. *The opportunity for young children to draw or paint something that comes from within helps in providing the basis for developing a self-concept. Here it seems that using more than one brush is important in the painting process.*

Art As an Important Element in Society

Art is often considered the highest form of human expression. It is certainly true that art is something that is cherished, sometimes valuable for the collector, and can even be stolen for ransom. Art is also a reflection of the society that creates it. The art of ancient Greece, or Egypt, tells us a great deal about the society in which it was produced. It is a little difficult to evaluate the present forms of art within our own society; although art critics enjoy tackling this task, the artists themselves seem to be less interested in the meaning of the art they produce.

For some people the field of contemporary art is a mystery. Apparently it has broken away from past traditions, and to some extent it seems more closely related to smashed automobiles or the stacked soup cans on the grocer's shelf. Sometimes it may resemble some of the bad dreams one does not speak about, or the nonsensical play of lights and forms. For some people today's art is distant from their interests and far removed from the refined cultural taste supposedly associated with "art." It may even seem unrelated to the scientific world in which we live.

C. P. Snow (1961) has written about these two extremes within our society: the artistic literary pull on one side as against the scientific on the other. However, it is interesting to note that art and science have somehow managed to keep forms that parallel the advanced state of knowledge in each area (Cassidy, 1962). The dissolving of space in science has been matched by the dissolving of space in paintings. Einstein's theory of relativity and the nonobjective movement in art developed about the same time. Although few people today claim to be scientific experts, many believe in the value of advanced scientific experimentation. At the same time, most people claim to know what they like in art and doubt the value of new experimental art forms. It seems strange to realize that one segment of our society is given approval but another segment condemned for their investigations. The physical scientist has gained control over parts of his environment through experimentation and manipulation of symbols. The artist also must come to grips with mass, energy, and motion, but in his field attitudes and values also play a part. Both scientist and artist continually try to fathom the unknown in their search for truth.

Art can have meanings within our society other than as the highest form of expression. It can be used in the most crassly commercial fashion to advertise, promote and sell a variety of products, candidates, and ventures. Many would object to calling this area art, but its use of color and form and concern about audience impact makes it a very evident part of our culture. It may be that this type of art is more truly representative of our culture than the art that is being produced for the connoisseur. It would be interesting to look at our society from the point of view of an archaeologist a few thousand years from now and guess at the kind of society he might piece together from the variety of art forms found in the drugstore, automobile showroom, or airport novelty shop.

Somebody has to worry about the future of our country. With poorly designed "builder" houses, glaring neon signs, big billboards proclaiming the virtues of particular kinds of beer, and local streams being used as garbage dumps, the prospects for the future beauty of America look very dim. Apart from the efforts of the art teacher and a few other truly concerned individuals, most schools do nothing about the problem of deciding what the world that we and our children are going to live in will look like.

Art has sometimes been looked upon as something one is born with, something that comes intuitively from a sensitive individual. There has been serious questioning whether art can really be taught. But there are also people who feel that art is so vital to our society that we must begin early in our educational system to teach good taste and to develop habits of care in selecting objects from the environment. Both these views seem too extreme. On the one hand is the opinion that nothing can be done to encourage or stimulate youngsters in their art experiences; it is almost as if a magic spark from heaven somehow alights on the chosen few. The other extreme tries desperately hard to develop a curriculum that, through proper rewards and appropriate disciplinary action, makes youngsters conform to the standards of the teacher. Somehow excluded from both views is the individual who should be free to reject or accept, to formulate his own opinions and to evolve new directions, but who should *not* be free to be a passive bystander in our society.

Art can play a meaningful role in the development of children. The focus of teaching is the developing, changing, dynamic child who becomes increasingly aware of himself and his environment. Art education can provide the opportunity for increasing the capacity for action, experience, redefinition, and stability that is needed in a society filled with changes, tensions, and uncertainties.

The Importance of   2
Creative Activity in
Education

Art As a Means of Understanding Growth

The picture that a youngster draws or paints is much more than markings on paper. It is an expression of the total child at the time he was painting. Sometimes children can become very engrossed in art and the product may have a real depth of feeling and completeness; at other times the drawing may be merely an exploration of a new material, but even in this case the picture shows the youngster's eagerness or hesitation in attempting a new task. Although it is stating the obvious to say

Figure 9. *A child draws from his knowledge, his observation, and his experience. This boy has often climbed trees and picked apples, as demonstrated in his drawing of a tree.*

that no two children are alike, it is also true that of thousands of drawings by children no two are ever alike. Each drawing reflects the feelings, the intellectual capacities, the physical development, the perceptual awareness, the creative involvement, the aesthetic tastes, and even the social development of the individual child. Not only is each of these areas reflected in the drawing that a youngster does, the changes as the child grows and develops are also clearly seen in his drawings. In order to better understand and evaluate the importance of these changes, an analysis of the significance of the different components of growth follows.

EMOTIONAL GROWTH

A drawing can provide the opportunity for emotional growth, and the extent to which this is accomplished is in direct relation to the intensity with which the creator identifies with his work. Although this is not easily measured, the stages of self-identification range from a low level of involvement with stereotyped repetitions to a high level where the creator is truly involved in portraying things that are meaningful and important to him and where, particularly in young children, he appears in the picture himself. It is here that there is the best opportunity for emotional release.

Frequent stereotyped repetitions are usually seen only in the drawings of children who have developed rigid patterns in their thinking. Every adjustment to a new situation implies flexibility, flexibility in thinking, flexibility in imagination, and flexibility in action. In severe cases of emotional maladjustments there may be real difficulty in adjustment to new situations. For one girl, the slightest change in situation called for a serious adjustment. For example, when she was unexpectedly asked to get a glass of water she withdrew into a cramped position, unable to respond to the request. For her, getting a glass of water meant changing her position, getting up, stretching, going, finding the way, locating the sink, finding the faucet, turning on the water, and many more changes from her present position. Unable to face these changes and to adjust to them, she withdrew into a stereotyped, cramped position. In her drawings, too (see Figure 10), she felt most secure by repeating the same meaningless, stereotyped patterns of the same schema of a figure. This expressed an escape into a world in which she felt secure. Only when her drawings became meaningful to her did her inflexibility gradually disappear; only when she was able to adjust to a new situation did her drawings show more flexibility. Emotionally maladjusted children frequently escape into such a patternlike representation.

Such stereotyped rigid repetition expresses the lowest type of emotional involvement. It is sad that adults often encourage this type of expression by asking youngsters to copy or trace meaningless forms, or, even as a teacher of arithmetic might do, ask a youngster to copy a symbol for a kite ten times. Most children are able to survive such imposition; however, a child accustomed to depending on such patterns and doing this type of copying well, and who also receives the praise of the teacher for his neat work, may lose confidence in his own means of expression and resort to stereotyped repetition as an escape mechanism. Such unthinking mechanical activity has no place in either art or arithmetic.

At certain stages of development the youngster may spontaneously repeat forms to insure his mastery over these forms. A stereotyped

Figure 10. *The schema for a man is drawn here again and again without variation. Meaningless repetition of a stereotype is symptomatic, in this case, of an evasion of reality.*

repetition does not show any changes, whereas a flexible use of a symbol can be readily seen by changes and modifications. A youngster drawing a flower garden will include flowers in a variety of positions, some tall, some short, some bent over, and maybe one that has been broken or stepped on. However, the stereotyped repetition of a flower will be repeated in a meaningless way without any involvement or experience shown on the part of the youngster. This may be an escape from facing a world of experiences and may in fact be satisfying to the individual who made it. Emotionally maladjusted children often feel disturbed when something interferes with their escape mechanisms.

Parents sometimes say, "But my child loves to draw from coloring books." An escape into a pattern is a protection from exposure to the world of experiences. Continued overprotection conditions children to rely upon others and to hide behind the overprotection. This deprives a child not only of his freedom but also of his ability to adjust to new situations. An overprotected child sent to camp may sit in a corner and cry for his protection, unable to use and enjoy the freedom that is available to him. A child who loves to trace or do copy work may gain individual satisfaction from such an occupation, but such satisfaction is based upon the feeling of security and the fear of being exposed to new experiences. The child escapes into a passive state of mind which is undesirable.

An emotionally unresponsive child may express his detached feelings by not including anything personal in his creative work. He will be satisfied by a mere objective representation. "There is a tree, there is a house." Nothing is included that will indicate his relationship to these objects. He is merely passively representing objects. This detached art expression can be seen at all ages. In the beginning stages of art such objective reports show neither action nor variety, but rather indicate only enough to signify an object. Figures usually are not included but if they are they show no action. The experienced artist may also show this lack of involvement in repeating a technically proficient piece of art or a certain mannerism without any changes or involvement of the self. He too is caught in the stereotyped repetition of his own techniques.

With the direct inclusion of the self, the child actually participates in his drawing; he may appear directly in his creative work or he may represent someone with whom he identifies. The tree he draws is a particular tree, the house is no longer any house but has certain characteristics that were important to him in the act of drawing. A child who is emotionally free and uninhibited in creative expression feels secure and confident in attacking any problem that derives from his experiences. He closely identifies with his drawings and is free to explore and experiment with a variety of materials. His art is in a constant state of change and he is neither afraid of making mistakes nor worrying about the grade he might receive on this particular project. For him the art experience is truly his and the intensity of his involvement provides for real emotional growth.

INTELLECTUAL GROWTH

Intellectual growth is usually seen in the child's growing awareness of himself and his environment. The knowledge that is actively at the child's disposal when he draws indicates his intellectual level. Drawings are sometimes used as an indication of the mental ability of children, particularly when verbal means of communication are not adequate. Such differences can be readily seen and measured (Harris, 1963). A child of five years who draws a man with only head and legs (Figure 11) is intellectually not as developed as a child who also includes the body and other features (Figure 12). The lack of details in a drawing does not necessarily indicate a child of low mental ability. There may be many reasons why the youngster does not include much in his drawing: emotional restrictions may block the child's expression, or he may lack involvement in a particular drawing. Usually, however, a drawing full of subject-matter details comes from a child with high intellectual ability. This may not

Figures 11–12. *There is a wide range of differences in active knowledge, as indicated in these drawings of a man by two five year old children.*

necessarily be a beautiful drawing, but apparently the development of artistic ability closely parallels a child's intellectual growth up to the age of ten years (Burkhart, 1967).

As a child grows, his use of details and awareness of his environment change. Those individuals who tend to lag behind this developing awareness are displaying a lack of intellectual growth. For example, a youngster who draws in ways that are similar to those of a five year old but who is actually seven will have the intellectual abilities of a five year old in spite of his chronological age. This is a significant factor for the understanding of children, for it provides us not only with a means of realizing that youngsters are drawing and painting from their total being, but also with an opportunity for the alert teacher to understand problems that may be arising in other areas of expression. This is not to say that anyone can estimate a child's intellectual abilities merely by looking at his drawings; a sensitive teacher, however, can gain from them insight into and an understanding of problems the youngster himself may not

CREATIVE AND MENTAL
GROWTH

be able to deal with. At the same time, helping this youngster develop a sensitive relationship to his drawing may be extremely beneficial in encouraging an awareness of differences in the environment that may help in the intellectual growth of such a child.

It is important that a proper balance be kept between emotional and intellectual growth. If a child is found to be restricted in his creative expression yet highly developed intellectually, he must be provided with the opportunity to achieve a balance. Art can perform this function through proper motivation. Our present educational system suffers from an overemphasis on intellectual growth. The acquisition of knowledge remains the aim of education. It may be more important for the child to gain freedom in expression than to gather factual information. Knowledge unused is meaningless until the child develops the urge and freedom to use it.

PHYSICAL GROWTH

Physical growth in a child's creative work is seen in his ability for visual and motor coordination, in the way he controls his body, guides his line, and performs skills. The changing physical growth can be easily observed in children at the scribbling stage, when the marks on the paper change from a few random marks to a controlled scribbling within a relatively short period of time. Also the desire to make more refined and minute changes in sculptural form can develop motor skills very rapidly at the junior high school level.

But it is not only the direct participation in body activity that indicates physical growth in creative activities, for the conscious and unconscious projection of the body are also indicative. This projection of the self into the picture is usually referred to as body imagery. Essentially, the physically active child will portray active physical motions and he will develop a greater sensitivity to his physical achievements. Often the unconscious presence of muscular tensions or body feelings will also be portrayed. Sometimes children with defects will project these defects into their creative work. The ear that aches or the knee that has been scraped will be given emphasis. Continued overemphasis or omissions of body parts may be tied to the physical growth of the individual.

PERCEPTUAL GROWTH

The cultivation and growth of our senses is an important part of the art experience. This is of vital importance, for the enjoyment of life and

27

the ability to learn may depend upon the meaning and quality of the sensory experiences. In creative activity the increasing perceptual growth can be seen in a child's increasing awareness and use of a variety of perceptual experiences. Visual observation is usually the most emphasized in an art experience. Here one develops a growing sensitivity toward color, form, and space. The early stages of development indicate mere enjoyment and recognition of color, whereas on the advanced level the ever-changing relationships of color in different lights and atmospheric conditions can be stimulating. Perceptual growth reveals itself in a growing sensitivity to tactile and pressure sensations, from the mere kneading of clay and touching of textures to sensitive reactions to clay modeling in sculpture and the enjoyment of different surface and textural qualities in a variety of art forms.

Perceptual growth also includes the complex area of space perception. A young child knows and understands the immediate area around him, which has significance to him. As he grows the space around him grows and the way he perceives it will change. Auditory experiences are often included in art expression (see Figure 13). This inclusion ranges from

Figure 13. *This is a pencil drawing by a six year old boy who has watched his father mow the lawn. Notice how very much aware he is of the sound, of the grass ahead of the mower that still needs to be cut, and of the mechanical features of the mower. See too that the boy identifies so closely with his father that he puts his own sneakers on him, with the important laces he has just learned to tie.*

mere awareness of sounds and their inclusion in drawings to sensitive reactions to musical experiences transformed into an art expression. Kinesthetic experiences that range from simple uncontrolled body movements to highly developed coordination can also be seen as the basis for a variety of art forms. Space, shape, colors, textures, kinesthetic sensations, and visual experiences include a great variety of stimuli for expression. Children who are rarely affected by perceptual experiences show little ability to observe and little awareness of differences in objects. Awareness of variations in color, differences in shapes and forms, smoothness and roughness, sensitivity to light and dark, are all part of the creative experience. Unaware children may be blocked for a number of reasons; the inability to utilize the perceptual experiences may be a serious indication of a lack of growth in other areas. Again the teacher may play an important part in developing in youngsters the eagerness to see and feel and touch their surroundings, and in providing a wide range of experiences in which the senses play an important part.

SOCIAL GROWTH

The social growth of youngsters can readily be seen in their creative endeavors. Drawings and paintings reflect the degree of identification the child has with his own experiences and the experiences of others. The very young child begins to include people in his drawings as soon as he leaves the scribbling stage. Usually, in fact, the first recognizable object drawn by a child is a person. As the child grows, his art reflects his growing awareness of his social environment. As he develops a greater awareness of people and their influence on his life, these assume a large percentage of his subject matter content.

The art process itself provides a means of social growth. To some extent the term *self-expression* may have limiting connotations, since the expression of the self onto a sheet of paper also means viewing that expression. This viewing and looking at one's own work and one's own ideas is a first step in communicating these thoughts and ideas to others. Art has often been thought of primarily as a means of communication, and as such it becomes a social rather than a personal expression. The drawing can then become an extension of the self out into the world of reality as it begins to encompass others in the viewing of the subject matter. This feeling of social consciousness is the beginning of a child's understanding of the larger world of which he will become a part.

The development of social awareness goes on also in the portrayal of parts of our society with which the child can identify. This includes those forces that are established to preserve society itself. Drawing the fireman,

Figure 14. *Art can provide the opportunity for social interaction with peers. The opportunity to develop an awareness of others and their creative efforts can be an important part of an art experience.*

the road crew repairing a hole, the nurse helping people in the hospital, or the policeman giving directions, all provide stimulus to develop this social awareness. The arts can also contribute, through cooperative work, a greater awareness of each individual's contribution to a large project. This is particularly effective when the opinions of peers are sought and when the need is developed for social independence.

For older children the art of other cultures provides a means by which a society or a people can be felt and understood, and the values of one generation can have some influence on the next. Studying the variety of contemporary art from today's cultures can give indications of the attitudes and feelings of these people. One such investigation, examining the drawings by children from a variety of societies, indicated that group values can readily be seen in children's drawings of men (Dennis, 1966).

To a large extent, the only chances of real social interaction with peers within the usual school system occur at recess and in art classes. Both of these activities remove the teacher as a guide and provide an opportunity for social growth and the development of an awareness of others. Many activities can be included as art experiences that can foster social growth, and these will be discussed in more detail later. The creative works of children who are cooperative and conscious of their social responsibilities show a close feeling for self-identification with their own experiences and also with those of others. Those who are socially handicapped, who are suppressed in their desires for social participation, show this isolation by a lack of ability to correlate their experiences with those of others. Their art work shows inconsistent, spatially uncorrelated items, and figures are often drawn in isolation, if at all.

It is important to stress the significance of the individual's ability to live cooperatively in his society. This ability cannot be developed unless the child learns to assume responsibility for the things he is doing, is able to face his own action, and by doing so identifies with others. Creative activities provide an excellent means for taking this important step.

AESTHETIC GROWTH

Aesthetic growth is often considered the basic ingredient of any art experience. Aesthetics can be defined as being the means of organizing thinking, feeling, and perceiving into an expression that communicates these thoughts and feelings to someone else. The organization of words we call prose or poetry, the organization of tones we call music, the organization of body movements is usually referred to as dance, and the organization of lines, shapes, color, and form makes up art. There are no set standards or rules that are applicable to aesthetics; rather, the aesthetic criteria are based on the individual, the particular work of art, the culture in which it is made, and the intent or purpose behind the art form. There is a tremendous variety of organization in art. We find that an aesthetic form is not created by the imposition of any external rule but rather that a creative work grows by its own principles.

In the creative products of children, aesthetic growth is shown by a sensitive ability to integrate experiences into a cohesive whole. This integration can be seen in the harmonious organization and expression of thoughts and feelings through the lines, textures, and colors that are used. Young children organize intuitively, whereas those in the secondary school can find pleasure in the conscious manipulation and organization of spatial relationships in paintings. Each art material has different demands in terms of its aesthetic use, as a block print, for instance, presents an entirely different concept of organization from a fine line drawing.

Aesthetics is also intimately tied up with personality. Painters are recognized by their organization of colors and forms; a Van Gogh can be picked out anywhere by one who is familiar with his style of organization. The same is true for children, the organizational framework used to portray experiences in art can often give us an indication of some of the unconscious ordering that is unique for each person. Lack of organization or the disassociation of parts within a drawing may often be an indication of a lack of integration within the individual. One of the methods sometimes used to assess the value of therapy with psychotic patients is a study of the cohesiveness of organization in the drawings they produce.

Education has been thought of as the cultivation of expression in an organized manner. That is, it is the organization of words to make verbal communication, the organization of numbers or symbols to develop mathematical thinking, and the organization of images to make the arts. Education can therefore be looked upon as the development of aesthetic behavior. The thesis that art should be the basis of education has been pursued in depth by Herbert Read (1958). The thought that some balance and organization must be built into the educational system could be reflected in the development of courses in the humanities, such as those that are offered in several school systems. Aesthetic development is certainly an integral part of education.

CREATIVE GROWTH

Creative growth starts as soon as the child begins to make marks. He does this by inventing his own forms and putting down something of

Figure 15. *Young children do not have to learn skills before they can create. To an involved child, scribbling is an important and meaningful activity.*

himself in a way that is uniquely his. From this simple documentation of oneself to the most complex form of creative production there are many intermediary steps. Within the drawings and paintings of children creative growth can readily be seen in an independent and imaginative approach to the work of art. Children do not have to be skillful in order to be creative, but in any form of creation there are degrees of emotional freedom: freedom to explore and experiment, and freedom to get involved. This is true both in the use of subject matter and in the use of art materials.

The literature on creativity is relatively new. This is an area that is becoming of increasing concern both to educators and to researchers. Art experiences have always been considered the basis of creative activity within the schools. However, an understanding of this literature avails us nothing unless we can relate it directly to the individual child. We will go into detail later about the importance of creativity for art. For now it is sufficient to say that every art product, if it is truly the work of the youngster, is a creative experience in itself.

Those children who have been inhibited in their creativity by rules or forces unrelated to themselves, may retreat or resort to copying or tracing. They may quickly adopt styles from others, constantly ask for help, or follow examples of work that has been produced by their peers. Needless to say, the mere command to stop copying and become creative accomplishes nothing. Art activity cannot be imposed but must come as a spirit from within. This is not always an easy process, but the development of creative abilities is essential in our society, and the youngster's drawing reflects his creative growth, both in the drawing itself and in the process of making the art form.

A SUMMARY OF GROWTH CHARACTERISTICS

The art products of children tell us a great deal. The child reveals himself directly and without fear. Art for him is more than a pastime; it is a meaningful communication with himself, it is the selection of those parts of his environment with which he identifies, and the organization of these parts into a new meaningful whole. Art is important for the child. It is important for his thinking processes, for his perceptual development, for his emotional development, for his increasing social awareness, and for his creative development. It is obvious that correcting drawings or imposing particular demands upon the child that have no meaning to him serves no purpose and may instead establish a pattern of dependency upon the adult for direction and support.

We usually think of knowledge as flowing from the teacher to the student. The teacher has the responsibility for organizing the environment, providing the instructional materials, deciding upon the best method of dealing with the information he is trying to convey, and developing a curriculum in which he tries to cover the syllabus materials. The child, on the other hand, is usually the one who is graded on his acquisition of this knowledge, and on his ability to deal with the structure of the classroom in a socially acceptable way. The students' responses are judged as though they were signs of growth, although they may be primarily mimicking the teacher's own values.

Art can bring a new dimension into this organization, a dimension that is concerned with the psychological processes that occur and are experienced and developed in the youngster as he is involved in learning. This may be a high-level intellectual process quite akin to the thinking carried on by adults at the frontiers of our knowledge. Art provides the youngster with a wide range of possibilities, and his growth is not limited to the areas that have been predetermined by the educational system. The answers he seeks and the solutions he finds are his, and the drawing, painting, or construction reflects his growing ability to deal with a diverse range of possibilities in a constructive manner.

Art As a Reflection of Development

The study of children's art can be fascinating. Through an understanding of the way a youngster draws and the methods he uses to portray his environment, we can gain insight into his behavior and develop an appreciation of the complex and varied ways in which children grow and develop. Working with children in the area of art necessitates both an understanding of the various developmental stages and a thorough knowledge of the possibilities for growth. Such awareness is necessary for the teacher to determine to what extent the youngster can comprehend and utilize the art experience.

Art is not the same type of subject matter as arithmetic. In arithmetic, as in many other subject matter areas, the teacher plans gradations in the difficulty and amount of new material presented so that the youngster can properly grasp and deal with the content involved. In art, however, there is no external subject matter that needs to be presented in small doses. Subject matter in creative activities has a different meaning from that in other fields.

SUBJECT MATTER IN ART

In artistic experiences, there is no subject matter that must be taught. The same content is used in art by the very young child as is used in art by the professional artist. A man can be drawn by a five year old child or by a sixteen year old youth. The difference between the two drawings is not in the subject matter but rather in the way or manner in which it is represented. What changes is the subjective relationship between man and his environment. It is this subjective relationship that becomes important and not the drawing itself. A five year old child portrays a man quite differently from the way a sixteen year old youth would portray the same man. The child will draw a head and legs, and this will be satisfying; the sixteen year old will represent the man with a conscious consideration of size and proportion, and include all of the visible body parts.

The content, or whatever we draw, such as trees, houses, plants, flowers, and people will vary depending upon who is doing the drawing. For the five year old a tree has a trunk and something indefinite on top; a ten year old would draw the tree with branches to climb on; whereas the sixteen year old would draw the tree as part of the environment, with concern for proper proportions. It is the same tree, but what has

Figure 16. *This eleven year old girl is painting a tree that is quite different from a tree that a five year old would paint. Art reflects the development of the artist.*

changed is the subjective relationship of the people to the tree. The tree, as in the example of the man, is understood in different ways and therefore will be drawn in quite different ways. It would be beyond the comprehension of the five year old to draw a tree in all its details as part of the environment. To say which tree is better would be ridiculous. For each youngster, we have a tree that is symbolic of his relationship to the subject matter. For the sixteen year old to draw like the five year old would be as unnatural as it would be for the five year old to draw like the sixteen year old. In a sense there is no subject matter in art, only different ways of portraying the artist's relationship to objects, people, feelings, and emotions about the world around him.

The drawing by a five year old does not really represent his knowledge of a man. Every five year old knows that we have fingernails if his attention is directed toward them, but no average child of this age ever draws fingernails. The child draws his subjective experience of what is important to him during the act of drawing. He draws only what is actively in his mind. Thus in such a drawing of a man we get a report of the active knowledge the child has of a man at the time. Therefore the drawing gives us an excellent record of the things that are of importance to the child during the drawing process. A child knows a great deal more in a passive way than he ever uses. Part of a teacher's responsibility is to make this knowledge more active.

We can understand that each child draws his environment differently from any other child. The sixteen year old, for example, may be concerned about distances and sizes and his role in society; his mental and emotional growth are reflected in the way he portrays these differences. The five year old, however, experiences everything through himself; his spatial relations are limited to his own immediate surroundings, which he can touch, feel, or experience kinesthetically.

Subject matter is really not important in children's drawings; it is how this subject matter is portrayed that becomes important. Knowledge of the changes in drawings that appear at various developmental levels and of the subjective relationship between the child and his environment are necessary to an understanding of the growth of creative activities.

DEVELOPMENTAL STAGES IN ART

As children change, so does their art. Children draw in predictable ways, going through fairly definite stages, starting with the first marks on paper and progressing through adolescence. Although we think of these stages as being different steps in the development of art, it is sometimes difficult to tell where one stage of development stops and another begins. That is, growth in art is continuous and stages are typical mid-points in the course of development. Not all children move from one stage to another at exactly the same time; except for the abnormal or exceptional child, these stages follow one another, however, and a description of each is valuable in understanding the general characteristics of the child and his art at any particular time.

The very young child begins drawing by making random marks on paper. This stage is usually referred to as the Scribbling Stage. These random marks become much more organized and controlled but it is not until about the age of four that youngsters make any recognizable objects in their drawings. Therefore we can say that the scribbling stage usually lasts from two to four years of age. Even scribbles go through various stages of development from random marks to controlled scribbles. Sometimes parents try to teach youngsters at this stage of development how to draw something like an apple. That these marks drawn by the well-meaning parent can have any relationship to a real apple is a mystery to the child. This can be a frustrating experience for both parent and child, whereas the scribbling activity in itself is usually pleasurable; having an adult interested usually makes it even more interesting to the scribbling child. Apparently showing an interest in scribbling, and providing opportunities to draw and encouragement in using materials, can speed up development, but not very much. At any rate, the child tends to scribble until he is about four, and he seems to have a good time doing it.

The next stage is usually referred to as the Preschematic Stage, where the child makes his first representational attempts. This stage usually starts at about four years of age and lasts to around seven. Here the child draws the typical head-feet representation of a man, and begins to draw a number of other objects in his environment with which he has had contact. These figures or objects appear somewhat randomly placed on paper and can vary in size considerably. These first representational attempts provide an opportunity for adults to converse with children about their drawings, and usually children of this age are eager to explain and show what they have done without self-consciousness.

The next stage is the Schematic Stage, which starts somewhere around seven and lasts until about nine years of age. Here the child develops a definite form concept. His drawings symbolize parts of his environment in a descriptive way; the child usually repeats the schema that he has developed for a man again and again. It is at this time that one interesting characteristic of children's drawings appears: the child lines up the objects he is portraying in a straight line across the bottom of his page. The house is followed by the tree is followed by the flower which is next

Figure 17. *"Connia," drawn by a twelve year old girl who shows her concern for her place in society by making her whole group look just like herself. The environment is drawn more naturalistically than it would have been if she were ten.*

to the person who may be next to a dog which is the end of this picture. These works of art look quite decorative.

It is usually the first three stages of development that attract the enthusiasm of adults. The freshness and the spontaneity of children's drawings make the adult somewhat envious. However, this spontaneous and fresh method of painting comes naturally to children; possibly adults wish that they too could enjoy the freedom of childhood, forgetting that growing is not always full of joy and happiness.

By the time a child reaches the age of nine he has entered the Stage of Dawning Realism that lasts from nine to twelve years. Here his peers become so important that this is sometimes referred to as the Gang Age. The drawings by children of this age still symbolize rather than represent objects. The youngster is much more aware of himself and this awareness shows in his drawings. They are more detailed than his earlier work, and he no longer places objects in neat rows across the bottom of the page. He is becoming interested in detail and no longer makes the large free drawings that he made at a younger age. Not only is he beginning to draw smaller, but he is no longer eager to show his drawings and explain them, but in fact he hides them from adult observation. The youngster is much more conscious of himself as a member of society (in a way we will describe in more detail later) and this is reflected in his art work.

Somewhere around the age of eleven or twelve the youngster becomes increasingly aware of his natural surroundings, and he begins to worry about such things as proportion and depth in drawings. This stage is referred to as the Pseudo-naturalistic Stage, the stage of reasoning. There is a great deal of self-criticism, and drawings are now hidden in note-books or are attempts at cartoons. The drawing of the human figure shows a great deal of detail and, as might be expected, an increase in the aware-ness of sexual characteristics. There is also a greater awareness of differ-ences and gradations in color, although some youngsters are not able to develop this visual awareness. For some, this stage marks the end of their artistic development and we often find that adults, when asked to draw something, will make a drawing that is very typical of the twelve year old.

At about the age of fourteen, or later, youngsters are at the age of development where a real interest in visual art can take place. They develop a conscious awareness of art and are often eager to develop artistic skills. Some high school students gain great competency in mim-icking art forms or styles that may be currently in vogue, and some youngsters develop what might be thought of as a talent for portraying their visual environment. This age is also somewhat shallow in its artistic form, particularly if the perfected style or technique has been laboriously copied from elsewhere. To some extent, the natural develop-ment of a youngster does not extend beyond this stage, but it is possible now to consciously develop artistic skills.

Apparently these developmental stages are fairly consistent with all children, wherever they happen to be. This is especially true of the beginning stages of representation before his culture influences a child in his artistic development. What he draws will differ, depending upon the environment in which he lives and the drawing instrument that is used, but all children scribble until about the age of four; the period of first representational attempts will continue until about six or seven regardless of where the child finds himself.

It also appears that instruction in drawing does not have much influ-ence upon these stages. This is particularly true of young children, but by the time the youngster is eleven or twelve some effects of training can be seen in the quality of his work. In encouraging children to look for information about contours of objects or patterns such as angles and curves, Salome (1965) found that this training had no influence over the drawings of fourth grade youngsters but apparently made some improvement in the drawings of fifth graders. However, in an experi-ment with fifth graders, Neperud (1966) found that only girls of high in-telligence were able to profit from instruction that emphasized visual elements.

A number of studies have attempted to document the various developmental stages in children's growth. These sometimes give different names to the stages, such as calling the scribbling stage a stage of manipulation, and so forth, but there is general agreement as to the stages themselves. Lark-Horovitz (1959) found that these drawing characteristics varied more as children grew older and that it was sometimes difficult to tell where one stage of development started and another stopped. Applegate (1967) found that those children who were higher in the stage of development than their chronological age would indicate were generally higher in mental age, whereas children lower in intelligence drew according to their mental age rather than chronological age. It is to be anticipated, therefore, that the developmental stages as listed above are primarily for normal children.

SIGNIFICANCE OF THE DEVELOPMENTAL STAGES

It is easier to see the changes in children's drawings as they grow than it is to explain why these changes occur. Children do not attempt to copy nature as adults know it. There is no straight-line progression from a very poor drawing or the scribble that a young child makes of an object to an advanced likeness such as an adolescent youngster might draw. Lewis (1963) gathered drawings from children from kindergarten through eighth grade in which they represented, among other things, a house. She found that kindergarten children actually drew a house that was more naturalistically correct than did children in older grades up through fourth. Children in the first, second, and third grades were concerned about drawing several sides of the house, which it would be impossible to view naturally.

Obviously youngsters are not trying to portray their environment in a natural way. It is not that they are unable to do this because they lack the competency or coordination, but apparently that they are satisfied with their own means of representation.

Some people believe that children portray what they know rather than what they see. However, any child can tell you a great deal more about his features, his limbs, or the clothes he is wearing than he will portray in his drawing of himself. Even very young children are able to name various parts of the body, even though they cannot portray these parts. Apparently the child shows what is important to him at the time he is drawing. Probably for a five year old a head is necessary for eating and thinking, and legs are important for running.

We may well have been led down the wrong road by comparing children's drawings to nature. If we look at drawing as being a process that

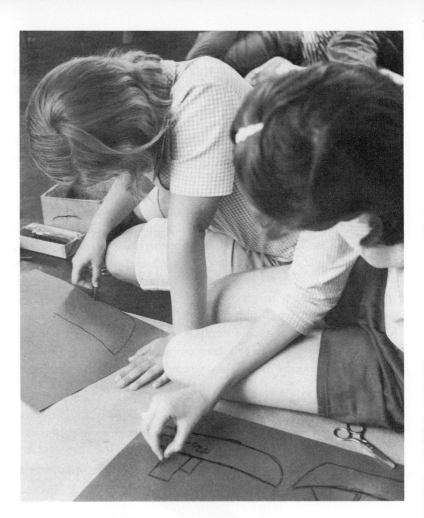

Figure 18. *Children do not attempt to copy nature as a camera would show it. These boats are more indicative of the youngsters' understanding of boats than of a naturalistic attempt.*

a child uses to signify and reconstruct his environment, the process of making a drawing becomes much more involved than a mere attempt at visual representation. That is, the child may be acting out or moving part of his environment around, and the parts are merely symbolized by whatever happens to be satisfying enough to connote the image or object. Looking at children's drawings from this point of view, it becomes apparent that the youngster himself is actually involved in every drawing. He is a spectator and an actor at the same time.

For example, one finds that drawings by five year old children have no space relationship except from the self. The five year old draws the objects around him and the finished picture looks as if the youngster had placed objects around the page. By the time a child is seven he begins to put the objects that he is drawing in a line, but each of these objects is drawn facing the child himself, as if they were lined up to be seen. These objects do not relate to each other but rather to the child artist himself. It is not until about the age of nine that we find drawings in which objects relate to each other rather than to the viewer. About the age of twelve or so, the picture starts to become a representation of space and objects within that space.

Drawings give us a good indication of the child's growth, moving from an egocentric point of view to a gradual awareness of the self as part of a larger environment. Even the scribbling child's drawing of undefined shapes may be essentially feelings of the self. Possibly the first man symbol is really not a man at all, but a representation of the self that slowly begins to take on the meaning of any person.

Piaget (1959), in studying children's thinking, discovered that there were stages in development that closely parallel the stages of development mentioned above. The first stage which lasts until about the age of two he calls the Sensory-motor Period, and this is followed by a Pre-operational Period which lasts until about the age of seven, followed by a stage of Concrete Operations which lasts from about seven to age eleven. A discussion of some of the implications of these stages of development and their relationship to art was completed by Lansing (1966). Lansing believes that Piaget's work shows that we will do the child no good by

Figure 19. *This youngster is involved in making an intricate design. This is a challenging activity for him, but the production of art makes sense only when the activity is meaningful for the youngster himself.*

criticizing the drawings or other visual forms that he makes; if it is important to change the shape of a youngster's work, then we must first change his concepts.

Drawings may reflect the ability of children to deal with parts of their environment in a very practical way. The teaching of particular skills becomes meaningful only when the child can deal with this information. For example, a five year old does not put shadows in his drawings. To try to show him that shadows exist, to teach him methods of shading and how a shadow is cast, would be meaningless. Lee (1968) asked youngsters of a variety of ages to make an actual shadow using rings of various sizes placed in front of a light. Younger children were unable to deal with the problem and believed that the bigger the ring the bigger the shadow, regardless of where this ring was placed. It was not until the age of eight that the youngsters began considering distance from the light as influencing the size of the shadow. At the age of thirteen both the dimension and distance factors were considered, but it was not until the age of seventeen that even half of the youngsters could verbalize the operating principles involved.

The teaching of art must start with the youngster and not be involved with externals. Changing or altering his drawing or painting to satisfy some whim of the art teacher will, in most cases, be incomprehensible to a child; it is the youngster himself and his interrelationship with his environment that becomes crucial.

Art and Creativity

Art and creativity have always been closely entwined. For years the art program in the public schools has been the bastion of creativity, and often art experiences and creative activity have meant the same thing. However, with the increasing interest in creativity and the great number of research studies in this area, it is becoming quite clear that it is possible to have an art program in the schools that is not automatically creative in nature. Creativity is becoming of vital concern to many people; we need to understand the process involved in developing the creative thinking abilities of children. There is no doubt that this area will be of increasing concern in the future as society turns toward the unknown, and schools will of necessity have to teach not only what is known but also teach *toward* what we do not know. Art can play an important part in this field. In fact, it has been suggested that intensive experience in the arts should be a basic tool of education to promote creative thinking (Hoffa, 1964).

To some extent the term *creativity* has become too popular. The words creativity or creative are applied like sparkling paint to book titles, do-it-yourself projects, or performance groups. Still, we must not lose sight of the tremendous importance that the development of creative thinking can have for us, both as individuals and as a society. It offers a change from what is and has been to what might be or what is yet to be discovered.

FOSTERING CREATIVITY

The definition of creativity depends upon who is doing the defining. Often researchers are rather narrow in their definition, stating that creativity means flexibility of thinking or fluency of ideas; or it may be the ability to come up with new and novel ideas, or to see things in new relationships; in some cases creativity is defined as the ability to think in ways that are different from other people. Usually creativity is thought of as being constructive, productive behavior that can be seen in action or accomplishment. It does not have to be a unique phenomenon in the world, but it does have to be basically a contribution from the individual.

Creativity has been considered the opposite of conformity, but this may not always be true. We have to conform a great deal in our society to rules and regulations that mean safety for ourselves and others. This kind of conformity, conformity to rules of physical behavior, is basic to society so long as these rules are able to be changed by those affected. There is another whole area of conformity, that of mental conformity, that may be of danger to our society. We need to differentiate between these two. This may be a difficult thing for young children to do, but as adults we must be sure that the pressures of conformity are limited to those areas that are necessary for the sake of society. One of the difficult tasks of a teacher of young children is to provide socially acceptable ways in which children can use and be encouraged to use their creative abilities while keeping to a minimum the areas in which they will have to conform. Probably the most crucial time in the encouragement of creative thinking is when the child is beginning his formal schooling. It is here that initial attitudes are established, all too seldom with the realization that school can be a fun place where the individual's contribution is welcome and where changes can be sought and made.

At one time distinct stages were suggested for the development of creative thinking. These consisted of an initial stage called Preparation,

Figure 20. *Each child has his own unique method of organization. The development of creative concepts comes from within and cannot be taught.*

followed by a thinking period called Incubation, which was background for the next stage of Illumination, which was followed by a period called Verification. These stages were looked upon as sequential, and the school's role seemed limited to the initial stage of preparation only. Nowadays it is considered outmoded to think of creativity in so limited a format. Rather, creativity is being more closely related to the thinking abilities and to attitude development. If there is any justification for saying that these four steps exist in the creative process, then they would have to be varied considerably to include both the many periods of illumination that a nursery school child goes through in building with blocks and the one sudden illumination that results in an invention by a research engineer. It is probably best to think of creativity as a continual process for which the best preparation is creativity itself. In fact, there is real joy in discovery—which not only is its own reward but provides the urge for continuing exploration and discovery.

Art can be thought of as a continual process of creativity, because each youngster works at his own level to produce a new form with a unique organization, with countless minor problems of adapting subject matter

45

to two- and three-dimensional surfaces. It is possible to maximize the opportunities for creative thinking in art experiences, and this opportunity should be a planned part of each art activity.

There are several factors involved in any creative process. These include the environmental factors over which the teacher has direct control. These include not only the physical structure of the room and the materials, but also the psychological environment, which may be much more important. Another factor is that of the social values involved. At certain ages the youngsters will become more dependent upon peers for direction and approval than upon the teacher, but even here the teacher can play an important part. Another variable is the personality of the child himself. The attitude that one has developed toward oneself and the worth that one feels about one's own contribution can play an important role in the creative process. In addition there is the problem of developing skills or the means by which creativity can become unleashed. It is this last area that is emphasized in most books and texts, but the teaching of skills or the development of competencies in art will bear little relationship to the development of creativity unless all the factors considered above are involved in the planning process.

Sometimes there is confusion between intelligence and creativity. The problem is compounded by the fact that creativity is usually considered an attribute that has positive value; because intelligence is also valued highly these two are often put together. Generally speaking, creativity may have little to do with intellect. The intelligence test is only an approximation of one small part of the total functioning of the mind. In some cases the individual who scores well on I.Q. tests may also do well on tasks of creativity; in other cases there may be no relationship. Children's drawings have been used as a measure of creativity (Trowbridge, 1967) with judges who apparently were able to distinguish between creativity and artistic competence. It is much more important to develop creativity than competence in children, because creativity cannot easily be learned at older age levels, whereas it is doubtful if one can teach youngsters of elementary school age very much in the way of artistic skills and competencies.

One theory about the structure of people's intellectual functioning supposes that there are five different operations in the mental process: cognition, memory, convergent production, divergent production, and evaluation (Guilford, 1964). Creativity would be considered a divergent production. This is the opposite of convergent production, which is usually stressed in school, where the outcome of thinking is one correct answer or the most approved solution. The creative arts are extremely important in our educational system if only because they stress divergent thinking, in which there are no right answers, and any number of possible solutions to problems or any number of outcomes in painting or drawing can be correct.

Some questions that are factual and demand specific answers might be, "What are the primary colors? What are the secondary colors? Give an example of a split-complementary color scheme." Open-ended questions that stimulate divergent thinking might be, "Which colors make you feel sad? How would you feel if you were purple? Which color would you like to be?" The importance of teaching toward divergent thinking is stressed by Burkhart (1962, p. 27): "The value of the divergent question is that it requires the student to look at a content area from a variety of viewpoints and to participate in an imaginative way in answering the question."

Creative growth seems to operate on a different set of patterns than do other areas of behavior. We are all familiar with the healthy child of about four who has a vivid imagination and a great deal of curiosity about things around him. Some researchers have found, however, that by the time the child is eight or nine he seems much less creative, and again in the seventh and eighth grades there is a dip in creative growth (Torrance, 1962; Kincaid, 1964). We have to be careful not to assume that children are creative in the same way that adults are, but even so, these leveling-off periods seem to exist. Certainly the demands of parents, teachers, and peers may put a high value on conforming behavior at these times. There is no doubt that adults considerably squelch what might be thought of as childish behavior and insist that their teenage son or daughter stop being "silly."

It is sometimes said that the public school discourages creative thinking, but the school has many tasks and we might be better justified in saying that creative thinking is not very high on the list of most teachers' objectives. Some evidence indicates that teachers do not like the creative child (Getzels and Jackson, 1962). There is reason to believe that the sweet, conforming child is rewarded in the classroom to the disadvantage of the development of imagination and creative thinking. This can happen in art classes too. The home influence is a significant factor in encouraging the development of creative thinking (Weisberg and Springer, 1967), but society in the form of parents, teachers, or peers undoubtedly rewards certain types of behavior at certain ages, and maybe this is why creative behavior develops in such an uneven pattern.

Creativity needs to be nurtured in a particular kind of environment. The "anything goes" atmosphere is apparently just as negative an influence as the authoritarian atmosphere where individuals are completely dominated. Creativity must be supported, but at the same time guided into socially acceptable channels. Curiosity has been thought of as one of the primary drives (Fowler, 1965), but strong forces may be working

Figure 21. *Children develop imaginative ideas in an atmosphere that encourages creativity. The classroom situation must be flexible enough to allow youngsters the freedom to express their own ideas.*

against creativity in many public school settings. Art experiences provide an excellent opportunity to reinforce creative thinking and to provide the means by which youngsters can develop their imaginative and novel ideas without censorship. There is no doubt that a certain amount of anxiety is produced in children who are afraid to rely upon their own judgment, but art is a good method to free the thinking of such children.

Probably the one most important factor in this area is to provide a model for the youngster to emulate. By model, of course, we are referring to the teacher himself. Although it is well accepted that art teachers value independence in thinking more than teachers in other fields (Davis and

Torrance, 1965), there is pressure for teachers to conform to the school standards of behavior. Youngsters need an opportunity to see teachers who admit that they do not know, who are willing to accept the thoughts of others, who can enjoy life and like having others enjoy theirs, who have lots of ideas and the flexibility to allow children to have their own, who accept every youngster on his own worth. Such attributes would make the art teacher an important person in the classroom, even if he were never to teach art.

WORKBOOKS AND COLORING BOOKS

There is general agreement that coloring books are detrimental to children's creative expression. These books usually have an outline of some form or other, such as a cow, or a dog, or a complete landscape. The youngster is supposed to color within the lines and some youngsters seem to enjoy this activity. This enjoyment may be because these youngsters do not have to think for themselves. The dependency upon someone else's outline of an object makes the child much less confident in his own means of expression. He obviously cannot draw a cow as well as the one in the coloring book. Parents, however, are becoming much more aware of these problems, and often blank pages can be purchased in book form for youngsters to use. The lines that a child makes himself are more meaningful, and children who mark all over a coloring book do not do the same type of marking over their own drawings.

We can decry the use of coloring books for children, but some of the same objections can be raised to the paint-by-the-number kits that adults use. Just as a poem can be copied without understanding the message, the rhythm, or the metaphor, painting a picture with a paint-by-the-number kit is an automatic procedure that merely reinforces one's own inabilities.

It may come as somewhat of a surprise to find that workbooks used in arithmetic often greatly resemble some coloring books. One of the many examples commonly used in one arithmetic book has a child draw seventy-six repetitions of a stereotyped rabbit, eighty-eight repetitions of a bird, sixty-two of a kite, eighty of a balloon, and so forth. Such repetition is meaningless. A study by Heilman (1954) indicated how dependent some children can become upon these workbooks, for the data revealed that the general growth pattern through creative work was seriously influenced by these workbooks. In some experiments conducted by Russell and Waugaman (1952), 63 per cent of all children who had been exposed to coloring-book birds lost their original concept of bird and

a

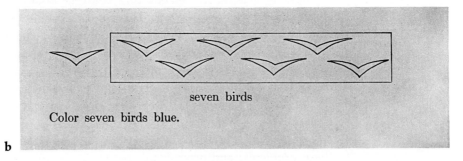

seven birds

Color seven birds blue.

b

Figure 22. *Coloring books affect a child's creative expression. (Courtesy of Dr. Irene Russell,* Research Bulletin, The Eastern Arts Association, *Vol. 3, No. 1, 1952).* **a.** *This bird shows one child's expression before he was exposed to coloring books.* **b.** *Then the child had to color a workbook illustration.* **c.** *After coloring the workbook birds, the child has lost his creative sensitivity and self-reliance.*

c

changed their drawings to resemble the workbook stereotype (see Figure 22).

Often the excuse is given that these workbook exercises are fundamental to learning arithmetical concepts or to developing recognition of a letter. However, a thesis by Johnson (1963) indicated that tracing over a letter up to ten times was of no value in recognizing that letter later. There is no evidence that these laboriously colored balloons and kites actually help to develop either number concepts or reading abilities. Although no one will admit it, one of the main reasons for using these workbooks may well be that they give the classroom teacher a chance to have some rest while the youngsters fill in the appropriate number of birds or color the proper kites green.

Surprisingly enough, we still occasionally see dittoed sheets handed out for youngsters to color that may have silhouettes of George Washington, a Thanksgiving turkey, a Hallowe'en pumpkin, an Easter rabbit, or even a Christmas tree outlined on them for the children to color in. One particular example showed Pilgrims standing in front of their log cabin holding blunderbusses. The fact is that the Pilgrims lived in huts made of sticks and vines until they built clapboard houses (Holbrook, 1945), and that "neither the English nor the Dutch built log cabins at first, and apparently did not even know how to do so . . ." (Stewart, 1954, p.152). Sometimes art projects also smack of the same absurdities, as when youngsters are given copper foil to press over some preformed design to mount for Christmas presents. Even May baskets preplanned by the teacher for the first grade youngsters to cut out fall into the category of being detrimental to creative expression.

Art instruction that includes these kinds of activities is worse than no art at all. They are predigested activities that force youngsters into imitative behavior and inhibit their own creative expression. These activities make no provision for emotional growth because any variation the child makes can only be a mistake; they do not promote skills, because skills develop from one's own expression. Instead, they condition the child to accept adult concepts as art, art that the child is unable to produce alone and which therefore frustrates his own creative urges.

RELATED ACTIVITIES

1. Observe the changes that take place in art expression by collecting drawings from children from kindergarten through high school age. Trace the development of the representation of a single object, such as a tree. Notice how the subject matter (child's portrayal of his reaction to the environment)

does not change, but the *manner* of representation changes as the child changes.

2. Observe in a classroom those children who look around, ask questions, and are easily distracted. Compare their products with those of children who are personally involved in portraying their experiences, noting stereotypes, simple objective reports, some inclusion of the self, complete self-identification with the product.

3. Work with a class of third grade youngsters. Plan one lesson emphasizing environment: trees, homes, school, and so forth. Plan a second lesson that emphasizes the imaginative: dreams, make-believe animals, strange creatures. Do the same children seem to enjoy both lessons?

4. Observe an elementary class for several sessions and list the number of opportunities for developing divergent thinking. Compare this with the number of times thinking is directed toward one "right" answer. Discuss the role of art in stimulating divergent thinking.

5. Collect drawings from a kindergarten class and list the various methods of portrayal of sensory experiences. Check especially for symbols for sounds and movements.

6. Compare the quantity and quality of drawings from several children you consider talented with several you do not consider talented in art. List the differences in drawings. Plan experiences you think would be of value to the talented children. Would these be of value for those not so talented?

Art in the Elementary Classroom

3

ART IS usually considered an important part of the program for the elementary school child. Art activities, however, are scheduled in a variety of ways. Sometimes there is a special art room set aside for the art activities and an art teacher to direct these. Sometimes the art teacher comes to each elementary classroom a couple of times a week or less, and sometimes the elementary classroom teacher himself is expected to provide experiences in art for the children in his classroom. Occasionally there is a flexible schedule where an art consultant will spend several days or parts of a month in one room and then move to another location to provide for a concentrated art experience.

There are many reasons for these different patterns, most of them economic ones. The most important consideration should be maximizing

Figure 23. *The atmosphere in a classroom that is engaged in art activities is quite different from the atmosphere that is present in the classroom when usual academic subject matter is taught.*

the value of the art program so as to provide a meaningful experience in the arts, with ample opportunity for the youngsters to express their own relationship to their environment. This provides an artistic outlet for their thinking, feeling, and perceiving.

Classroom Procedures

Art is not a subject where there are specific answers, for here the teacher does not have a book with the right solution to every problem on his desk. In the usual academic subjects the teacher and the books are the authority. There may be many approaches to teaching academic subject matter, but the correct response to a multiplication problem, the date of some exploration, or the proper spelling of a particular word are all known by the teacher. In the area of artistic expression, however, the teacher neither knows nor is looking for right answers. Classroom procedures are focused upon encouraging each child in his own very personal way. A teacher's function becomes one of developing children's self-discovery and stimulating depth of expression.

The atmosphere that is conducive to artistic expression, an environment that will foster inventiveness and exploration, is not the same type of atmosphere that is favorable for memorizing arithmetic tables. In the latter activity the student must concentrate on areas outside himself; he is dependent upon the teacher for recognition of his efforts and he must, with the rest of his classmates, deny giving vent to his own feelings. Creative expression is the direct opposite of memorization. Where individual inventiveness, expression, and independence of thinking are crucial, an entirely different classroom atmosphere needs to be established.

A teacher who wants to foster individual expression in the classroom, who wants to encourage initiative and spontaneity, and who wants to have children motivated to produce freely, will have to accept and reward creative behavior. We wish to encourage the child to be full of curiosity, to poke fun at himself and others, to have original ideas of his own, even to question the teacher's direction, and at the same time we discourage children from feeling withdrawn, quiet, retiring, and dependent upon the teacher for direction and approval. The child who looks upon learning as a self-initiated activity is the type of student we are trying to encourage, and he is the type of individual that is the backbone of our society. Children who are personally involved in an activity may be oblivious to those around them and are not easily distracted. Sometimes a whole class will become so involved in an activity that a classroom will be surprisingly quiet. At other times there may be a great deal of activity and noise as youngsters share ideas and materials.

An art class is often confusing to the outsider anyway, because of the problem of having numerous materials distributed and picked up. A great deal of responsibility can be assumed by the children themselves in handling the art materials. Actually the art experience is more than merely using the art materials in the drawing or painting process; learning takes place in finding how paint is stored, learning how to mix the paint so that it is of proper consistency, and learning how to clean up after the painting is completed. Cleaning and storing the brushes and putting the painting itself away to dry are all part of the experience. Although very young children will have difficulty with paints, even nursery-school children can help and there is no reason why the responsibility for paper distribution or putting away crayons cannot be assumed by the youngsters. The teacher who prepares the materials and then assumes the responsibility for cleaning up afterward puts himself in the position of a housekeeper rather than a teacher. There is some danger in encouraging students to think and do for themselves. But this danger exists only for the teacher who feels insecure within himself.

Classroom procedures should be kept flexible enough to allow each child the opportunity to deviate from the group activity. Specific suggestions for motivating children to express their feelings and emotions will be included in later chapters; however, if a particular project does not appeal to some of the children, there is no law that says that all children must be occupied in the same activity. Working with paper in a variety of ways, such as cutting, tearing, crumbling, or using paper to express some particular feeling by piercing the surface or folding it, might very well lead some children into escaping from the artistic investigation and using the paper for making folded airplanes. This might be a particularly interesting way to upset a teacher, but the use of paper for airplanes can be an interesting project in itself; certainly encouraging such children in making changes in the design of the folded paper—by adding a paper clip to the nose, by using a different type of fold, by trying a variety of weights of paper, and by experimenting with these forms in the hall—can challenge the energies and independent thinking of the creative child into a constructive art project. Denying the desire to make such airplanes by treating the child as disruptive and taking disciplinary action against him, would not only be frustrating for him, but would also deny the rest of the class the opportunity to deviate in the future from the prescribed procedures that the teacher might arbitrarily assign to the class.

Although undoubtedly every teacher would like to work with small classes, apparently there is no reason to believe that the size of class has much influence over the quality of the drawings of children. Lansing (1956) in working with fifth grade children found that class sizes ranging from eighteen to forty produced no significantly different effects upon the creative drawings of these children. Apparently the teacher and the motivation are more important in what and how youngsters do in their creative activities.

Any procedures used in the classroom should encourage rather than discourage creativity. Children seated in rows with hands folded, waiting for something to happen, waiting for the person in front to pass the paper back, waiting for someone else to use the paint, lining up to wash hands at the sink, or patiently waiting for their turn at the easel may experience long enough delays to make real creative expression difficult when the time finally comes to put a line on paper. In some cases, putting supplies in several locations, grouping youngsters with four or five others who share the same interests, not having everyone working at the same project, and encouraging children to change activities without waiting for

Figure 24. *It is important that the teacher involve each youngster in the activity, whether the class is involved in a group project or in individual art expression.*

teacher approval will provide a means by which greater flexibility is possible.

Those children who have a good deal of energy and who are freer in their responses may need to have these energies channeled into acceptable form; at the same time the passive, quiet child may need real encouragement and the opportunity to develop independent thinking and to discover the joy of self-expression. Providing encouragement for creative behavior and rewards for independent thinking can go a long way toward developing an atmosphere of creative activity. The classroom procedure can help in this respect, but it is only one factor among many that can provide the background for a meaningful art experience.

The Teacher of Art

THE TEACHER'S BEHAVIOR IS IMPORTANT

In teaching art to children the most important factor is the teacher himself. If we could imagine a very poor teacher in the elementary school —though this may be difficult to imagine—we would undoubtedly feel sorry for the children under his charge. At least we would know that the children could get a great deal from the reading material in the class, the history book and the English reader would be there for them to use, and they would probably be able to develop some competencies in arithmetic. In art, however, there could be some real damage done. The basic ingredient of art comes from the child himself. This is essentially true whether we are talking about an elementary school child or a high school senior. The teacher has the important task of providing an atmosphere conducive to inventiveness, exploration, and production. In art, then, a poor teacher might be worse than no teacher at all.

There are ways that teachers can provide a proper atmosphere for creative activities. There are ways that the environmental conditions can be organized to provide optimum conditions for art activities. The teacher of art should be a warm and friendly person. Cogan investigated the relationship between teacher behavior and the amount of required and self-initiated work performed by pupils. Nearly a thousand junior high school pupils were surveyed, and it was found that in almost every classroom positive relationships were found between the extent to which the student described the teacher as warm and friendly and the amount of self-initiated and required work produced. Averaging the amount of work that students did for each teacher clearly showed that the more friendly and warm teachers had pupils who produced more work (Levin, et al., 1957).

There is some basis, then, for saying that a warm, friendly attitude toward students does foster productivity. In a study done with eleven year old children, Lippett and White (1960) tried to find out what effects adult leaders had upon the behavior of children if the leaders behaved in ways called *authoritarian*, *democratic*, and *laissez-faire*. The authoritarian leader was one who issued orders and directions and gave praise or criticism; the democratic leader gave guiding suggestions, asked for children's opinions and judgments, and joked on a friendly basis; the laissez-faire leader gave out information when he was asked, but did not take an active part in giving out directions nor in stimulating self-guidance. Leaders changed groups part way through the experiment; the group behavior included a great outburst of horseplay by those children who were released from the authoritarian leader. But one interesting point was the finding that the children under a democratic leader showed the greatest expression of individual differences while at the same time showing less irritability and aggressiveness toward fellow members.

In checking the creativity test gains of elementary classroom pupils, Wodtke and Wallen (1965) studied seventy-seven female teachers' method of classroom control. Some of these teachers preferred a highly ordered and controlled classroom and could not tolerate behavior of youngsters that did not fit into the pattern of order and control. They found that a high degree of control by the classroom teacher had a detrimental effect on verbal creativity.

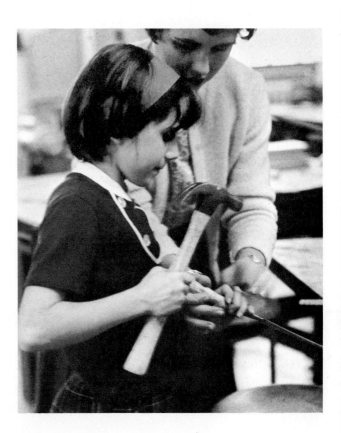

Figure 25. *A warm, friendly teacher motivates and supports individual creative expression.*

A work of art is not the representation of a thing but rather the representation of the experiences we have with that thing. Because experiences will change not only from year to year but from day to day, art expression becomes a dynamic, ever-changing process. The teacher, too, must be a flexible person, able to throw away his plans and to capitalize upon the enthusiasm and interest of the children. It is the ability to be warm, friendly, and democratic in nature that will provide the opportunity for youngsters to express themselves freely, both in words and in artistic expression; but it also is vital that the teacher be able to provide the flexible format so that the expression can be formed into an art product. To some extent this becomes a two-way exchange. Not only is the supportive atmosphere necessary, but flexible channeling of the youngster's feelings and emotions and perceptual skills must culminate in an artistic form for the process to be meaningful.

IDENTIFYING WITH THE CHILD

Art must be important for the artist. This is obvious at the adult level, but it is also true for children. The youngster must feel that what he is doing is important and that this activity is relevant to his needs. One of the main difficulties that a teacher can face is a discrepancy between his own way of thinking and that of his pupils. What can be an exciting experience and a learning situation for an adult might not be relevant for children's needs. The teacher, therefore, must be able to identify with those students with whom he is working. It is important that the art activity be theirs and not the teacher's.

A child who shows signs of inhibitions in art or lacks the self-confidence for his own expression cannot be helped by a teacher who limits himself to instruction in the use of art materials, or in the problems of space relationships or color harmony. For example, a three or four year old child who is afraid of becoming involved in scribbling may just put a few lines down in the corner of the page. Telling him to draw larger will not be of much value, even if accompanied by threats such as, "You may flunk nursery school if you do not draw larger." Instead, the teacher

Figure 26. *Most nursery school children enjoy scribbling and look upon painting activities as one of the good things about going to nursery school.*

needs to identify with this child in such a way that the teacher too can feel the big blank piece of paper as a threat.

The scribbling must become meaningful, and in this case one could ask the child, "Suppose you were in a big empty room. Would you stand in just one corner or would you run all around the room? No one is there and you can do what you like. Wouldn't it be fun to run all the way to one side of the room and then to run back to the other? Now, look, here is a red crayon and suppose this sheet of paper is a great big empty room, how do you suppose the red crayon will act? Do you think the red crayon will just sit quietly in the corner? I don't think so either. Let's see how the red crayon runs around the paper." The tiny motions would thus become enlarged meaningfully because the reason for the large motion would become important. Few children could avoid the temptation of making large strokes all over the paper.

Although this may be an example that is obvious on the scribbling level, the identification with the youngster and the problems that he is facing is true at any level. A fourth grader who says he cannot draw himself throwing a ball does not need the mechanics of figure drawing or an example that the teacher might make for him to copy, which might even widen the gap between his experience and his ability to express it. He needs an understanding of his own experience: "Show me how you throw a ball. What did you do with your arms, your legs? Let's try it again. Now you threw it up high. What did you do with your hands? Where did you look? Now throw the ball to me again." Such questions will develop in the youngster confidence to express these experiences, and the urge for such expression will be strong enough to overcome his lack of confidence.

It is also important for the teacher of art to identify with the youngsters who are successful in their achievement and who can express themselves easily. It is more important to recognize and share this joy of expression and pride in accomplishment than it is to point out that there are some corrections needed in proportion or that the hand has six fingers instead of five. The product is important for the child while he is drawing. One teacher was observed who told her second grade charges that the drawings would not be saved on this particular day, and that they should throw their papers in the wastebasket on the way out. Obviously this teacher did not identify with these children, and it must be confessed that this observer felt that the attendance sheet she had been working on ought to join the youngsters' drawings in the wastebasket. The self-identification of a youngster's own work can be a meaningful experience only when the teacher can identify with his pupils so as to provide the proper motivation and environmental conditions for meaningful expression.

IDENTIFYING WITH THE MEDIUM

A teacher who has never experienced the qualities of wood, who has never run his fingers over the grain or sanded a board to a smooth finish, a teacher who has never been frustrated with the splintering of wood or been pleased with a joint well made will never be able to motivate and inspire the youth who has failed to solve a poorly conceived problem in working with wood. To think in terms of the material is an important part of the creative process, especially during the adolescent years. A teacher who has never gone through the process of creating in a specific art material may never understand the particular type of thinking that is necessary to work with clay, paint, or whatever. This means that the teacher must have been truly involved in *creating* with materials, not in dealing with them in an abstract way by reading or mechanically carrying out some project. The material and the expression should be as one.

This does not imply that the elementary school teacher needs to be an artist. But a teacher of children should have been involved in a real creative experience and feel competent in some area of expression. In some cases the introduction of new material can be worked through with the teacher himself becoming involved in the activity. However, as the child grows, the final product becomes increasingly important to him, and with the increased emphasis being placed on the product itself, thinking in terms of art materials becomes an integral part of the teaching process. It then becomes impossible for a teacher who has never gone through the experience in a specific material to understand the significance of thinking in terms of that material, whether it is wood, clay, pencil, paint, plastic, or any other medium.

An artist would seem to be the most logical person to teach art. It might be simpler if we said that a painter should teach painting, since art encompasses a great number of vocational areas. Most painters are striving to make some sense out of what they have experienced; that is, they try to put some feelings or emotions into a new configuration or try to place some visual matter in a pleasing, or in some cases a shocking, relationship. Each artist has his own point of reference and because of this we find that each artist paints in quite a different way. It is probably true that some artists are striving for recognition and tend to follow any current fad, even if this means making hamburgers out of an old pair of pants, or taking one's book shelf and painting it gold. However, the artist is supposedly attempting to make sense out of our strange and twisted world.

Now this sounds surprisingly like what the child is doing in the elementary school. He too is using himself as a reference point for his artistic creation. He too is trying to make some sense out of his own

environment and is putting things into new relationships. Essentially, then, the child painter and the adult painter are both striving for the same goals, the main difference being that each has his own reference point, or his own experiences to draw upon.

There is no suggestion that a painter would be the best teacher for elementary school children. Nor is there the suggestion that a painter should even help the classroom teacher guide the art experiences of grade school children. There may be some reason to believe that a painter might give some real assistance with a high school class, but even here the evidence is not sufficient. There would seem to be certain qualifications for a person who is going to be working with children in the area of art, qualifications that have nothing to do with his occupation. Essentially, what is needed is a person to give confidence and support to each child in his own mode of expression. The essential ingredient in any artistic creation is the artist himself. This is true at any level. Without the urge to create, the development of self-confidence, the enjoyment and frustration of achieving an end product, the teaching of art becomes a meaningless ritual.

Since there is no body of factual knowledge in art necessary for the child to learn and retain, a painter's technical knowledge is not needed in the elementary school. At the secondary school level this technical knowledge could be valuable. There may be some point in saying that a competent painter might help throw out some of the tricks and busy work that are often called art at both levels. Looking at what galleries are presently exhibiting, the painter would probably cherish and support the spontaneous, free expression of children and look down upon triteness and repetition. However, what might seem spontaneous and free painting by young children might just as easily be random exploration, and as a child grows older he develops a real need for order and repetition, which is reflected in his drawings and paintings. This decrease of spontaneity is actually a step toward the development of abstract thinking, an important factor in creativity. Therefore, a classroom teacher might seem better equipped than an artist to understand the developmental differences. But the education and training of the usual elementary school teacher does not include a real understanding of children's art as a prerequisite to receiving an education degree. In fact, an understanding of the normal development of children's art is often sadly neglected. Instead a new teacher may have several projects up his sleeve for every occasion: Thanksgiving, Christmas, Easter, Mother's Day, or Friday afternoons when he and the children are both tired—projects that have no relation to a live, thinking, feeling child.

Whether or not a person working with young children calls himself an artist or a teacher may be incidental. An artist may be autocratic, know what is important to teach, and be sure what the paintings of children should look like. An elementary school teacher may be like this too. What is needed is an artist or a teacher who is warm, friendly, and democratic, someone who wants to help children develop their own concepts, is generally interested in what children paint, and has no preconceived notions of what each project should be like. The focus should be on developing the sensitive, aware child.

Art has a greater potential in the development of children than is now accorded to it. Until we can shake loose from tradition, until we can stop giving approval to what we, as adults, would like to do, until we can shake ourselves out of the grasp of habit and the *status quo,* we shall assign a meaningless role to art education in the elementary school.

Motivation in the Classroom

One of the most important elements in any art experience is the degree to which children are truly involved in the experience itself. The urge and excitement that children can bring to an art experience is dependent to a great degree upon their motivation. This motivation may come from several sources. In some instances there is a natural drive for expression, which can sometimes be seen in children when they are filled with enthusiasm for a particular topic. At other times it falls upon the shoulders of the classroom teacher to stimulate the interests of the children and to provide such a motivational framework that each child can believe that the art experience was designed especially for him.

It would be quite impossible to say that any one approach to motivation is good for all children. At some times it might be best to have the children divided into interest groups or working on small projects; at another time the children might work with a variety of different materials but on one topic; at another time, children might be working individually on a variety of topics. The approach depends upon individual needs, and a sensitive teacher should be aware of when these differences are important. First grade youngsters often have group experiences, such as visiting a fire station, and often an experience like this may excite a whole class so that everyone wants to put down on paper his reactions to such an experience. However, even here some individuals will become involved in particular parts of this experience. Some boys may be excited about the big fire truck, others about the size of the wheels or length of the hose; whereas girls may be much more interested in the sleeping arrangements, or in the pole that is used to slide down to the waiting truck. Although group motivations can be used effectively, it is still the individual and his mode of expression that is important.

At times the motivation within the classroom can develop an enthusiasm that becomes contagious, and occasionally fifth grade youngsters can develop such enthusiasm over a group project that it seems like the most important event in the world. Probably a variety of approaches best insures that each youngster is free to use his own mode of expression and

Figure 28. *These youngsters have become enthusiastic over the project of decorating the room for a party. Sometimes such art activities can be the most important thing that happens in school.*

at the same time free to reject a suggestion if he already is motivated in another direction. The purpose of motivation is to make the creative process meaningful to the child, not to force a particular topic upon him.

EXTENDING THE FRAME OF REFERENCE

The principle of extending the frame of reference constitutes an important learning device in education. Basically, the principle is to start where the youngster is and extend his thinking, feeling, and perceiving one step farther. This provides the opportunity for an expansion of possible directions in which he can move and which would be a logical extension of his own thinking. If, for instance, a kindergarten child has drawn a picture of his mother and, as is usual, shown this off with pride, it is possible to extend his thinking into the environment in which the mother might find herself. "Where is your mother? Is she all alone? What is she doing?" Needless to say, such questions are aimed at enlarging the experience that the youngster has with the subject matter and are presented with warmth and interest in what has been accomplished. All relationships with youngsters should be supportive.

If Johnny at the fourth grade level draws only airplanes, the important fact is to start with Johnny and his interest in airplanes and to make these meaningful, to make the drawing experience important by extending the child's frame of reference. Again we have to start on the level of the child. If Johnny draws all airplanes alike, it will be a discovery for him to distinguish between big and small planes. "Where does your plane fly? Where does it land? Do you have people in your airplane? Where are they going? How will they get off?" To make the plane and its environment meaningful to the child, the teacher has to identify with the child's needs, which in this case means identifying with his relationships and feelings toward airplanes. In this way it is possible to extend the child's frame of reference from an airplane symbol that may have been repeated many times to an expression with meaningful variety, in which the airplane becomes a flexible part of the youngster's knowledge. In some cases it is possible to involve the youngster in the technical aspects of an airplane, in which case an interest in how a plane actually functions might be more important than a so-called artistic expression. It may also be possible to forget about drawing for a while in order to develop a greater technical knowledge through reading or by having the child actually climb into an airplane and watch its dials and operating mechanism. Sometimes, transferring the interest in airplanes to a different material, from pencil sketches, for instance, to paint, wood, or folded paper can also extend the child's thinking into other art forms. Obviously the command, "Stop drawing those silly airplanes!" will not contribute to the child's greater flexibility and understanding of his environment, but will only make him realize that his own interest and desires cannot be accepted in the framework of the classroom.

To some extent every drawing or painting becomes a natural means of the youngster's extending his own frame of reference. The elements in a drawing tend to be additive, that is, they provide an extension of thinking to related objects which are then combined into a new form. The drawing of a person can often extend into the drawing of the ground, trees, houses, roads, and so forth. It is this relatedness that can sometimes lead youngsters to continue their drawings on the reverse side of the page as though the paper were continuous but folded. It should be

Figure 29. *We cannot expect every child to be thoroughly engrossed in every art activity; however, every child should occasionally be totally involved in some art experience.*

mentioned that a child ought to be in a position to reject any adult effort to get him to include a greater number and variety of objects in his drawing or painting. Every child does not have to be totally involved in every drawing, but every child should sometimes be totally involved in some drawings. We will discuss later how to involve the child who seems continually uninterested in art activities, for it may be this child who most needs the motivation of the teacher.

MOTIVATION AND DEVELOPMENT

A teacher must know the child whom he is trying to motivate. There are certain characteristics of each age that make it different from any other. Not only is it important to realize that what may be an exciting art material for the twelve year old can be a confusing material for the scribbler, but it is also important to realize that at each stage of development the youngster actually has a different relationship to his environment. The interest that a high school youngster may have in the structural design of a building will not be shared by a first grade youngster even though this topic is of interest to the teacher. The pleasure that a junior high school youngster may get from making a poster protesting new dress regulations in his school will obviously not be shared by a third grade boy who gets great pleasure from close examination of a caterpillar. To identify with the needs of a particular youngster may not always be easy, but it is important that the teacher subordinate himself and his desires to the needs of the children with whom he is working.

A child who is scribbling at the age of four may begin to name some of the parts of his picture and relate this to objects outside himself. Lines may move up and down across the page and the child may identify this as a dog running. The youngster has made a big discovery: that the motions of running are similar to the up-and-down line that he can see on the page. A sensitive and aware teacher must understand that this can be a satisfying experience, identify himself with the youngster, and share in the discovery. This line is of kinesthetic origin and it would be ridiculous for the teacher to try to motivate the child with visual imagery. To talk about a dog in visual terms, discussing his color and size and the proportion of the head to the body, would be meaningless. The well-intentioned teacher may seize upon this discovery as a chance to show the child pictures and illustrations of dogs, and may even try to point out the differences between breeds of dogs. But this will all be wasted effort because the teacher has not made himself acquainted with the physical and psychological needs of the child.

Not only is it necessary for the teacher to identify with the general needs of a youngster, but he must also be able to discover the specific needs of a particular individual. He may find out that one child lacks freedom in his motions and feels inhibited in his motor activity. Another child may appear particularly timid and fearful of using materials. Still another child may have a very short attention span and never get truly involved in the art process. It is important that the child's general as well as specific needs are understood, for without this background the teacher may never really reach the child with his motivation.

MOTIVATION AND THE INSECURE CHILD

Most of the children in our classrooms are free and willing to express themselves in art activities. Occasionally, however, we find a child who is so insecure that he has a fear of even putting a line on a page unless it is given prior approval by the teacher. These children often express the feeling that they cannot draw, or that they do not know how to do it; often they want the teacher to show them how or draw something for them. Obviously, these are the children who need the art experience the most; to ignore this plea for help or simply to say that the youngster really *can* draw is no motivation whatever. If a child says to the teacher that he cannot bring himself to express his feelings or emotions on paper, it is obvious that this is a statement which should not be contradicted. There may be children who go through life so withdrawn from their own world that they feel at a loss unless they are given clear guidance and direction. This reliance upon adults can in some instances have a very negative influence upon the youngster's thinking; in other cases the child may have been rebuffed by his own attempts at self-direction and may retreat into a world in which his sensitivities and emotions will not be hurt further.

Sometimes a child will have difficulty in identifying with what he does. Usually such a child laughs nervously and self-consciously about his own products, for he is continually dissatisfied with his achievement. For this child the end product itself has become so important that he has to please others or himself. His own experience is less important to him than the product itself. The loss of confidence in one's own ability is seen in the method by which the youngster approaches the art experience. The final product is only the result of the process, which is a complex learning experience that brings together the thinking, emotional, and perceptual processes resulting from preceding experiences. If the child cannot identify with his own experiences, the final product will show this.

A third grade boy who says, "I can't draw" knows he cannot draw. "What can't you draw?" Perhaps he cannot draw a camel because he has never seen one, which would be quite understandable. But often the problem is deeper than that. "What do you want to draw?" If this third grade youngster says that he does not want to draw anything, then the teacher must find out what experience has been meaningful to him, or in some cases sensitize him to experiences he has had so that these can become meaningful. "What did you do yesterday?" The problem is one of making the youngster more actively aware of himself as part of the environment, and of stimulating this awareness. Some youngsters actually feel that they have done nothing interesting and can go through life partially sealed off from the outside world.

Figure 30. *Most children are anxious to paint, but occasionally a child will passively put color on the paper in an uninvolved manner. Then the teacher must actively involve the child in his own experiences.*

"What did you do yesterday? Did you just stand up all day? What did you do? Remember, remember exactly where you were yesterday afternoon. Oh, you had to work around the house. What did you do? Oh, you helped wash the car. Was your father with you?" Now here is something definite to talk about. The child has indeed had some experiences that you can discuss and share. Although to him this may be just another boring day, the washing of the car can be a focal point for a discussion that needs to be carried on with warmth and interest on the part of the teacher. It is important that all of the senses be involved in such a discussion so that the youngster can relive the experience in even more detail than he experienced this originally. "Did you take the car to one of those car wash places? Oh, you washed it at home. Was it very dirty? Did you use a hose? Oh, you used a bucket and a sponge. Was the water cold? Did you get yourself wet? Was the car so dirty that you had to change the water? Did you draw any pictures on the dirt before you washed it? Did your hands get all puffy from the water? Did your back ache when you were through? Did you have to change your clothes after it was finished? Let me see your hands—I can see that your fingernails are clean, you must have gotten them well soaked. Did your father do very much? Did the bucket of water spill? Were your feet cold when they got wet? Did the car look better when you were finished?"

The particular motivation will vary depending upon the age of the child. The younger child will need more physical stimulation, and sometimes with young children it is a help to have them go through the motions of how they washed the hubcaps. The older child will be able to identify more with the father and share with him the pride of having a clean car. In any case, it is important to make this motivation meaningful to the youngster himself and to stimulate the sensory experiences, what he has seen and felt, as well as stressing his own contributions to the activity.

Although we do not have many very insecure children in our classrooms, it is of vital importance that children who are completely bound up in themselves and have difficulty interacting in any meaningful way with their environment be given special attention in art. This is one area of the school program that can truly be based upon the youngster's own experiences, and any motivation should be of such a nature that it provides the opportunity for a flexible, meaningful growth.

Numerous experiments have been done to assess the effectiveness of various motivational methods upon children's drawings. There is no doubt that the intensity and personal involvement of the motivation plays a most important part in the quality of an art product (McVitty, 1954; Lansing, 1956; Clements, 1964). To a great extent there is a parallel development between the quality of experience that the youngster is try-

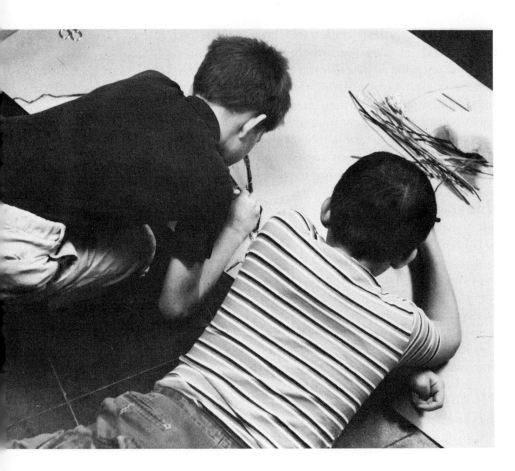

Figure 31. *The motivation for art should not always have to come from the teacher. Often youngsters have projects of their own that merely need to have a place to happen.*

ing to portray and the quality of the final product. The higher the quality of the one, the higher the quality of the other. The motivation is a vital part of this process.

Integrated Learning Experiences

Too often within the school learning program, experiences are isolated. At 9:27 the arithmetic books come out, at 10:14 it is time for recess, at 10:23 the music teacher arrives, at 11:05 it is social studies time. This fragmentation of the learning process into isolated segments creates an artificial situation. A child does not grow in single subject matter areas, nor does each area remain isolated in life outside school. This early specialization has isolated some of the subject matter areas from life to such a degree that the subjects have lost contact with society. We can even see this at the upper levels of education, where there is great discrepancy between social and scientific achievement.

Sometimes art is used as a means of correcting this difficulty, usually with superficial results. Integration in learning means that the single subjects lose their identity and form a new integrated unit within the student. Teachers often think that if history is illustrated an integration between these two subjects takes place. This is sometimes referred to as correlation, as, for instance, where the students may be studying the American Indian in social studies and drawing wigwams in art. Sometimes this is successful. When third graders draw a picture before they are instructed to write something they produce an increased amount of work (Cecere, 1966). All too often, however, an injustice is done to both areas. Because art is usually looked upon by the child as an attractive experience, and some of the social studies, arithmetic, or writing exercises are less favorably viewed, the correlation of these subject matter areas with art may have a negative value for the art experience. It is a little like mixing medicine with orange juice—both can be rejected.

It is possible that an integrated experience can develop from a school setting, but the separate parts must lose their identity and the individual child must feel that there is a meaningful whole with which he can identify. Integration occurs within the individual. The child is influenced by his emotional responses and perceptual sensory experiences. If the youngster can become totally involved in the learning process, then real integration takes place.

For example, history is often taught only in terms of dates and events. The Pilgrims landed in 1620. Plymouth Rock is somehow important in the event, and a ship called the *Mayflower* was there, too. A request for children to draw this event is a meaningless activity. On the other hand, if children can empathize with the experience itself and focus upon this involvement, the activity can be a meaningful one.

"Have you ever been on a boat? On what kind of a boat? Were you ever in rough water? How did it feel? Do you know how big the *Mayflower* was? That's really pretty small! Did you realize that they had to come all that distance by relying on sails? How many sails were there? Do you know what happens when it is windy? The boat tilts way over and where do you go? Yes, all the people have to go to the other side! Do you get wet? Do you think you would like to stay down below deck? Do you know how long the Pilgrims were on this little sailing ship? That's a long time! Just suppose you had been on that ship all that time! Then you finally see land! Is everyone anxious to get off the ship? Are there any docks built? Oh, you have to get into a little rowboat! How do you go over the side? Hold on, don't slip on the way down! We still have to row to shore! Stay all together! What shall we do when we first land? Build a fire? So we can all keep warm!"

The children must feel the air and the waves, and even taste the salt on their lips. The experience must be their experience. The Pilgrims are no longer figures marching across the history book, but are re-created in the child's own experience. The picture that may result from such an experience can be anything that is of particular interest to the child. It may be the motion of the ship itself, with lines going up and down, or it may be the portrayal of a particular incident with which the child particularly identifies. Meaningful integration occurs in the youngster through such a motivation in which an atmosphere is created that is conducive to self-identification and self-involvement. To have the child involved in the learning process and to make these isolated subject matter segments important to him must be an important goal for the teacher. The art experiences that the youngster has had can provide the means of accomplishing this. To some extent, then, art can be the core of the learning environment within the school. Integration does not happen by merely shuffling subject matter around—such integration can take place only through the child himself.

The Importance of the Art Product

For the child the value in an art experience is in the process. A discussion of the art product must be primarily concerned with the experience that motivated a child's picture rather than with the picture itself. Yet the product itself, whether it be a painting, a construction, or a drawing, does have great importance. How the drawing looks is unimportant for the four year old, and the child usually will not recognize his own drawing the following day. On the other hand, the high school student may be actively aware of what his product looks like and concerned that it portray the intentions that he was trying to express. However, our primary concern here is the importance of the art product for the teacher.

In studying the creative products of children, we must first of all consider the purpose in doing so. There are different reasons for examining a child's drawings. Too often this is done solely for the purpose of evaluation, showing him his strengths and weaknesses, his skill or lack of skill, and his degree of artistic ability—in other words, to classify him. On the other hand, a child's drawings may be valuable for the purpose of gaining insight into his growth, understanding his emotions, getting a feeling for his problems, interests, and experiences. If our purpose is only to classify the child, this had better be left undone. Classification has no educational value, and to say that this child has weaknesses or that that one has strengths, based upon one teacher's opinion, helps neither the child nor the teacher. If the purpose is to understand the child and to give him support for his expression, to find out how we can involve him more fully in life, then it is a legitimate one for teachers.

One important factor to be kept in mind is that creative work must be understood individually. We can only appreciate the significance of creative work by understanding the child and seeing his picture as part of his life. For example, it may happen that a child portrays an emotional event that has great significance to him, such as a fire that has burned down his house, or an accident in which he was involved. To the adult these may be ordinary paintings; they may even be ugly from an aesthetic point of view. Yet the work produced may be an important resolution within the child's own life, and to direct attention only to the painting and to be concerned only with technical abilities would be an injustice. It is also true that an insignificant and timidly executed work may provide insight for the teacher so that he can plan activities that will give the child the opportunity to develop confidence in his expression. Each art work must be considered on its own basis, and this is true for all levels of teaching.

The understanding of children's creative works does not only differ from one individual to another; great differences can be seen from one stage of development to another. An experience that is meaningful to a child of twelve may be meaningless to a child of seven. It is not the content that becomes the important consideration in children's drawings, but the way in which youngsters portray this content. A child will draw and paint from what he is. His feelings, desires, thoughts, his explorations with paint and subject matter will all appear in the painting. Particularly a young child, but to some degree everyone, paints in a direct manner with no thought of hiding or concealing true feelings. Some psychiatrists use art as a major way of diagnosing neuroses, and interpretations are often made of the drawings and paintings of individuals under psychiatric care. But most teachers are not in a position to make inferences from children's drawings, and it is far better to look at drawings as examples of classroom work than it is to make conclusions based upon a limited understanding of the field.

Sometimes children's drawings are analyzed by individuals with little or no background in understanding children's art; the results would be quite funny if these people were not sometimes taken seriously. Often what happens is that the individual will see forms or shapes in children's drawings that have meaning to the person looking at the drawings,

Figure 32. *The product assumes greater importance for the fifth grade child, and he enjoys the chance to experiment with a new medium, such as printing. As the experience progresses, new possibilities become apparent and the product can grow in unforeseen ways.*

Figure 33. *An adult might see this second grader's drawing as being full of aggression, with a large axe form, a hanging child, and a youngster shielding his eyes. Actually, it is a drawing of favorite activities, such as climbing a rope and riding a bicycle, with only the necessary parts of the tree shown. The child's regular schema for a man did not provide two hands for riding the bicycle, so one arm extends over the head to the other handlebar.*

though not to the child who painted them. To some extent, then, we get a better understanding of the person making these interpretations than we do of the child who made the picture.

For most teachers, however, the painting or drawing is not looked upon as being anything other than a painting or drawing. But a difficulty sometimes arises when some standard of quality is placed upon this work. These standards, which are based upon arbitrary aesthetic criteria, attempt to label these paintings as good or bad with little if any understanding of the process that gave rise to the picture itself. The use of these standards can lead to grading or giving a youngster a mark for art.

GRADING THE CHILD'S ART

Probably no child has ever failed a grade because of his poor marks in art. One often finds, however, that marks are required in art for report cards at various times. These report cards may take many forms, such as a letter to parents; at other times the grade is actually a numerical score, which is supposed to show the percentage of achievement in art. The usual practice is to use some sort of external standard, but this deals only with the product and completely neglects the individual child or the effect that the creative process has had on him. At the high school level, each project may be graded and the teacher goes through the process of averaging the grades, which may make it sound somewhat more objective.

This is probably not the place to question the value of giving any grades to children, but it is important to state that grading in art has no function. This is particularly true in the elementary school, where the youngster has no conscious awareness of making art in any manner other than that which is natural to him. At this level it would make more sense to grade the teacher, for it is the teacher who has been able to motivate the children to do excellent work, or has not been able to motivate some youngsters, or who may have failed to involve a few youngsters at all in the art activities.

Unfortunately, many teachers do try to grade art, which throws added importance upon the end product. This is harmful to the child because it turns his attention away from creating to concern for the picture itself. It can be particularly discouraging for a youngster who is beginning to find himself in his creative activity if he fails in the art work that he has been doing.

Often the grading system is decided by a teacher who puts a high mark on the works of art that he himself enjoys, and will grade other works of art lower on the same arbitrary basis. Neatness and fine line control are frequently important in such a grading system, so that the youngster who paints more freely and who is bolder in his drawing tends to be penalized. Sometimes, of course, a teacher who is very aware of trends in contemporary art may reward children who accidentally produce the type of art that is currently in vogue. Both methods are equally meaningless to the child.

There should be one place in the school system where marks do not count. The art room should be a sanctuary against the school system, where each youngster is free to be himself and to put down his feelings and emotions without censorship, where he can evaluate his own progress toward his own goals without the imposition of an arbitrary grading system.

EXHIBITS AND COMPETITIONS

Exhibits in the classroom are usually held for the children. A youngster enjoys seeing his own work displayed, and for some children this becomes particularly important. The child who is not able to achieve in other ways can see himself as a member of the class in good standing when his art products are displayed with everyone else's. Generally, the work to be displayed should be selected by the child himself. The preparation for an exhibit can often be an exciting occasion, and when properly guided, children can take over most of the work of hanging the pictures. Classroom exhibits should be frequently changed, for a youngster quickly loses the intimate relationship to his own work, and it is senseless to display work that was done weeks or even months earlier.

An exhibit for parents may be a different problem. Here the reason for the exhibit should be clear. Often the purpose is to educate the viewer rather than to display pictures for parents to admire. It is possible to combine these two functions, but such exhibits take a good deal of planning. Often carefully lettered signs help in conveying the message; a carefully labeled exhibit will be able to explain itself. It is better to have a small exhibit stressing one theme such as individual differences, the variety in expression of a particular topic, developmental differences from a variety of ages, or a sequence of drawings showing changes in development, than to have an exhibit that is too large to be easily seen and that may be too hastily put together.

Competition in art is of two types. Natural competition is inherent in every classroom situation, where a youngster has a natural desire to improve upon his own achievements. Forced competition is usually imposed upon a class or a group of children, and prizes are often given as rewards. Growth is a continuous competition with one's own standards

Figure 34. *The stimulation children receive from one another can contribute to a creative atmosphere. This sharing of thoughts and enthusiasm is quite different from copying from one another.*

and achievements, and this is a most natural and healthy form of competition. Children in the lower elementary grades are usually unaware of any competition in art, for their drawings and paintings are merely a means of expression. Each child differs from his classmates, and usually there is no feeling that one drawing or painting is better than another. The situation changes somewhat as the child grows older and as the final product becomes more and more important. In the upper grades of the elementary school the stimulation children receive from each other's creative work is a valuable contribution to their own flexibility. The youngster is usually exposed to many different styles and modes of expression. These he can evaluate in terms of his own experiences, and reject or adapt them as he chooses. Such natural competition is not based on standards outside the youngster himself. This sharing of ideas is not to be confused with a copying of forms by the insecure child, where the problem is quite different because the youngster is copying a configuration without any understanding of the process behind it.

Plate 1. *"Cow," drawn by a four year old girl. A naturalistic representation is not important to the child; rather, this picture represents her concept of a cow. She has drawn the face as she would a human face. The large number of legs is probably due to the child's realization that the cow has more legs than a person, and not to a knowledge of the actual number of legs a cow has.*

Plate 2. *"Mommy and Daddy," painted by a four year old child who has just left the scribbling stage. There is no relationship between the colors the child uses for Mommy and Daddy and their actual physical appearance: that is, unless Mommy is an Indian and Daddy is a Martian. The entire mode of representation is quite rudimentary; heads are indicated by circles, and household objects appear as ambiguous shapes.*

Occasionally forced competition is unwittingly brought into the classroom. Sometimes the teacher himself may state that the best pictures will be saved for an exhibit, or sometimes the local P.T.A. or chamber of commerce will offer a prize in a good-hearted manner to the best picture illustrating how our town can be made more beautiful. Michael (1959) found in an experiment with high school art students that giving a prize for the best painting significantly decreased the aesthetic quality of students' work. A judge of an annual competition of children's art said that each year some children copied the winner of the preceding year in the hope that they would be awarded a prize too. To a great extent, this type of competition is bad for the winner and the loser. The losers know that they do not have the artistic ability to achieve and they therefore lose interest in art expression. The winner has achieved recognition in art and therefore loses the incentive to investigate and explore other means of art expression. Some schools pride themselves on the number of prizes that their high school has won in various art exhibits. The results tend to be superficial, with a stress on techniques and an overemphasis on outcome. All this overpowers serious involvement by the youth with his own creative experiences. No jury can take into consideration the meaningfulness of an art work to its creator. Even on the adult level the winner of a competition may not be looked upon as a great artist ten years later. Such forced competition has no place in our school system.

Child art is highly individual. No two children express themselves entirely alike. One of the vital aims of art education is to bring out the individual differences that make up each child's personality. To suppress these individual differences, to emphasize the final product, to reward one youngster over another, goes against the basic premises of creative expression.

The Importance of Materials and Skills

The proper materials and the development of skills play an important part in the expression of art. It is only through the use of the art material that any expression can evolve. Just as words are important in verbal communication and the structure of sentences and paragraphs are important in written work, in art the artist must develop the skills and techniques necessary to communicate, and he must have an understanding of the materials that he is using in order to be able to utilize their intrinsic qualities.

Important as skills and techniques may be, however, they must always remain the means to an end and never become ends in themselves. It is not the skills that are expressed, but the feelings and emotions of the artist. To concentrate only upon the materials that are used in art, or upon developing particular skills to utilize in an art expression, ignores the fundamental issue, which is that the art springs from human beings and not from materials. Exercises in penmanship were once popular in our school systems, and children would spend a considerable length of time making neat ovals or copying from meaningless poems so as to perfect their writing abilities. This is no longer true, and a great deal more concern is voiced over the fact that youngsters need to develop a will to express and a need to utilize the written word before these exercises can become meaningful. Even then the proper writing method is no longer based upon some arbitrary standards.

In art the same factors hold true. The mere understanding of the differences between art materials, and the development of particular skills will avail the child nothing unless the need and urge for expression is there first. The expression of the self, the urge to put down experiences that are meaningful, the desire to put into artistic form the frustrations or joys of life must all be present before skills can be developed. The teaching of this expression is the crux of an art education program; the mechanics of art are secondary and can be explained simply when the demand for this knowledge comes from the youngster. Once the desire for expression is awakened the urge for greater knowledge about the use of materials will follow.

Figure 35. *The procedures in working with new materials should be explained briefly. Even in working in the woodshop youngsters are much more anxious to do than to learn how to do.*

TECHNIQUES AND PROCEDURES

Often an artist's work is recognized by the particular technique that he uses. This is often an unconscious approach to the use of materials and is highly individual. With children this can also be true. Some youngsters will paint boldly with a great deal of spontaneity, whereas other children will be more concerned with detail and may concentrate on the outline of the forms they are making. A technique develops according to the individual's own needs. A procedure, on the other hand, consists of the different steps necessary in using a specific material. There are, for example, general procedures in making an etching. These are the preparation of the plate and the acid used for etching, the methods of controlling the etching process, the ways in which the ink is applied to the plate, and so forth. These procedures can be explained to students, and it is often necessary to develop considerable experience before the procedures become so automatic that etching can be used for expression. Needless to say, a procedure such as this would be too complex for children.

Any material that is used with children must fit their needs for expression. The procedure in using these materials can often be discovered by the children themselves, but occasionally simple explanations or demonstrations of certain procedures may facilitate the use and care of art materials. For example, ten year old children will find pleasure in a discussion of a variety of ways that tempera paint can be used. Colors can be mixed either in a tray or directly on the page, colors will mix on the painting if the undercolor is still wet but not if the undercolor has dried, paint has a different quality depending on whether it is thick or mixed with water; these suggestions may open other possibilities to the ten year old. The facts that brushes store better with the handle down, that jar tops must be tight so that the paint will not evaporate are also part of the painting procedures. Much of this is not particularly appropriate to the nursery school child, who needs the paint thick so that it does not run down the paper in uncontrolled mistakes, and the tightening of his jar lids is probably best done by the teacher. A sensitive teacher can constantly take clues from his children as to when particular procedures would be valuable to discuss or when these children would benefit from finding other ways of using familiar materials.

ART MATERIALS AND DEVELOPMENTAL STAGES

There is an almost unlimited range of materials that can be used for art. Some of these are the traditional materials such as pencils, clay, paint, and so forth. Then there are other materials that are often used for art although their main purpose is for some other function. These include wood, collage materials, and plaster. A third category might include materials that are unrelated to art but which sometimes have a unique contribution to make and can be utilized in various ways in art experiences. These include such things as broken bottles, rusty tin cans, and pieces of discarded pipe.

Artists, seeing beauty or a message in almost any material, have given the impression that anything can be used for art expression. However, when working with children, materials are not sought out for their unique characteristics or the qualities that make them particularly expressive for the professional artist. Rather, the youngster sees these materials as being what art is all about, in somewhat the same way as he accepts a pencil to write with and a book to read. Therefore, much harm can be done to a child unless his developmental level is taken into consideration in the selection of the materials he is to use for art expression.

Let us look, for example, at watercolor as one art material. Watercolor is transparent, it has a flowing, merging quality, it mixes easily and can be made into fine gradations. Watercolor also changes easily in its characteristics, and it has a vibrating quality that lends itself to atmospheric effects. This material would be used quite differently by a scribbling child, a child of eight years of age, a youngster of twelve, or a sixteen year old.

A three year old who is scribbling would have real difficulty with watercolor. Because scribbling is primarily a motor activity he would quickly become discouraged and frustrated. If he scribbled with watercolor, the lines he produced with the wet brush would have to be interrupted frequently, as he would need to dip his brush into the water and paint. As he continued to scribble, his paper would fill with brush strokes and the lines would run into one another, merging into a blur, into an indistinguishable mass of colors in which kinesthetic sensation and the child's urge for control would become invisible. For a child who is beginning to name his scribbles this blurred mess would be frustrating.

An eight year old child has developed symbols that he repeats, which signify the order that he has developed within his environment. This structuring is important in that it indicates the development of abstract thinking. He paints objects definite colors, such as green for grass and trees and bushes. He knows that these objects are green and continues to paint them this way with satisfaction. Differences in light or shadows do not influence these colors, and the unintentional shading or running of colors will interfere with his satisfaction. These unintentional changes are meaningless and only frustrate him in his desire for mastery. An accident cannot be repeated and an unintentional change is a mistake.

What often seems of aesthetic quality to adults would mean a spoiled picture to an eight year old child.

A child of twelve years has found himself as a member of society and a part of the environment in which he lives. He may still be a member of a gang, and he loves to discover new things, and to read fantastic stories. He enjoys the opportunity to experiment, and what formerly appeared as an accident in painting might now be considered stimulating. The flowing, merging quality of watercolor is well suited to this age, and the youngster may experiment with the accidents that occur when wet paint runs on the paper and merges with other colors in unexpected beauty. A colorful sky will be made more so by the introduction of reds and greens which can be quite dramatic.

A sixteen year old has become much more critical of himself and the work he produces. Usually he will have definite intentions about what he wants to produce; in some cases the changing effects of distance and atmosphere will be the primary intent, in which case watercolor may be an excellent medium. Another student may not find the same interest in portraying nature, but may want definite concepts expressed in flat tones. Watercolor may be an obstacle to this kind of expression. Not all students will have the desire to use watercolor. For some it may be frustrating, but for others it may be an excellent art material.

The teacher should know the variety of choices available in art materials and introduce them at the appropriate time. Every material must make its own contribution, and if a task can be done more easily by using something different, then the wrong art material has been used originally. The teacher should know that every child must develop his own technique and that any help from the teacher can only be valuable if it provides the opportunity for greater awareness and greater flexibility. The procedures in using materials should be kept to a minimum. Often several materials can be used at one time within a classroom, and this provides an opportunity to develop various possible approaches to expression. It is not the material itself that needs emphasis, for art materials must be seen as avenues for expression and not as ends in themselves.

SOME COMMENTS ABOUT ART MATERIALS

Certain mechanical, routine methods of handling art materials make the art program much more effective. Children at all levels can take a great deal of responsibility for their own art materials. Occasionally a teacher will become so involved with the distribution and cleaning-up processes that he has little time to stimulate the children to depth of expression. Having children take over some of this responsibility not only frees the teacher from the routine of passing out paper, distributing scissors, and cleaning up paintbrushes, but it also provides an opportunity for children to become more aware of an art activity as a total experience that is primarily theirs. A violin virtuoso handles his violin like something sacred not only because it is of material value, but because it is the means by which he can express himself. A true artist develops a kinship to materials, and some of these feelings can certainly be developed within children.

Some materials should be placed where children can obtain them freely. Spontaneous drawing or painting should be encouraged, and the paper, crayons, or paints should be readily accessible not only for the kindergarten child but for all children through secondary school. The older child should be able to gather and put back materials without supervision. Although art materials in daily use should be left within easy reach of children, certain materials should be stored out of sight. These are not necessarily the expensive materials but rather those that can have special meaning at special times (styrofoam balls for mobiles, shiny paper for Christmas decorations) and those that are potentially dangerous (large glass jars, thin strands of wire, sets of cutting knives).

In no instance should the lack of materials stand in the way of a good art program. This is not to say that such basic materials as clay, tempera paint, and paper can be dispensed with. What is meant is that adding

Figure 36. *Easels, oil paints, expensive brushes, or other costly materials do not make an art program. Sometimes the floor and large white paper can be just as effective as more costly materials.*

sheets of copper foil, gummed paper, clay glazes, and cans of spray paint do not in themselves insure a good art program. Often children can provide many inexpensive or free materials, such as old newspapers for making papier-mâché, cloth for making collages or banners, boxes for making animals or dragons, and bottle caps and straws for making decorations. The art materials are important to an art program, but they play a secondary role; the materials are not as important as the way in which they are used. Because children of each developmental level have different needs and different capacities for using various media, specific suggestions for art materials will be included in following chapters.

A vital part of any art motivation is the moment of tension before the transition into expression. If this gets lost, we lose an important part of the creative atmosphere. A child who is stimulated in terms of shopping in the grocery store, and who is eager to portray his feelings about the canned goods stacked way above his head, the smell of the produce, or the excitement of picking out his favorite cookies, should not have to wait for six children in front of him to pass the paper back before he can get started. The materials should be ready for immediate use once the child is ready for them. Sometimes if the presence of the material would be a distraction, children can be gathered in a circle in a different part of the room for a discussion.

Although children should be given the feeling for the quality and wealth "buried" in every bit of material, no undue concern should be shown if the child uses this material in unexpected ways. If a second grader crumples his sheet of paper, do not condemn him to inactivity. A question like "Didn't you like that piece of paper?" may be better than trying to condemn his actions, and the child himself may not be able to understand why he felt like crumpling paper. A material like clay might be more appropriate, for it can be twisted and crushed without destroying the material itself. Every material should be thought of as meeting the needs of children and not as dictating a particular type of art lesson.

RELATED ACTIVITIES

1. Collect the drawings from an elementary school class. Ask a teacher, an art teacher, a college student, and a child to grade these drawings, as for a report card. Ask how these judges determined the best and poorest. How do the various ratings compare? Which, if any, seems to be the most valid approach? How does this compare with the discussion in the section "Grading the Child's Art"?

2. Plan and display an exhibit of children's art work with a definite purpose. Organize the exhibit so that it presents a feeling of unity. Identify and label the specific age, grade level, medium, and subject matter or motivation.

3. Observe two separate classrooms of the same grade. Predict on the basis of the teacher's interest and enthusiasm in art activities how the products will differ. Collect drawings from these classrooms on two occasions and compare. Note differences in amount of detail, color use, amount of action indicated, and extent to which the total area of the page is used.

4. Make a survey to determine what competitions are presently being sponsored in a local school in music, art, and so forth. Gather information from teachers and students and discuss the effects of these competitions upon the classroom behavior, the time consumed, and the results of the competitions.

5. Check to find an elementary school that divides its classes according to achievement levels. Compare the drawings of children in the "fast" classes with those in the "slow" classes. Are there any differences in method of representation? In the number of details used?

6. Pick out one child who does not appear gifted in art. Over a period of several months give special attention to his art performances. Show an interest in his products, encourage him, praise changes in his expression, exhibit his paintings, show him you enjoy what and how he draws, give him confidence to explore new materials, ask him if he would like to be an artist. After the experimental period is over compare his products with those done previously. Do you still consider him not particularly gifted?

The Beginnings of Self-expression: The Scribbling Stage, 2-4 Years

4

The Importance of Early Childhood

The first few years of life are probably the most vital in a child's development. It is during this period that he begins to establish learning patterns, attitudes, and a sense of himself as a being, all of which will color his entire life. Art can contribute a tremendous amount to this development, for it is in the interaction between the child and his environment that learning takes place. Although we usually think of art as starting with the first mark that a child puts down on paper, it actually begins much earlier when the senses first contact the environment and the child reacts to these sensory experiences. Touching, feeling, seeing,

Figure 37. *Although the early marks that children make on paper may not make much sense to adults, these scribbles are an important part of growth and need encouragement. Touching, feeling, and manipulating the art materials is learning in itself.*

manipulating, tasting, listening, in fact any method of perceiving and reacting to the environment is essentially background for the production of art forms, whether it is on a child's level or on that of a professional artist.

Although the child expresses himself vocally very early in life, his first permanent record usually takes the form of a scribble at about the age of eighteen months or so. This first mark is an important step in his development, for it is the beginning of expression which leads not only to drawing and painting but also to the written word. The way these first marks are welcomed may have great importance to his continued growth. It is unfortunate that the very word "scribble" has negative connotations for adults. The word may suggest a waste of time or at least a lack of content. Actually the very opposite may be true, for the way in which these first marks are received and the attention that is paid to them may cause a young child to develop attitudes that will remain with him as he starts his formal schooling.

The Development of Scribbling

Scribbles tend to follow a fairly predictable order. They start with random marks on a paper and gradually evolve into drawings that have content recognizable to adults. But between the ages of about eighteen months and about four years, when the first visual image appears, a great deal of development takes place. It is rather surprising, therefore, to find that comparatively little research has been done on these early drawing attempts. Generally speaking, scribbles fall into three main categories. These are disordered scribbles, controlled scribbles, and named scribbles.

DISORDERED SCRIBBLING

The first marks are usually random, and the child does not seem to realize that he can make these do what he wants. They vary in length and direction, although there may be some repetition as the child swings his arm back and forth. Often a child may look away while he is making these marks, and still continue scribbling. The line quality often varies considerably with somewhat accidental results. A typical disordered scribble is shown in Figure 38. Various methods are used to hold the crayon or pencil. The crayon may be held upside down or sideways, it may be grasped in the fist or held between clenched fingers. The fingers and wrist are not used to control the drawing instrument. It is important to realize that the size of the motions shown on the paper is relative to the size of the child. If an adult swung his arm back and forth, he would cover an arc of about three feet; a child would tend to draw an arc only about twelve inches long. Because scribblers have not yet developed fine muscle control, usually only the larger sweeps will be repeated. We have to remember that the child scribbles with what are big motions for him, although to an adult the result may appear to be on a small scale.

The two year old typically cannot copy a circle, although some two year olds are able to copy a line. It is important to mention that scribbles are not attempts at portraying the visual environment. To a great extent the scribbles themselves are based upon the physical and psychological

Figure 38. *This disordered scribble was made by a two and a half year old child. Notice how the lines go in random directions.*

development of the child, not upon some representational intent. The haphazard array of lines that he makes, however, is extremely enjoyable for him. A child will be fascinated with this activity and enjoy these marks both as motions and as a record of a kinesthetic activity. It is very important that he have the opportunity to scribble. Sometimes scribbling will be done in the dirt, on the walls, or on furniture if the proper tools and place are not provided.

Parents may try to find something in these early scribbles that they can recognize, or sometimes a well-meaning grandparent will attempt to draw something for the child to copy. While a child is still in the state of disordered scribbling, drawing a picture of something "real" is inconceivable. Such attempts would be similar to trying to teach a babbling baby to pronounce words correctly or to use them in sentences. Rarely would a parent ask a babbling child to repeat the Gettysburg Address, even though this may become important to a child when he reaches fifth grade. The stick figure or apple drawn by an encouraging parent can be just as ridiculous. Such imposed ideas are far beyond the ability of a child at this developmental level and may even be harmful to his future development. However, an interest in what the child is doing is important, because the child has to feel that this avenue of communication is an acceptable one.

The child at this age has no visual control over his scribbling, which parents should regard as an indication that he is not yet ready to perform tasks that require fine motor control over his movements. He is going to be a sloppy eater; he is going to have trouble with his buttons; and he will not be able to follow visual directions. As long as the child has not established visual control over his scribbling motions it is senseless to require him to have control over other activities.

A very young child may find a crayon more interesting to look at, feel, or even taste. However, the two year old usually has no such problems, and scribbling activity quickly becomes a real means of expression, one of the first other than crying. All children begin with scribbling, whether they are Chinese or Eskimos, Americans or Europeans (Kellogg, 1967). It is quite apparent that scribbling is a natural part of the total development of children which reflects their physiological and psychological growth.

CONTROLLED SCRIBBLING

At some time a child will discover that there is a connection between his motions and the marks on the paper. This may occur about six months or so after he has started to scribble. This is a very important step, because now the child has discovered visual control over the marks he is making. Although a casual glance may show no difference in the drawings themselves, gaining control over the motion is a vital experience for the child.

Most children approach scribbling at this stage with a great deal of enthusiasm, because this coordination between their visual and motor development is a very important achievement. Enjoyment of this new discovery stimulates the child to vary his motions. Now the lines may be repeated, as they are in Figure 39, and sometimes they are drawn with a great deal of vigor. These lines may be drawn horizontally, vertically,

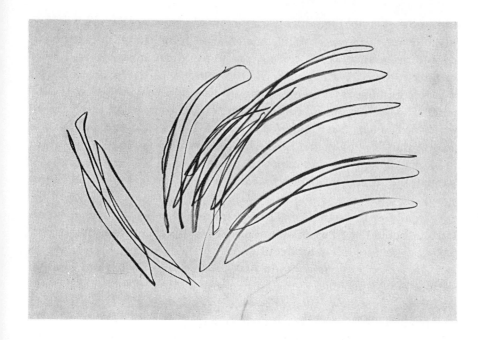

or in circles (see Figure 40). Rarely do we find dots or small repeated patterns, because this means the child would have to take his crayons off the page. Children can become very engrossed in scribbling, as the girl is in Figures 41, 42, and 43, sometimes with their noses practically glued to the paper.

Figure 40. *This controlled scribble shows a repeated circular pattern. It was made by a three year old child.*

Figures 41–43. *Scribbling is a serious, meaningful activity for young children. Notice the determination and concentration that have gone into this drawing.*

The child will now spend about twice as long drawing and occasionally likes to try different colors on his paper. Also he often likes to fill the page, while earlier he even had trouble staying on the paper itself. He still experiments with a variety of methods of holding his crayon, though by the time he is three he usually comes close to an adult grip. He now understands more about trying to copy a line or a cross, but he will not refer to the model given him and usually strikes off in an unpredictable direction. By the age of three he can copy a circle but not a square (Holladay, 1966).

The scribblings now become much more elaborate and often the child will excitedly discover a relationship between what he has drawn and something in his environment. There may still be very little relationship between what he has drawn and a visual representation of the subject to which he refers.

This control over the scribble is also reflected in the child's control over other parts of his environment. The mother who, six months earlier, could not get this child to button his jacket now finds that he insists on doing it for himself. The child understands and enjoys the practice of this new ability. Because the control over his motor abilities is an important achievement, we can certainly understand that calling attention to interesting patterns in a child's drawing would not be particularly helpful; at this stage the child's intentions do not go beyond the movement of his crayon, and his enjoyment is essentially from the kinesthetic sensation and its mastery.

The adult's role is increasingly important now, because children will often run to an adult with these scribbles, eager to share their excitement. It is this sharing of an experience that is important and not the scribble itself.

THE NAMING OF SCRIBBLING

This next step is an important one in the development of children. This is the point when the child starts to name his scribbles. He may say, "This is mother," or "I am running," although neither mother nor himself may be recognized. This naming of scribbling is of great significance, for now the child's thinking has changed. Before this stage he was satisfied with the motions, but now he has connected these motions to the world around him. He has changed from kinesthetic thinking to imaginative thinking. This stage usually occurs at about the age of three and a half years. The importance of the change can be simply understood if we realize that, as adults, most of our thinking is in terms of mental pictures. If we try to think back in our own memory as far as we can,

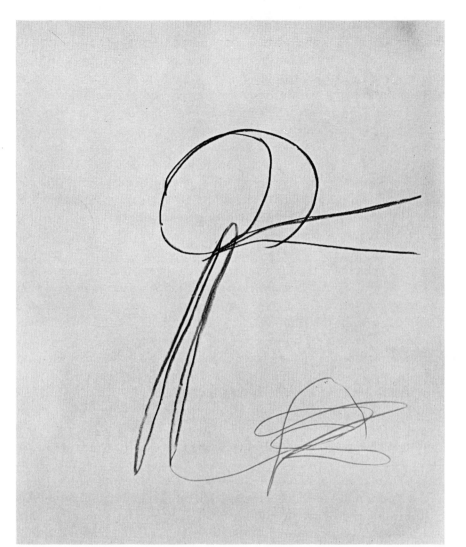

Figure 44. *A four year old's drawing, which he called "Mother Goes Shopping." This indicates that he is now in the naming of scribbling stage.*

our memory will carry us no further than this naming of scribbling stage. It is at this point, then, that the child develops a basis for visual retention.

The drawings themselves have not changed remarkably from early scribbles. Although the child may now start with some idea of what he is going to do, he is also influenced by what he has done. So, as the child makes marks on the page, these marks may have a visual reference for him, which in turn affects the drawings. Whereas earlier he sometimes could see a relationship between what he had drawn and some object, now he draws with intent.

Although the child at three and a half has usually arrived at the stage of naming of scribbling, he will often enjoy the sheer physical motion, and if he is given a new drawing tool, he spends a considerable length of time in trying out his instrument to see how it feels, in much the same way as an adult would do. The amount of time that a youngster spends on drawing will increase even more, and the scribbles become much more differentiated. They may be well distributed over the page, and the marks will sometimes be accompanied by a verbal description of what is going on. This conversation is not directed at any particular adult, but often seems to be a communication with the self. Not all children do this by any means, but it seems apparent that the drawing now becomes a record of how the child feels about parts of his environment, and the method or way in which he is drawing makes the scribbles an important means of communication.

Sometimes at this stage a child will announce what he is going to draw, or sometimes the drawing will evolve from the first exploratory marks on the paper. It is quite clear that although parts may have some intent as they are being drawn, the child has no preconceived notion as to what his finished scribbling will look like. A line that is drawn at the top of the page may be called a tree but may end up being given a different name before the picture is completed. The wavy line may be a dog running or himself making giant steps. These lines are not always visual representations, but can also be representations of a nonvisual nature; smoothness, roughness, or hurry-up lines are just as important as the visual impression of an object. The important point is that the scribbles and lines that may be looked upon as meaningless to adults do in fact have a real meaning to the child who is making these drawings. Some of the circular motions and longitudinal lines may seem to tie together to make a person in the child's drawing, but adults should not try to find a visual reality there or try to give scribbles their own interpretation. There may be a real danger in parents or teachers pushing the child to find some

Figure 45. *This is obviously a meaningful scribble for this four year old boy. However, an experience is expressed in quite a different way from the reality of an adult representation.*

name or some excuse for what he has drawn. Rather, teachers and parents should give confidence and encouragement in this new kind of thinking.

The Meaning of Color

The experience of scribbling, then, is mainly one of motor activity. At first satisfaction is derived from the experience of kinesthetic motions, next from a visual control of these lines, and finally from the relationship of these lines to the outside world. Color, therefore, plays a decidedly subordinate role in the scribbling stage. This is particularly true in the first two levels, when the child is establishing motor coordination. The choice of many colors, in fact, can sometimes divert the child from scribbling to the activity of playing with the colors. It is of great importance that the child be able to distinguish his marks from the rest of the page. Therefore, a strong contrast is necessary in the selection of the drawing materials. Black crayon on white paper or white chalk on a blackboard are to be preferred over colors that may not give this contrast.

Only when the child enters the stage of naming of scribbling does he have the desire to use different colors for different meanings. One of the first stages of color perception is to distinguish between colors. This in no way indicates that a child should be expected to name colors, but rather that he should be given the opportunity to have some choice of color at this stage.

Some work has been done in attempting to relate color and form to the personality of children of nursery school age. A well-known study by Alschuler and Hattwick (1947) attempted to relate the paintings of some one hundred and fifty nursery school children to certain of their behavioral characteristics. In a two volume report, support was given to the assumption that in painting children express their emotional experiences and adjustments. Those children who consistently painted in warm colors manifested free emotional behavior in warm, affectionate relations; children who preferred blue tended to be more controlled in their behavior; and children who used black tended as a group to show a dearth of emotional behavior. More recent research, however, has raised some questions about these conclusions. Corcoran (1954) found evidence that three year old children used colors in sequential order when painting at an easel. That is, the colors were used from left to right or right to left on the easel tray, regardless of what the colors were. Apparently, Alschuler and Hattwick did not control for the placement of colors in their study. In a doctoral study by Biehler (1953) it appeared that nursery school children again tended to apply colors in direct relationship to how they were placed on the easel tray. This might indicate that painting at this level is more a mechanical activity than an emotional one. At this age scribbling apparently tends to be more concerned with a striving for visual control. Color as part of the scribbling process in painting is mainly exploratory, and the use of particular colors may be related more closely to the physical arrangement of colors than to deep-seated emotional problems of the child.

Changes in color can sometimes be significant in the naming of scribbling stage, for here colors may have some meaning for the child. Colors can also be fun for the child to work with and to explore occasionally. However, it is of far greater importance in the scribbling stages that the child be given the opportunity to create lines and forms, to develop mastery of his coordination, and to begin his first pictorial relationship to his environment.

Scribbling As a Developmental Process

With increased attention focused upon early learning and a good deal of concern being shown over the need for developing methods of working with young children, the art experiences of young children take on added significance. The very young child, before the age of eighteen months, expresses himself with his voice and body. It has been shown that even during the first few months of life children exposed to an enriched visual environment develop faster than children who do not have anything interesting to focus on, such as mobiles hanging over their cribs (White, 1964). Children raised in an atmosphere of sterility and deprivation apparently fall far behind normal development in all phases of their growth (Bronfenbrenner, 1968). The interaction between the child and his environment is the crucial element in learning. A passive, neutral, sterile environment for young children is not the ideal setting for development.

Programs for disadvantaged children are often started at a very young age. Some experimental programs have been concerned with mothers; others have started when the child arrives at the age of three or four in the nursery school setting. Some of these programs are called enrichment programs, in which children are exposed to a great number of activities that hopefully will provide some of the background that youngsters

Figure 46. *It is important during the scribbling stage that children have the opportunity to develop a pictorial relationship to their environment with drawing instruments that they can control.*

in nondeprived homes would normally experience. A number of these activities are essentially art activities, with youngsters involved in painting, drawing, manipulating clay, or working with two- and three-dimensional forms. Some programs go even farther and force the child into learning situations (Bereiter and Engelmann, 1966). The theory behind most of these programs is essentially the same: that the interaction between the child and his environment needs to be increased so that the child actually sees, hears, smells, tastes, and uses all of his senses to make this interaction process meaningful.

One study on the drawing development in preschool children (Goertz, 1966) found that experience in working with art materials increases the development of the child's drawings. Probably the attitude of the parent toward the child's drawing behavior is indicative of the attitude of the

Figure 47. *Children often enjoy seeing their own motions take on definite form. Here children finger paint directly on the table. Occasionally finger paint can be used to advantage with nursery school children.*

parent toward the child himself. An interest in the child's drawings may indicate a real interest in supporting his development in all spheres.

In a study of preschool children's attention Helen Bee (1964) expected that children who were not easily distracted would have parents who would leave them alone to solve problems. However, this was not borne out. What she found, in fact, was that children who were easily distracted had parents who offered children ready-made solutions, whereas the children who were not easily distracted had parents who gave them suggestions only for means of finding their own solution. Apparently, there may be some advantage in interacting with the child and helping him to find ways to solve problems rather than in leaving him alone or providing specific answers for him.

Art in itself is a constant problem-solving situation. This is true at the preschool level as well as at older ages. The parent or teacher who provides the task and the solution may be doing as great a disservice to the child as the teacher who stands back and lets the child create on his own. What seems to be needed is a teacher who can provide alternate suggestions, give encouragement, and make the child feel that his end product is worthwhile.

The Scribbling Child and His Environment

There is a direct relationship between how a child approaches scribbling and how he relates to the rest of his environment. His scribbles with crayon, paint, or clay exhibit the same type of characteristics that he exhibits in other situations. This can be readily observed. Children who tend to be delicate and timid usually have a similar approach to art materials. The scribbles themselves reflect a delicate and timid personality. A child who has lost confidence in his ability to adjust to new situations will tend to scribble in stereotyped repetitions (see Figure 48). Lack of confidence can readily be seen in these repeated patterns, which are drawn over and over again as a measure of security. This harmful security can inhibit the growth of a child because it tends to block any further development. It is therefore important for the emotional growth of the child that he be encouraged to develop concepts and to realize the possibilities of scribbling.

It is apparent that an adult artist uses his senses to acquaint himself with his surroundings and also to translate these reactions to his environment into paintings and constructions. The growth of sense apparatus is a vital necessity for everyone. The opportunity to examine the common materials of our environment provides a variety of both kinesthetic and tactile experiences. By encouraging the exploration of a variety of tactile

Figure 48. *This scribble drawing shows repeated stereotype motions. This indicates a lack of self-confidence in the drawing activity.*

sensations, an adult can stimulate the child who approaches clay through the use of the finger tips only. A child who does not enjoy tactile sensations may avoid contact with different textures. Encouraging children to experience and become aware of a variety of tactile differences can help develop this area of perceptual growth. Noticing the differences between hot and cold, hard and soft, or just enjoying the tactile differences between feathers and glass or between metal and velvet can be an exciting experience.

Scribbling itself is primarily a kinesthetic activity, and the enjoyment of this activity is usually seen in the vigorous and large motions of the young child's drawings. However, it is important to point out that not all children have to make large motions. To force them upon a child is just as senseless as to try to change a delicate child into a robust one. Any imposition creates unhealthy reactions. Providing the encouragement and freedom to enjoy a variety of kinesthetic experiences can lay a firm foundation for future development.

Creative children scribble independently of outside influences. Even when they scribble in a group they seldom inquire, ask questions, or look at their neighbors' work. For them their own work provides all the stimulation necessary. But there are also children who constantly ask questions, wondering how to use the material, asking the way in which things should be done. These are also the ones who are most easily influenced by the work of others. If one child starts with big round motions, they will start to imitate him. Lack of self-confidence and of independence in thinking are responsible for such easy influences. These are the children who lack confidence in their own creativeness. They are the ones who most need a boost in their creativeness, and they are also the easy victims of coloring books and of people who promote the use of patterns.

When a child names his scribblings his originality and creativeness become especially evident. He will develop his own interests and will not need to be motivated. This is no way implies that the creative child is not influenced by things around him. Rather, the creative child is one who enjoys and gets satisfaction from his own work independently of the teacher's continuing approval. Because scribbling is the beginning of creative expression, it is especially important at this time to develop self-confidence in the child and to give him independence and responsibility for his own work. Ideally, each child should be self-motivated to express himself and to feel satisfaction with the process. It is sad but true that projects planned for the scribbling child occasionally undercut his confidence: projects that develop dependence upon the adult, projects that are too difficult for a young child to accomplish by himself, projects that are conceived by and for adults.

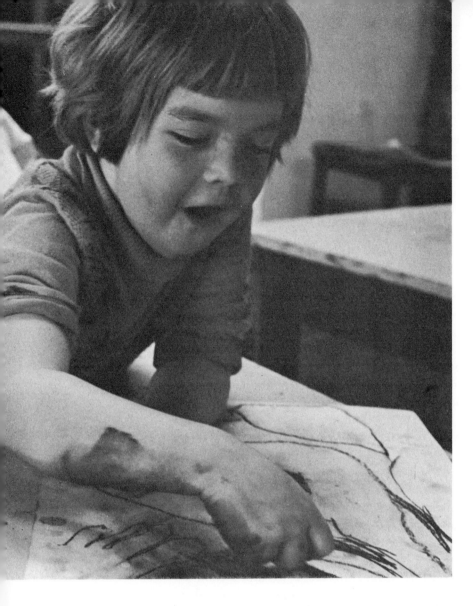

Figure 49. *Nursery school children enjoy the opportunity to scribble and derive great satisfaction from this activity.*

Scribbling As a Reflection of Growth

The growth process is continuous, but not smooth. This can be seen in the physical growth of children. Although we can say that children of a certain age have an average height of so many inches, we find great differences in individuals; sudden spurts of growth, especially during adolescence, make us realize that growth is extremely uneven. This same holds true for the development of young children. We have said that art is a reflection of man's reactions to his environment; in the scribbling stage this is easily seen, for scribbling can be considered a reflection of the physical and emotional development of children. Just as we find differences in growth we also find great individual differences in the scribbling of children.

Teachers can look at the scribbles of children as being part of the total child. There is some danger in looking at scribbles from the point of view of making interpretations of them. The beauty that we often see in preschool children's art may be because, as adults, we see these markings as a free, uninhibited approach to painting, whereas actually this beauty may have very little to do with the child's intent. Some individuals even go farther in this interpretation and look at children's drawings as an indication of inner feelings and inhibitions. When an adult looks at an ink blot, he can often see within this blot figures or forms that remind him of certain aspects of his own life. Adults can also look at scribbles in the same way and see certain forms or shapes, but this has very little to do with the child's meaning. We may get a better understanding of the adult, but very little help in understanding children. Circles and vertical lines should be looked upon as being circles and vertical lines, and not as being symbolic or as having meaning other than scribbles.

To a great extent the differences in levels of scribbling reflect physiological and psychological changes in the child. On the average, we expect children to start scribbling at about the age of two and to continue until they are about four years of age. If there is a marked discrepancy, the child is either above or below average for his age. If we find a child in kindergarten who is still scribbling, we could normally expect that this child is below average for his age. This is not a lack of talent but rather a stage of development that is a reflection of the total child at the time. In some cases a child may regress if he is afraid or unsure of himself. That is, he may scribble for a short period of time even though his normal development has gone beyond this stage. However, if we find a child of seven who has never done anything but scribble, we must assume that this child is not functioning at the level normal for children of his age.

The whole concept of intelligence as used within our society is essentially that of relating one child's performance to that of all children of the same age. A child who performs tasks typical of an older child tends to be considered more intelligent. Since scribbling is a reflection of the child's total development, we have here an indication of the child's intellectual growth, particularly at a time when the usual group-type intelligence tests are not usable. Therefore, a kindergarten child who is still in the scribbling stage will not be able to perform at the level usually expected of kindergarten children. In first grade the same child could not learn to read. It is obvious that the understanding of scribbling can help us to understand children.

Art Motivation

Usually in the first stages of scribbling no special motivation is needed except to provide the child with the proper materials and the encouragement to go ahead with the activity. Most children will eagerly cover two or three sheets of paper with scribbles. Do not expect the very young child to continue at this activity for more than a few minutes. The child of three may be involved for as long as fifteen minutes. The four year old child, if he has arrived at the naming of scribbling stage, or if he has been introduced to a new material, may keep at this activity for twenty to thirty minutes. However, no clock should dictate the length of time a child may spend in expressing himself on paper.

Scribbling should not be interfered with. Sometimes a nursery school teacher will see a child painting a picture that accidentally turns out to look quite like a piece of modern art. It is a great temptation to stop the child at this point and "save the picture." However, the child will not understand this interruption to his scribbling. The child himself should decide when a picture is completed. We have already mentioned the inhibiting effect of trying to see some respresentation in scribbles, for this may interrupt the normal growth of the child's motor activities at a time when he is developing visual control over his movements.

Occasionally one finds a child who seems to be afraid of scribbling. Certainly a parent or teacher should encourage this important developmental activity. There may be several reasons for this hesitancy to engage in a creative activity, from being told "No" by parents when he has started to scribble in the past to a more deep-seated problem of anxiety or fear in a particular situation. Establishing mutual trust is important, and it is sometimes necessary to make the art experience into a tempting activity. Providing the child with a mound of easily workable clay about the size of a grapefruit might be a good start. "Is it cold? Can you squeeze it? How high can you make it? Can you push your finger through it? Can you make it smooth? Can you make it lumpy?" Once a child gets involved in the clay, other means of expression will come more easily as the child develops confidence. Colored chalk or a new felt pen may be enough to make a youngster eager to draw. Most children will scribble quite eagerly after motivation.

After a child has named his scribbling, we have, as observed earlier, a definite clue to his thinking. This new direction, the relationship of his scribbles to the environment, should be stimulated. We are not talking about improving drawings now, for the drawings themselves do not look very different from earlier scribbles. We can, however, stimulate the child's thinking in the direction he has already indicated. For example, when the child says, "This is Daddy," it is possible to stimulate a greater awareness of Daddy. "Is your Daddy tall? Does he have big feet? Does he ever lift you up? Do you ever feel his whiskers? Do you like your Daddy?" The purpose here is to encourage imaginative thinking. We will be perfectly satisfied with the motions that are made on the paper, although they may not be recognizable to adults; some lines may represent a feeling of lifting or the texture of whiskers, or even be symbolic of being held. The inclusion of many senses is important. If the child says he is going shopping, such things as smells, sounds, and personal involvement, his own part in the shopping experience, his likes and dislikes for this activity, can all be included in the stimulation. But the child should also feel free to ignore these comments and be satisfied simply with the relationship between his scribble and his imaginative thinking.

During the very first stages of scribbling no particular motivation is necessary, whereas any topic the child suggests during the last stage of scribbling is suitable to extend his thinking process. Most important in all stages is the adult's understanding and encouragement.

Art Materials

Any art material used with children must fit their needs. Since during scribbling the child needs to practice and experience kinesthetic sensations, the materials used should encourage free expression without the intrusion of technical difficulties. Watercolor, for example, is a very poor medium at this age because the colors tend to run and flow easily. The child is unable to gain control over his motions or to follow his motions on the paper and is therefore discouraged by the material. The usual type of pencil is also unsuitable for the scribbling child because sharp points prevent gliding along the paper, and of course the points break easily.

There are numerous art materials that *do* lend themselves to the needs of the child at the scribbling stage. A big, black, unwrapped crayon is excellent and easily obtained. However, white chalk on a blackboard or a felt- or nylon-tipped pen with black ink are also excellent materials. Any art material should facilitate expression rather than be a stumbling block, and at this age the need to control kinesthetic motions should be uppermost.

Because of some adults' feeling toward scribbling, we sometimes find

Figure 50. *Tempera paint must be a thick mixture so that it can be controlled if the youngster will be painting at an easel. Here we see a two-fisted approach to painting.*

that old newspapers, the back of wallpaper samples, or wrapping paper is used for the scribbling child. Although these materials may have a real place in the art program at a different developmental level, these materials have no place in the nursery school or in the kindergarten. Drawing a dark line over a printed news page is much too confusing, the back of old wallpaper tends to be rough and prevents the easy flow of a crayon, and wrapping paper does not provide good contrast with the drawing medium. A 12 by 18 inch size light-colored or white paper is best for crayon; a larger 18 by 24 inch size is best if paint is going to be used.

Tempera or poster paint can be used to advantage (see Figure 50). The paint must be mixed to a fairly thick consistency so that it does not dribble or run down the page. The opportunity to use paint can satisfy some of the emotional needs of the scribbler better than a crayon. The result is obvious joy in exploring a range of colors. A flat surface is best for a child to paint on, since the problems of running paint are thus

Figure 51. *Clay is an important material to use since it provides the opportunity for manipulating a three-dimensional material which can be pushed, stretched, squeezed, and pounded.*

minimized and the child can work from all sides of his paper. However, in situations where space is at a minimum, it is better to use an easel, or even to fasten paper on the wall, than not to give a painting experience at all. Large fairly absorbent paper, three-quarter-inch bristle brushes with the handle not too long, and some variety of thickly mixed tempera paint provide a wonderful opportunity for an emotional outlet and a truly artistic experience.

Clay is also an excellent material for this age (see Figure 51). Handling a three-dimensional material provides the opportunity for the child to use his fingers and muscles in a different way. Beating and pounding the clay without any visible purpose is a parallel stage to disordered scribbling. The forming of coils and balls without attempting any specific object is parallel to controlled scribbling. At some point the child may pick up a lump of clay and, perhaps with accompanying noises, call it an airplane or say, "This is a car." Psychologically, this is exactly the same change in the process of thinking as we discussed under "The Naming of Scribbling." Also here, the child has changed his kinesthetic thinking to imaginative thinking. The clay should not be so hard as to be difficult to work with nor so thin that it sticks to the fingers. Clay of proper consistency can be stored in a plastic bag for an indefinite length of time. Since the scribbling child does not have good control over his small muscles, the clay chunk he works with should be large enough to be grasped with both hands. A grapefruit-sized piece of clay is probably adequate. Since the child is exploring and manipulating the material in a kinesthetic way, there is no need to let the clay harden or even to think of firing these products.

Providing an opportunity for children to become aware of color and texture by the handling of various collage materials is of value (see Figure 52). Although it is interesting for the child to select some materials he enjoys and then put them into some sort of assemblage, the continual use of collage materials may stand in the way of the development of motor-visual experiences. However, the occasional use of collage materials is certainly worthwhile for the scribbling child.

In some nursery schools and kindergartens finger paint is a favorite material. There is some real reason to doubt the advantages of using this medium with the scribbling child. Just as we would hesitate to have a very young infant handle and use a crayon, if the prime enjoyment from the crayon was scratching it or chewing on it, we should hesitate to use finger paint with the scribbling child who tends to be concerned with its sticky consistency. If we think of art materials as primarily providing the opportunity for the child's self-expression, then the misuse of materials may interfere with the activity for which the finger paint was originally planned. Instead of improving control over their muscular

Figure 52. *A child enjoys exploring a box of materials of various colors and textures. Selecting pieces of scrap materials, cutting them, and pasting them on a piece of cardboard provides the opportunity for comparison and selection.*

activities, children can become involved in the pastelike consistency. We also have evidence from experiments and direct observation that the young child may sometimes regress into an earlier stage of behavior. Finger paint, because of its very consistency, may remind children of these former stages and retard development temporarily. You may easily see this effect by watching children. If they are more concerned with the sticky consistency and with smearing the paint all over than with using it for expression, then they are not using finger paint to satisfy the desire to control their kinesthetic movements. However, for tense, timid, or fearful children finger painting may provide an important outlet even when used in such a manner.

There is no place in the art program for those activities that have no meaning for the scribbling child. Occasionally a nursery school or kindergarten teacher may plan certain art activities such as pasting, tracing, folding, or cutting; these are designed for a particular end product, such as May baskets, Pilgrim silhouettes, cute snowmen, or projects for Hallowe'en, Christmas, or Mother's Day. Such activities are worthless

Plate 3. *"I Am Playing in the Leaves" is a typical head-feet representation, drawn by a kindergarten youngster. This drawing includes only the child's active knowledge of a man. His increased physical control would distinguish his picture from one by a gifted, younger child, although the concepts might be similar. Notice that the leaves were colored in with such eagerness that the hands and feet were painted too.*

Plate 4. *"I Am in a Lightning Storm," painted by a six year old child. The use of color is completely subjective; colors are used according to their emotional or aesthetic value rather than an attempt at naturalism.*

and should never be included in a program planned for scribbling children, because they only point out the inability of the child to perform on a level foreign to his understanding and ability. Sometimes teachers have an interest in discovering new and novel activities for children. Any new material should be looked upon with a great deal of care to make sure that it can further the natural development of children. It must not obstruct the opportunity for the child to gain control over his material; rather, it should promote his own creative expression.

Summary of Growth Characteristics of the Scribbling Stage

For an understanding of the child, it is of great importance that scribbling be recognized as part of the total growth pattern. A child during this stage will reflect his intellectual and emotional development in his creative work. He will pursue his scribbling vigorously and yet be flexible enough to change his movement whenever new experiences demand such changing. He will enjoy his kinesthetic development through his scribbles and will gradually gain visual control over these markings. Creatively, he will be independent and free from disturbing influences.

The young child will freely explore his environment through a variety of senses, and some of the experiences will appear in his scribbles when he begins to name these. The drawings themselves will have a healthy variety, starting at about two years of age with a series of random markings, changing to continuous or controlled motions about six months later, and becoming much more complicated when he begins to name what he has drawn. In working with paint, these stages will closely parallel work with crayon, and he will particularly enjoy the use of color when he begins to name his scribbles. He will also enjoy working with a range of three-dimensional materials.

This period of life is extremely important for developing attitudes about oneself and in establishing the feeling that the world is an exciting and interesting place to live in. The roles of the teacher and of the parent become very important in helping the child develop these attitudes. The nursery school teacher is in an excellent position to provide the opportunity for a child to grow by means of his art experiences, to help him develop the confidence and sensitivity important for self-expression, and to provide a range of materials and the environmental setting for creative

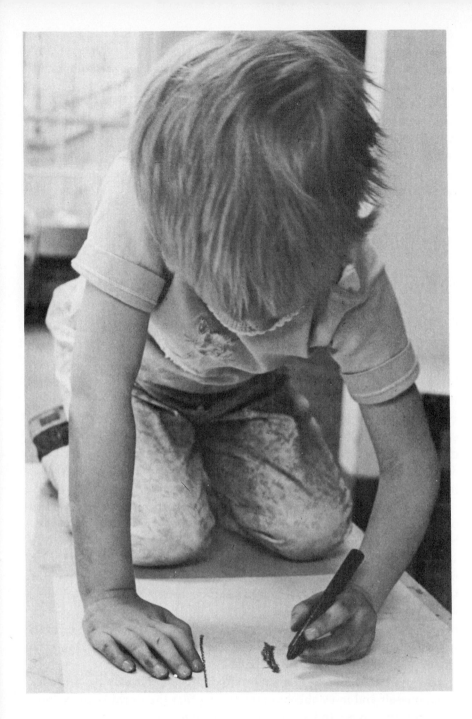

Figure 53. *This child, eager to scribble, has climbed right up on the table to better reach the paper.*

activities. Most important of all is to provide the stimulation and motivation necessary for developing an increased awareness of the environment and to provide the encouragement and approval for the creative act. All these responsibilities rest squarely upon the shoulders of the parent or teacher.

RELATED ACTIVITIES

1. Collect examples of art work from a nursery-school or preschool group of children. Observe the variety of expression. Try to classify the scribbles according to disordered, controlled, or naming of scribbling stage. Compare the drawings for use of space, control of line, boldness or timidity of motion.

2. Collect the scribbles of one child over a period of several months. Date each drawing and note any remarks the child made while drawing. Keep a notebook in which you record observations on length of attention span, materials used, amount of concentration or diversions, motions and technique used, and the emotional reactions of the child. Compare these notes with the child's motor coordination when eating, dressing, and so forth. Draw conclusions from the three sources of information (the scribbles, the notes, and the behavior) as to the child's growth during this time.

3. Find out the effectiveness of your motivation during the period of naming of scribbling by comparing one scribble done when the child was left completely alone with another made when you motivated the child in the direction of his thinking.

4. Observe children working with clay. See if those children who make forms or shapes also give these forms names. How does this relate to the scribbles of these same children?

5. Watch children paint at an easel several times. Make a list of the amount of paint used and the order of use. Shift the order of paints in the easel trough and see if there are any changes. Experiment with two or three different consistencies of paint each week. Repeat this for several weeks to see if the children make any comments or if there is any relation between paint consistency and length of time spent in painting.

6. When a child starts to name his scribbling, does he introduce certain lines or motions for certain objects or experiences? Collect scribbles and keep notes on the changes in the scribbles when naming begins. Observe the development of a form for man.

First Representational Attempts: The Preschematic Stage, 4-7 Years

5

The Importance of the Preschematic Stage

A different method of drawing has begun, the conscious creation of form. This stage grows directly out of the last stages of scribbling. Although the drawings themselves may not look particularly different to the adult, to the child this stage of development is very important. Now he is consciously making forms that have some relationship to the world around him. This conscious creation of form takes on great meaning when we realize that this is the beginning of graphic communication. The marks and scribbles have lost more and more of their relationship to bodily movement, and these marks are now controlled and related to visual objects (see Figure 54). In scribbling the child was mainly involved in a kinesthetic activity, but now he is involved with the establishment of a relationship with what he intends to represent. This gives him a great feeling of satisfaction.

These new drawings are important not only for the child but also for the parent or teacher, who now has a tangible record of the child's thinking process. This not only gives the adult a concrete object he can see and discuss with the child, but it also provides clues about what is important in the child's life and how he is beginning to organize his relationship with his environment. Usually by the age of four, children

Figure 54. *A child in this stage makes definite forms, although these may not look like a naturalistic represen-tation to adults.*

are making recognizable forms, although it may be somewhat difficult to decide just what they are. By the age of five these marks are usually quite distinguishable as people, houses, or trees, and by the time the child is six these shapes and forms have evolved into clearly recognizable pictures with subject matter. However, there is much variation among children, and even the material that the child uses influences how he draws. Several factors may influence the kind of drawing that is done at any particular moment, and these will be discussed later.

Characteristics of Preschematic Drawings

It is possible to think of drawing by children of this age as evolving from an undefined collection of lines into a definite representational configuration. The circular motions and longitudinal motions turn into recognizable forms, and these representational attempts have grown directly from the scribbling stages. Usually the first symbol achieved is a man.

Typically, the man is drawn with a circle for a head and two vertical lines for legs. These head-feet representations are common for the five year old child. It is not surprising that the first representation should be

Figure 55. "A Man," drawn by a four year old child. The first representational attempts develop naturally from the child's scribbles.

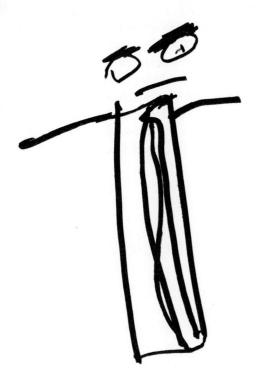

Figure 56. *This child's concept of a man is unusual. The separate features are shown, but there is no outline for the head. Arms and legs are also indicated.*

a person. The importance of people in children's drawings is quite evident throughout childhood. It is not as clear why the head-feet representation should be the first method that the child uses to portray people, but there is general agreement that a child of this age is not trying to copy a visual object in front of him. We have found that showing five year old children pictures of people or having them look at people while they draw does not change the way they draw a person. It may be that the child is actually drawing himself; if we were to try to draw what we see of ourselves as we look straight ahead, the representation would probably be a somewhat nebulous round circle for the head with legs and arms attached. This assumes that the child is involved primarily in the self; his egocentric view of the world is actually a view of himself.

Another point of view is that the head-feet representation is what the child actually knows about himself and is not a visual representation at all. The head is where all eating and talking goes on. Piaget (1960) found that some six year old children thought that the thinking process goes on in the mouth. Certainly the eyes, ears, and nose make the head the center of sensory activity. The addition of legs and arms makes this center movable and may indicate a really functional being. There is no doubt that children know a great deal more about the body than they portray, for most children can quickly identify most of its parts.

Another view is that the first representational attempts result neither from visual stimulation nor from a concept, but are a representation of the method by which a child perceives. For example, the sense of touch in actually running the hands over an object may be as important at this stage as visually seeing this object or understanding its function. At any rate, the first representational attempts at a man should not be looked upon as immature representation, for it is fairly obvious that a drawing is essentially an abstraction or schema from a large array of complex stimuli and is the beginning of an ordered thought process.

The head-feet representation becomes elaborate with the addition of arms sticking out of the sides of the legs, the addition of what seems like a belly button between the legs, and the eventual inclusion of the body. There are many variations in this development, and by the time the child is six he often has a fairly elaborate drawing of a man.

During this stage of development, the child is continually searching for new concepts, and his representational symbols are also constantly changing. He will represent a man differently today from the way he will represent a man tomorrow. This is not only true of his drawings of a man but also of his representation of houses and trees. But, by the time

Figure 57. *No two children paint alike, and at this age the representational symbols of each child are also constantly changing.*

the child is seven, he will have established a schema; drawings by children in first grade can usually be identified by the way in which an object is drawn the same way again and again.

The Meaning of Color

During the stage of the first representational attempts, more interest and excitement are stimulated through the relationship of the drawing to an object than between color and an object. The child has begun consciously to create forms and it is those forms themselves that become important. Young children in the scribbling stage often use color to match objects, but once youngsters start using lines to portray form in their drawing, they begin to match objects by form rather than by color. One study (Corah, 1966) tried to teach the matching of geometric shapes by color but found that kindergarten children matched the shapes on the basis of form, whereas younger children quickly identified shapes on the basis of color. This does not mean that children in the preschematic stage are not aware of color, but it indicates that the ability to make forms of their own choosing dominates their thinking.

In drawings and paintings done by this age there is often little relationship between the color selected to paint an object and the object represented. A man may be red, blue, green, or yellow, as in Plates 2 and 4, depending upon how the various colors appeal to the child. To an adult these color relationships may seem a little crazy. In fact, one study (Marshall, 1954) compared adult schizophrenics with normal five year olds and found the use of color with these two groups quite comparable.

This does not mean that these colors do not have significance to the child who is using them. Lawler and Lawler (1965) found that nursery school children of about the age of four selected yellow crayons to color a happy picture, whereas the same picture was colored brown if the child was told a sad story about it. It would not seem strange, then, for a child to select a favorite color for painting a picture of his mother, especially if he feels a warm emotional attachment. There are often other reasons for the particular selection of a color for an object. Some of these are simply mechanical in nature. That is, the color selected may be thicker and less likely to run, or perhaps the red has not been used, or maybe the brush used for one of the colors has a longer handle. Children may have deeper psychological meanings in their color choice, but these meanings tend to be highly individualized, and adults would be put in a difficult position to try to interpret what these colors mean.

The use of color at this age can be an exciting experience. Although the child has no desire for exact color relationship, he can and does enjoy using color for its own sake. This is particularly true when using paint where rich masses of color can be painted quite fluidly. It is obvious that criticizing a child's use of color or pointing out the correct color for objects would interfere with his freedom of expression. Ample opportunity should be provided for the child to discover his own relationships with color, for it is through continued experimentation that a child establishes a relationship between his own emotional involvement with color and the harmonious organization of color on the page.

The Meaning of Space

The representation of space in drawings or paintings by adult artists differs widely, depending not only upon the individual artist but also upon the culture in which he finds himself. Our own society tends to look upon the representation of space as being appropriately shown by the use of perspective, a mechanical perspective with vanishing points and horizon lines. This has not been true for other times or other cultures; for example, an Oriental concept of space shows objects in the distance drawn higher on the page. Many contemporary artists have rejected mechanical perspective of space in favor of placing subject matter honestly on a two-dimensional surface. It can be readily seen, then, that there is no right or wrong way to portray space in a drawing.

A child's drawings in the first representational level show a concept of space quite different from that of an adult. At first glance objects in space tend to be put down in a somewhat random order. However, closer inspection will show that the child conceives of space as what is around him. That is, objects will appear above, below, or beside each other in the way the child understands them. He does not see himself standing on the ground with other objects also on the ground beside him. Possibly this could be better understood if we were to quickly look around the room and list the things we have seen. "There is a table, there is a light, here is a chair, and I am in the middle." No spatial relationship has yet been established outside the child's concept of himself. Space, therefore, is conceived of as revolving around the child. A boy aged five and a half drew the picture in Figure 58. Here he thinks, "There am I. There

Figure 58. *"I Am on the Street," painted by a five and a half year old child. Notice the ambulance and airplanes. Space and objects are revolving around the child.*

is an ambulance. There are airplanes. There is the sky." No relationship between the objects has been established. The child does not think, "I am standing on the street. The ambulance comes along the street. Above, there is the sky. The airplanes fly in the air." Notice the four wheels on the ambulance.

Of particular interest is the meaning of the child's spatial concepts at this age. He conceives space as being primarily related to himself and his own body. This is sometimes referred to as *body space.* We will later see how the concept of space changes in his drawings to what is sometimes termed *object space.* We find that children's drawings show markedly different spatial organization from that usually conceived of as correct from an adult point of view. Just as children draw what is around them in an apparently random fashion, their comments tend to be loose-jointed and disconnected. If a child of five is asked what he did at a birthday party, his reply does not follow any logical sequence. In fact the importance of his remarks may be more closely tied up with their emotional significance to him rather than with any orderly array of events.

As long as a child is still in the preschematic stage, there is no advantage in trying to teach this child how to read (Sibley, 1957), or in getting

C R E A T I V E   A N D   M E N T A L
G R O W T H

him to reason in an abstract way the logical relationships of numbers. Although children can learn early how to count (Pentz, 1965), or to recognize words, there is no genuine understanding of content.

Since experiencing oneself as part of the environment is one of the most important assumptions for cooperation and for visual coordination, the child's inability to relate things to each other in space, in his drawings, is a clear indication that he is not yet ready to cooperate socially and that he does not have the ability to relate letters to each other or to learn to read. A kindergarten teacher can readily tell from a child's drawings whether the child is ready to participate in tasks that require spatial coordination. Forcing a child too early into tasks that he is not yet ready for may lead to undesirable actions and attitudes, and these may last longer and be more important in the end than doing the task at the moment. Since the child himself is the center of his environment, in what might be called a stage of egocentrism, those experiences that are directly related to himself become the most meaningful. A child's conception of his world may be so bound up with himself that he may even confuse his own thoughts and feelings with those things around him. If a chair falls over, he is concerned about the chair's being hurt (Piaget, 1960). It is almost as though he were the chair. We can say, therefore, that the child at this stage is emotionally involved in his spatial relationships. The size of objects and the subject matter he selects from his environment, and the way in which these are placed in this early stage, are to a large degree conditioned by value judgments. We can see that the way in which a child portrays space is intimately tied up with his whole thinking process. To teach an adult's concept of space to children at this age would not only be most confusing but might actually damage the child's confidence in his own creative work.

The Development of the Preschool Child

Some children start school at the age of three or four in either a community- or church-sponsored nursery. The kindergarten child is usually five or sometimes six years old, and formal schooling for all children usually begins with first grade. The preschematic stage, then, tends to fall between the time when some children enter nursery school and the time when all children begin formal education in the first grade.

Children differ tremendously during this age. Each child is a product of his background, and just as parents and the environment vary so will

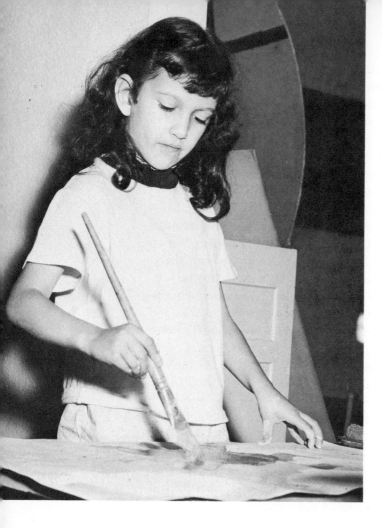

Figure 59. *Most five year old children are eager to try new tasks, to manipulate materials, and to express themselves. Here a girl enjoys mixing various colors on her paper.*

the child himself. The background that the child comes from, then, cannot be ignored. However, all children of this age tend to be generally curious, full of enthusiasm, eager to try tasks, particularly those that involve manipulation of material, and they are often anxious to express themselves, although not in logical ways. Apparently, the preschool child has developed a logic of his own, and although he may be full of questions, of "Why?," he seems to see the world as being how it is without realizing that he himself can make changes in it. The world tends to revolve around him, and his experience is limited to firsthand contact with his environment. The preschooler plays by himself or alongside other children rather than with them, and often his conversation is more a reflection of his own thinking than the development of a social grace.

We can expect that the art of the preschool child will follow the same developmental patterns as other aspects of his growth. In fact, the study of children's drawings can give us great insight into the method and reasoning behind his actions. It may be well to mention that although there are general trends and a clearly definable developmental path visible in drawings, these do not come automatically. Rather, they evolve slowly in spurts, and at times the children will regress to an earlier stage. Growth is never a smooth process.

Preschematic Drawings As a Reflection of Growth

It is important to remember that a child's art is a reflection of himself. A child cannot, nor should he be expected to, draw or paint like someone else. Although this may seem like an obvious statement, it is well to keep it firmly in mind. There are great individual differences in children just as there are great individual differences in children's drawings. Children also have some general growth characteristics that are common to their developmental level, and we find this also true in their art work.

Drawing is much more than a pleasant exercise for the child. It is a means by which he develops relationships and makes concrete some of

Figure 60. *A child's art is a reflection of himself. He learns as he organizes his experiences. The drawing is an opportunity to put thoughts into concrete form.*

Figure 61. *The child's concept of the world may be puzzling to the adult, but obviously these forms have significance of a very personal nature.*

the vague thoughts that may be important to him. Drawing becomes in itself a learning experience. Although children can recognize and name numerous objects around them, these objects can be somewhat peripheral to the child's functional thinking. One study attempted to compare how five year olds recognized missing or deformed arms and legs in incomplete pictures of people (McPherson *et al.,* 1966). They found that five year olds drew anatomical parts with much more accuracy than they recognized them. Apparently a picture is not as important to look at as it is to draw. It may be that through the drawing experience the child is beginning to establish some sort of conceptual organization, and this experience is not one that can be imposed (see Figure 61). That is, the teaching of certain artistic skills or techniques to a child of this age has no relationship to the use of drawing and painting as a means for the child to understand himself and his own relationship to his environment.

The development of concepts in art and their relationship to reality can help us understand the thinking processes of these children. Because this is an age where we find great flexibility and change in drawings, it is also an age at which we find rapid changes in the mode of thinking. We are not discussing thinking here as the quiet contemplation of a problem but rather considering total intellectual development, which at this age is nicely infused with fantasy, reality, and biological responses to the environment.

A child who has reached the chronological age of four or five and who still thinks in terms of motions has not advanced intellectually to an average stage of growth. In looking over a series of drawings by a five year old child, we would normally expect some representational attempts. The more differentiated these attempts are, the more highly the intellectual processes have been developed. Generally, the more details included in a drawing, the more aware the child is of those things around him. Our whole concept of intelligence is based primarily upon this assumption. One well-known test of intelligence is based upon how completely a child draws a man (Harris, 1963). The more a person knows about his environment, the more he is actively aware of and can utilize the various factors within it, the more intellectually developed he is. It is fairly obvious, then, that the child who has not yet developed concepts of his environment at the age of five is retarded in his intellectual growth.

One of the most important indications of this preschematic stage is the flexibility of the child. This can best be seen in the frequent changes in his concepts. A child whose drawings are merely repetitions of the same symbol without any deviations uses that symbol to hide behind, and will exhibit in his other behavior a tendency to withdraw or to hide behind social stereotypes. A child who reacts toward meaningful experiences in an emotionally sensitive way will show this emotional sensitivity in his art work. In his drawings he will exaggerate those things or parts with which he has become emotionally involved. For example, in Figure 62 John walked barefoot in the grass after the rain; the obvious delight

Figure 62. *"Walking in the Grass after the Rain," drawn by a six year old boy. The picture shows the intense feeling of wetness from the grass on the boy's toes.*

of this kinesthetic experience shows in his emphasized toes, almost to the extent that we, too, can feel our toes in the cool grass. A very sensitive child who becomes too bound up with one part of his drawing may easily lose connections with the rest of his subject matter. This can sometimes be seen in greatly overexaggerated details.

Sometimes adults can be misled by words children use, but drawings reflect a child's development honestly. Adults may mistake the use of words for an understanding of these words and try to carry on a conversation with a youngster, teaching him according to what an adult would mean by the use of these words. One teenager recalls that a song he learned in nursery school about springtime had a phrase in it that warned him to "watch out for the first crocuses popping up from the ground." The teenager remembers that he was scared stiff for weeks because he was afraid that crocuses popping up from the ground might bite. In fact, he still doesn't like crocuses.

The way things are represented is an indication of the type of experiences the child has had with them. The image a person has of himself and of the things around him will change as he becomes more aware of the significant characteristics of these objects. *Perception* means more than just the visual appearance of objects; it includes the awareness of all the senses, such as kinesthetic or auditory experiences. Later when a child establishes more than the mere meaning of an object, visual perception will begin and a child will use lines other than crude geometric ones. For example, look at the drawing in Figure 63; we find that only geometric

Figure 63. *Notice in this drawing the beginnings of the use of geometric lines and forms for symbolizing the parts of the face and the legs. Even the bodies are rectangles.*

CREATIVE AND MENTAL
GROWTH

Figure 64. *Plan and elevation are combined in this drawing of the manger scene by a six and a half year old girl. Notice how the basket with the handles on each side has been tipped up so we can look inside.*

forms are used. All such geometric details convey a meaning only in context. The same situation exists in color at this age. Looking at Plate 1 and Plate 4 we find that a child uses color for the sake of color itself. It does not relate to the subject matter. We can see here purple rain and a green body and head that obviously express very little of a visual percept.

One of the most vital areas of growth with which we should be concerned is the area of creative growth. During the first representational attempts the creative child expresses independent concepts, and will not ask how to draw a mouth or a nose. He will, without hesitation, draw on his own. The child's own concepts can readily be distinguished from those taken from other sources by the free and flexible use and frequent changes that he makes. Copied symbols are usually repeated in a stiff inflexible fashion. In a group the creative child remains uninfluenced, although he may show interest in what others are doing. The creative child spontaneously paints or draws or manipulates materials and does not create only when motivated to do so. The development of creative growth within the context of art education is one of the prime considerations and justifications for inclusion of art experiences for any age group. A creative first grade girl was stimulated by the Christmas story to paint the manger scene in Figure 64. Notice how she has shown the top view of the basket so we can look inside, but has shown the side view of the stable. An angel is just arriving on the scene from the left, carrying the star. At the level of first representations, early patterns of behavior are established by which a child can develop into a creative adult or by which he can develop a dependence in thinking. It is essential, therefore, that at this crucial time great consideration be given to the creative development of children.

ART MOTIVATION

Any art motivation should stimulate a child's thinking, feeling, and perceiving. To be successful, the motivation should make the art experience much more than just an activity; it should stimulate a child's awareness of his environment and make him feel that the art activity is extremely vital and more important than anything else. A teacher, too, must feel that this is an important activity, and he himself must be a part of the motivation and identify with it. As long as the adult remains outside the motivation and merely directs an art activity, we should not expect children to be interested. To merely follow an adult's instructions for working with materials, or to be handed paper and told, "Draw what you want," or even to have a range of material and activities to do over a period of time—any one of these can result in busyness yet fail miserably in being a meaningful learning experience. One cannot expect a child to gain in knowledge and confidence and in sensitivity toward his environment if there is a barrier between adult and child. The teacher as well as the child needs to feel that this is an important, meaningful, and stimulating experience.

The atmosphere for art experiences is also important. The way something is said can be more important to the child than what is actually said. In a study of the influence of a nursery school environment upon children's drawings (Reichenberg-Hackett, 1964), it was found that children in what was termed a supportive-permissive atmosphere made drawings that were rated higher than drawings by children in either an authoritarian atmosphere or in a *laissez-faire* atmosphere. Other studies have tended to support these conclusions: that the attitude of the teacher is vital to the learning experience. When the adult shows an interest, provides an atmosphere of support for the activity, and acts as though there were nothing more important in the world than the drawing experience, then the environment is ready for art. The two other extremes, that of standing back and not particularly caring what a child does or the authoritarian role of dictating what must be done, apparently have a negative influence upon drawing and therefore a negative influence upon children.

A child should become involved in, and identify with, his art experi-

Figure 65. *This is a drawing by a boy from a rural area. See how he has enlarged the hands of himself driving a tractor. The steering wheel takes on special importance.*

ences. Since all contact or communication with the environment is established through the self, it is of great importance to stimulate the sensitivity toward the self. Therefore, any art motivation at this age ought to start directly with the child himself. We know that a child's development in art follows general growth patterns. He has certain needs, which should be considered in any good motivation. First of all, he needs to discover a relationship between his own marks and the outside world. Now for the first time he relates to his own work and to his concept of his environment (see Figure 65). These concepts originate with the child himself and therefore are related to the "I" and "my."

There will be differences in perceptual sensitivity between children at any age; some children will be more aware of sound or touch while another child may be more sensitive to visual stimulation. Because we acquaint ourselves with our environment only through our senses, the development and cultivation of perception are a prime concern of art education.

One of the best means of stimulating the child's relationship to things around him is to start with the function of the various body parts. This stimulation of a child's concept of his body parts will show readily in the drawings of children at this age. For example, a class of six year olds who draw only a line for a mouth can be motivated to include teeth and other facial features by stimulating an awareness of teeth in a topic such as "Brushing Your Teeth in the Morning."

"When do you get up in the morning, children? What time do you get up? At seven? How long does it take you to get dressed? Does your mother call you? Do you have an alarm clock? How long does it take you to get dressed then? Does your mother have to help you? Do you have to catch a bus? Where do you have your bedroom? On the second floor? Why? All by yourself? After you are dressed are you ready to catch the bus? No? Oh, you haven't eaten your breakfast yet? But you forgot! You went to breakfast without brushing your teeth! Oh, you brush your teeth after breakfast? Don't you have to hurry? Especially if it's raining? Oh, you brush your teeth anyway! Why? You mean it's bad to leave all that food in between your teeth all day? Do you brush your teeth every morning, Johnny? How do you hold your toothbrush? With just two fingers? Oh, you hold it this way! Do you brush your teeth back and forth? Oh, no; you mean you do it up and down? Why? Did you ever get your toothbrush caught in between your teeth? Does it hurt? You have to be a little careful when you brush your teeth, don't you! But, Johnny, did you forget the toothpaste? Some people don't use toothpaste! Do you? Let's think how we brush our teeth. Let's really brush them good and clean! Now are we all set to go to school? Oh, no; not with all that toothpaste still there!

"Now, children, we are going to paint a picture about how we get up in the morning and go to the bathroom and brush our teeth."

Every child should now have a feeling for brushing his teeth and one may even have a pain where he got his toothbrush caught between

Figure 66. *Here a six year old girl shows how she lost a tooth. The exaggerated size of the mouth, the great number of teeth, in fact, the whole picture, all show how important this experience was.*

his teeth. But every child will be conscious of his teeth, and each drawing will include teeth as an active part of the child's awareness. We can compare former drawings with those drawn after the motivation; if an enrichment of the form concept has taken place, the teacher was successful. In this topic, "Brushing Our Teeth," an enrichment of the form concept of mouth and a closer coordination between mouth and arm may also be expected.

In some cases the motivation for a lesson such as the one above can be achieved by actively engaging the child in an actual experience. One example might be to pass out a bag of hard candy for the children to munch on. "Is it hard? Do you really have to bite with your teeth?" Actual experiences are sometimes very helpful. The activating of the child's knowledge of himself in his immediate environment, the development of his concept of the environment through his own body self, are what matter. Any such motivation should include as many senses and sensory experiences as possible, and should include the total child in terms of his thinking, feeling, and perceiving.

The length of motivation may depend upon several factors. If the children have just engaged in an actual experience, a short discussion may be quite sufficient. However, in some cases the motivation may take longer than the actual drawing or painting experience. Discussing how a child feels in the rain, how the rain feels on his face, or what clothes the child has to put on, and stimulating an awareness of the sensations of walking with boots on or even how his feet feel if they are wet inside his boots, may take a longer time.

In some cases the motivation may be concerned primarily with the material itself. When first working with clay or collage material, the experience with the actual qualities of the material will be most important. "How does the clay feel? Is it hot or cold? Can you push your finger into it? Does it bend easily?" This type of question may be the only motivation necessary to stimulate a child to a greater awareness of his own senses and to help him to identify directly with what he is doing.

A motivation based primarily upon recall of something in which the children have all been involved should provide the opportunity for each child to express his own feelings and emotions in his own individual way. No attempt should be made to censor the child's creative expression, but rather we should try to stimulate the greatest variety of responses. The general atmosphere for the particular topic should be generally established by a discussion of the *where* and *when*. "Where do you go to school? What time do you go to school? Do you walk?" The *what* should usually follow. In this case it might be catching the bus. After a discussion of catching the bus the motivation should culminate in a thorough discussion of *how*. "How do you get on the bus? Do you hold on to the door when

Figure 67. *In some schools, the opportunity to paint is a special treat; then no motivation may be necessary, even if the only material available is watercolor, which is of doubtful value for small children.*

you climb in? Is the first step a high one?" Topics for motivation should therefore include first the *where* and *when*, second the *what*, and third the *how*.

SUBJECT MATTER

The most important consideration in the selection of topics for children in these first representational attempts should be the meaning of the activity for the children. The more involved the child becomes in the art activity, the more he identifies with what he is doing, the more he is actively using his senses, the more the project is really his own, the more meaning it has for him. At this age it is particularly important that any motivation or any subject matter be related directly to the child himself. To emphasize this, the "I" is placed first in the following suggested topics. A greater awareness should evolve for body parts, size, and emotional relationships.

I and My Mother (sizes)

I and My Family (sizes)

I and My House (sizes)

I Am Brushing My Teeth (teeth)

I Am Drinking My Milk (mouth)

I Am Blowing My Nose (nose)

I Hurt My Knee (knee)

I Am at the Dentist (teeth)

I Am Picking Flowers (hand, arms)

I Am Eating Breakfast (mouth)

I Am on the Swing (body)

I Have a Stomach Ache (body)

I and My Doll (emotional relationship)

I Get a Birthday Present (emotional relationship)

I and My Pet (emotional relationship)

Children often have subject matter within themselves, requiring no motivation or further encouragement for it to spill out. Every kindergarten teacher realizes that if Johnny's cat has had kittens, this news will come out in arithmetic class, during social studies, or maybe when the child bursts into the room first thing in the morning. Ample opportunity should be given children to express on paper their feelings and emotions. Some of these feelings will be quite apparent to any adult. Such topics as "The First Snowfall," "The Storm," "An Approaching Holiday," "A Big Fire" are all subject matter that cannot be ignored. Some subject matter will be a great deal more personal to the individual child. Such topics as "My New Baby Sister," "I Got Hit by a Car," "I Got Lost in the Store," "My House Caught on Fire," or "I Have a New Dress" all make appropriate subject matter for any age. The child who produced Figure 68 eagerly explained that his teacher, represented by an armless figure, watched while he played on the new slide in the kindergarten play yard. When the child is eager for expression, art should certainly not be limited to a specific time of the day or regimented to a particular topic.

Figures 68. *"I am Playing in the School Yard," drawn in chalk by a five year old boy. Apparently the teacher only watches while the youngster plays on the slide, for the child has drawn the teacher without arms.*

Figure 69. *This boy is pounding nails into a board for sheer enjoyment. Children need to develop a positive attitude toward materials without concern for artistic quality of the outcome.*

CREATIVE AND MENTAL GROWTH

Another topic area that is suitable for subject matter during these first representational attempts is an art material itself. Any art material should play a subordinate role in an art experience, and the child's own expression should be of predominant importance. However, at this age children have been exposed to only a few art materials, and in some cases their experience with these materials may have been limited to a restricted use. The prime reason, then, for using an art material as subject matter is to provide the child with a positive attitude toward these materials and to insure the greatest amount of exploration and flexibility in its use. Such experimentations with art materials should be related directly to the child himself (see Figure 69) and should not be concerned with any adult consideration of "artistic qualities." The use of an art material as a subject matter should therefore take the form of exploring and experimenting with the various qualities of clay, or finding out about the qualities of tempera paint.

Any topic for art expression, whether it is an experiment with art materials or an expression of a real or vicarious experience, should not only be tied closely to the child's body self but should also provide the opportunity for the child to establish a relationship between his drawing and his own environment.

ART MATERIALS

Because the child at this age is excited by his ability to represent what is meaningful to him, any art experience should provide the opportunity for developing mastery of the material itself. The process of creation is of greater significance than the final product, which means that an art material should be selected that meets the need of the age group for which it was planned. Constantly introducing or changing art materials may actually stand in the way of a child's mastering the material enough to express his own feelings, his own reactions to his sensory processes, and his own intellectual concepts of his environment.

Another consideration is that any art material should truly be an art material. Expression itself is not limited to any age group, and any material used with children should be of such a nature that a child may use this material throughout his life. There should be no "cute" art materials for nursery school or kindergarten children to use, because these provide no opportunity for continued growth.

For developing great freedom, thickly prepared tempera paints, used with a bristle brush on a somewhat absorbent large sheet of paper, are excellent material for this age level. Absorbent paper (about 18 by 24 inches) is recommended because it prevents the paint from running. A low, flat table provides the best surface on which to paint; the floor can also be successfully used. If the limitations of space do not allow painting on a flat surface, easels or a bulletin board can be used. Here, however, the paint should be of a thick enough consistency so that the child can control his painting without the frustration of dripping accidents.

Good-quality colored crayons and smaller sheets of paper (12 by 18 inches) are also excellent materials. The quality of the crayon can be determined by the amount of surplus wax that can easily be scratched off the paper. The more surplus there is, the poorer the quality of the crayon. The crayon should be large and unwrapped. Too often a new set of wrapped, sharply pointed crayons is looked upon as a treasure to keep rather than as a material to use. Unwrapped crayons can be used on the sides and ends, and their use is less likely to be confused with the function of a pencil.

Pencils may provide the opportunity for some children to draw in detail. The usual large kindergarten pencil works quite well. A study comparing crayon and colored pencils used by children in kindergarten indicated that drawings made by crayon tended to be rated higher on several measures, but some youngsters spent more time and were able to include more detail with pencils (Salome, 1967). It is more important that the child be given the opportunity to draw, even if he has to use a pen or poor pencil, than that he not be given the opportunity at all.

Figure 70. *"Indians," drawn with a felt-tipped pen by a seven year old girl. This material lends itself to a bold, direct presentation of thought. Every art material has its own characteristics and specific values.*

In addition to these basic materials there is a range of other materials that are quite suitable for this developmental level. These include colored chalk, fiber-tipped pens (see the Indians in Figure 70), colored papers, collage materials, and other materials that truly give the child an opportunity to explore and manipulate his environment and provide for a flexible development of his concepts. Cute or tricky use of materials should be avoided, such as dripping paint, pasting cereals, printing, and using stencils, or using materials in methods that are foreign to the child's own intentions. Purposely, no decorative projects have been suggested, because on this level no child feels the conscious need for decoration. As long as the search for a concept of form and space is predominant, the desire for decoration generally does not develop.

There is no place at this age level for cutting out paper flying angels or Pilgrim hats. A nursery school or kindergarten teacher should not be concerned with mass-producing little stereotypes for holidays or seasonal events, because such activities can only make the child feel inadequate and tend to reduce his confidence in his own means of expression.

Clay is an excellent three-dimensional material for the preschematic stage. As in drawings we find a search for a definite concept of form; in clay this search is seen in a constant change of modes of representation and in the representations themselves. Pulling out all meaningful parts from the lump of clay and the action of adding parts together to make a form can both be observed. A child who starts with a lump of clay and pulls parts out from the whole usually does not go into as much detail as a child who starts with separate parts and then puts these together. But either method comes naturally from the child and is acceptable. Moist clay can be easily stored in plastic bags, and water can be added as needed to maintain the proper consistency. Plasticine, which is essentially clay with an oil base, is much more expensive than clay, and the consistency cannot be altered.

Summary of Growth Characteristics of the Preschematic Stage

The art of children in the stages of first representation can be seen as a direct reflection of the child himself. Not only are the drawing and painting of a child a record of his concepts, feelings, and perceptions of his environment, but these drawings and paintings also provide the sensitively aware adult with the means for a better understanding of the child. In our discussion the concern has been primarily to see art as one of the essential components in a child's total development.

The art of children provides us not only with understanding of a child but also with an opportunity to promote growth through the area of art education. Here we mean something a great deal more significant than changing the outward appearance of the drawings themselves; we are concerned with the total process of creating. We cannot positively affect a child's behavior by providing him with patterns or procedures to follow in order to achieve a "better-looking" product. The change in the product itself should come about through the changes in a child's thinking, feeling, and perceiving. It is through the *process* that changes in behavior or changes in growth patterns develop. It is also through the process that meaningful changes take place in the product itself.

The art motivation for this particular age group concentrates upon the experiences the child himself has had, either in his own physical self, or in fantasy, or in vicarious experiences. We are all composed of both hereditary and environmental factors and because we can do little about the heredity of those children with whom we are working, we must concentrate upon the environmental factors within a learning situation. Art can play a vital role in providing the environment in which the

Figure 71. *These five year old boys are enjoying using adult tools. The opportunity to explore, investigate, and invent new forms through art activities is an absorbing experience.*

various growth patterns can develop. Art plays a crucial part in our educational system, particularly in the area of perceptual growth, the developing awareness toward those things around us through all our senses; through creative growth, the development of characteristics of flexibility, imaginative thinking, originality, and fluency of thinking; and also through emotional growth, the ability to face new situations, the ability to express both pleasant and unpleasant feelings. To a lesser extent at this age art also provides the opportunity for growth in the intellectual, social, and aesthetic areas.

The majority of children who are beginning to attend school will be in the stages of first representational attempts. It is therefore imperative that their introduction to art experiences be a meaningful one. A great deal of what goes on within school is dictated by the adult society in which we live; however, as we have discovered, the child is not a miniature adult nor does he think in adult terms. Art can provide not only the opportunity for growth in several vital areas but also the opportunity for a child to investigate, invent, explore, make mistakes, have feelings of fear and hate, love and joy. Most essential, he should have all these experiences of living for himself, for himself as an entity—an individual who can, should, and will think for himself.

RELATED ACTIVITIES

1. Collect drawings over a period of time from a child who is scribbling, and trace the evolution of the first representational symbols. Check to see which technique (drawing, painting, or modeling) is most satisfactory for this development.

2. Collect drawings that include symbols for the mouth. Stimulate these children by a motivation built around chewing peanuts. Compare the drawings done before and after the motivation to see what changes, if any, have taken place in the symbol for the mouth.

3. Observe the activity of a group of kindergarten children during their free play and during organized games. Relate the amount of parallel play to the preceding discussion of the use of space in drawings. What are the differences or similarities between these two segments of a child's growth?

4. Compare the development of representational symbols in drawings with symbols in clay. Photograph the clay products to keep a record of the development in clay to compare with the drawings.

5. Compile a list of the various art materials used in several kindergarten classes. Rank these in order of value for the child. Are there any materials used that cannot be justified as being of value for development? Explain your reasons.

6. Observe a child who is making his first representational symbols. Keep a verbatim record of his comments for several different fifteen-minute periods. What relationship is there between his verbal and his graphic expression?

7. From a collection of paintings by five year olds list the objects that are painted with a visually established color-object relationship. List those objects that are painted with no visually established color-object relationship. What might cause some of these choices of color?

Plate 5. *"I Am Standing in My Back Yard," painted by a six and a half year old girl. Notice the first signs of the child's awareness of the relationship between objects and color: the grass is green, the sky is blue, and the girl's hair is yellow. She has painted herself much larger than the tree; the relative sizes show the child's egocentrism at this stage of development. She is holding a doll in the picture, and a doll carriage is on the right.*

Plate 6. *"Lightning and Rain," drawn by a seven year old girl. Here the relationship between objects and color is more firmly established: sky is blue and lightning yellow. Large hands grasp the umbrella, which does an effective job of keeping the child dry.*

The Achievement of a Form Concept: The Schematic Stage, 7-9 Years

6

The Importance of the Schematic Stage

After much experimentation the young child arrives at a definite concept of man and his environment. Although any drawing could be called a *schema*, or symbol, of a real object, here we refer to schema as the concept at which a child has arrived and which he repeats again and again whenever no intentional experience influences him to change this concept. The difference between the repeated use of a schema and the use of stereotyped repetitions is that a schema is flexible and undergoes many deviations and changes, while stereotyped repetitions always remain the same.

Figure 72.

These schemata are highly individualized. For some children the schema can be a very rich concept while for others the schema can be a fairly meager symbol. Differences in schemata depend upon many things, but just as no two children are the same, we find that no schemata are identical; rather, they depend upon personality differences and upon the degree to which a teacher was able to activate the child's passive knowledge while he was originally forming his concepts. Although there is no magical time for the formation of a schema, most children arrive at this stage at about seven years of age. The schema may be determined by how a child sees something, the emotional significance he attaches to it, his kinesthetic experience with or touch impressions of the object, or how the object functions or behaves.

We find a pure schema in a child's drawing whenever a child's representation confines itself to the object. "This is a tree." "This is a man." However, when intentions are present that alter the forms, we no longer speak of a pure schema. Thus, a pure schema, or schematic representation, is a representation with no intentional experiences included. When intentional experiences are represented, or when there are modifications of the schema, we know that the child has portrayed something of importance to him. A study of the kinds of modification undergone by the schema allows us to understand the intention underlying the representation. This is of special importance to the teacher, who can then study the effects of his teaching by comparing the schema with its deviations.

The schema of an object is the concept at which the child has finally arrived, and it represents the child's active knowledge of the object. The schema can also refer to space and figures just as it refers to objects. For example, a child may usually draw a house with roof and windows only. For a particular experience the door may be of special significance; he will then change his schema and add the door. Through this change of the schema the child has shown his particular experience.

Characteristics of Schematic Drawings

HUMAN SCHEMA

We use the term *human schema* to describe the concept of a figure at which the child has arrived after much experimentation. Younger children in their first representational attempts draw the human figure in many different ways, and a child's drawing of a man may change from one day to the next. As a child gets closer to the achievement of a form concept he gradually develops a symbol for a man that is repeated again and again, so long as he has no particular experience to influence him to change this concept. Each child's schema of a man will be quite different from any other child's.

At about the age of seven the drawing of a human figure by a child should be a readily recognizable symbol. The child will portray body parts depending on his active knowledge of them. Not only should there be a head, body, arms, and legs, but also some of the various features. The eyes should be different from the nose, the symbol for nose should be different from that for the mouth, and there should be hair and even a neck. Usually, the child includes separate symbols for hands and even fingers, and of course a different symbol for feet. Often clothing is drawn instead of the body, but the average schema for a seven year old includes most of these items. The opinion that the profile represents a more advanced stage in a child's creative concept is, according to experiments, incorrect (Harris, 1963). Apparently, for some children the symmetry of the body, the two arms, the two legs, the two eyes, the two ears, is of most importance. In some cases the side-view, or profile, concept is the first schema. Some schemata can have a mixed profile and front view that includes a representation of two eyes and profile nose. The schema consists of geometric forms and when separated from the whole these lose their meaning. Sometimes ovals, triangles, squares, circles, rectangles, or irregular shapes are used as schema for the body, though all kinds of shapes are used for legs, arms, and clothes. In Figure 73, "My Family," notice how the boy repeats his schema for each member of his family. It is quite clear in the human schema that a child is not attempting to copy a visual form, but rather, that his concept is arrived at by a combination of many factors: his process of thinking, his awareness of his own feelings, and his development of perceptual sensitivities. The human schema is therefore highly individualized and may be considered a reflection of an individual's development.

SPACE SCHEMA

The great discovery during this age level is that there is a definite order in space relationships. The child no longer thinks, "There is a tree, there is a man, there is a car," without relating them to one another as he has done during the preschematic stage. A child now thinks, "I am on the ground, the car is on the ground, the grass grows on the ground, mud is on the ground, we are all on the ground." This first

Figure 73. *"My Family," drawn by a seven year old boy. Here the schema is repeated for each member of the family. Notice that he uses the same irregular shape for the body, the same system for fingers, and even the same symbols for ears.*

conscious awareness that a child is part of his environment is expressed by a symbol which is called a *base line*. From now on, this consciousness, which includes all objects in a common space relationship, is expressed by putting everything on this important base line (see Figure 74).

At this stage of development the child has not developed an awareness of how to represent the three-dimensional quality of space. We find,

Figure 74. *"Picking Flowers" shows how everything is organized along a base line. The hands are enlarged in size because of their importance for picking.*

Figure 75. *"Milking Time" shows a part of the barn cut away so that we can see the important cows and farmer. We see a sky above and a base line below the barn, with air in between.*

therefore, that the schema is usually a representation of two dimensions. Occasionally some abstract lines are substituted for depth, but the biggest discovery is that there is a definite order in spatial relationships. The space schema is almost entirely abstract and has only an indirect connection with nature as adults know it.

The base line is universal and can be considered as much a part of the natural development of children as learning to run or skip. In a study of over five thousand drawings, it was found that only 1 per cent of the children included the base line at age three, that by the age of six more children included the base line than did not, and that by eight years 96 per cent of the children included the base line in their drawings (Wall, 1959). The base line appears as an indication of the child's realization of the relationship between himself and his environment. He places everything on this base line; this line can apparently represent not only the ground on which objects stand but can represent a floor, a street, or any base upon which a child is standing.

It is quite obvious that in nature neither objects nor persons standing on the ground are in actuality standing upon a line. When questioned, children invariably identify this base line as being the ground. A counterpart to the base line appears in drawings as a sky line. This is usually drawn at the top of the page and the space between this and the base line is identified by children as being air (see Figure 75). As adults we usually think of the sky in pictures as coming down to ground level; however, this is actually an optical illusion. Not only does the sky never actually meet the ground, but of course there is no tangible sky, only an accumulation of air over a dark background. The concept of the sky above, ground below, and air between is just as valid as our concept that the sky and ground meet. Both are illusions.

In creative products of primitive stages of mankind the base line is often used as a means of indicating motion. Drawings made by Australian aborigines or by Arctic tribes all use the base line to indicate motion. It may be that the origin of the base line is the kinesthetic experience of moving along a path. The use of the base line is also very apparent in the art of some advanced cultures, such as in the carvings on the tombs in ancient Egypt, or the vase decorations of ancient Greece. In the latter two instances pictorial matter is arranged on a line with a narrative purpose. If children use their art as communication, it may be natural to think of objects coming one after another on a line.

THE BASE LINE AS PART OF THE LANDSCAPE

When a child is drawing or painting an outdoor picture, the base line is used at one time to symbolize the base on which things stand and at another time to represent the surface of the landscape. In the painting in Figure 76 one base line symbolizes the level ground while another base

Figure 76. "I Am Climbing a Hill," painted by a seven year old boy. The hill is an upper base line which is bent, representing the experience of climbing up and down.

represents the mountain. Apparently, the child wishes to indicate that this second base line is elevated over the plain. It can readily be seen that the mountain is still meant as a base line from the fact that the flowers stand perpendicularly to the mountain. Even the figure is bound to its base line. We can realize this experience most clearly if we consider the base line to be a length of straight wire with flowers attached to it. If we bend the wire according to the kinesthetic experience of going up and down, the flowers attached to the wire stand out perpendicularly, just as we see them in this drawing. Clearly, it is not the mass of the mountain that is of significance but the line itself, which goes up and down.

If we look at the illustration in Figure 77, entitled "Fruit Harvest," we will see two base lines that represent an orchard. The child himself is shown on the lower part of the paper picking apples off a tree. Above him is the sky and above that another base line upon which his father appears driving a wagon full of apples. Notice the schema the child has for apple tree. Notice also the size of the apples on the tree as compared to the size of the apples in the basket. The apples have great importance on the tree, but once they are in the basket they become less important. One can get a real feeling for the freshness of children's expression from this, and it is this freshness that many adult artists strive to emulate. The bird in the upper corner becomes important, too, for apples pecked by a bird must be discarded. The showing of two base lines is a later development, and is a step toward perspective as we know it in drawings. However, this is strictly a two-dimensional representation, as can clearly be seen by the fact that the sky is represented in both halves of the painting. Children rarely draw anything that is not directly related to the base line, even if two or more base lines appear in one picture. A better understanding of "Fruit Harvest" may be had by seeing the top portion as a more distant row of trees in the orchard, beyond the lower or closer trees.

In this picture everything functions and has meaning. The child wants to say, "There is an orchard," therefore he is not satisfied by merely drawing one tree. "The apples on the tree are the most beautiful ones, because I want them, but I have picked some into the basket. I am just now reaching for one. Those in the basket are no longer single apples, they are the dozens of apples I have collected. Daddy is carrying them to town. Birds are pecking on the apples. We don't want the birds." We can see how the child relates himself actively to his environment. He is on the ground, the basket is on the ground, the apples are in the basket, the tree is on the ground; and farther away, the wagon is on the ground, the horse is on the ground, and the bird is in the air with the sky above. The picture signifies the child's understanding of himself and his environment.

Figure 77. *"Fruit Harvest." The child has used two base lines to represent the orchard.*

Figure 78. *"Galloping Horses Followed by a Dog." Although this pencil drawing was done by a gifted younger child, it illustrates how two base lines are used in drawings.*

THE ACHIEVEMENT OF A
FORM CONCEPT

Figure 79. *"Norfolk Ferry," painted by an eight year old boy. This painting is an imaginative example of representing space by "folding over."*

OTHER MEANS OF SPACE REPRESENTATION

Although the base line is the most common means used by children to represent space in their drawings and paintings, occasionally an emotional experience forces a child to deviate from this type of schema. These are subjective space representations. The frequently used process of *folding over* belongs to this category. By folding over we mean the process of creating a space concept by drawing objects perpendicular to the base line, even when these objects appear to be drawn upside down.

The illustration in Figure 79 is a typical painting by a child, which shows the process of folding over. Here we see that the child has depicted himself as waving to the ferry. After the child drew himself waving with his handkerchief, standing on one side of the bay, he decided to draw the boat. He drew it apparently upside down. But it isn't really upside down. This child was leaning on the floor and after drawing himself on one side of the base line, he walked around his paper and drew the other side of the bay and the ferryboat. You can even see where the ferryboat is landing. This concept can best be understood if we fold the paper along the base line on which the boy is standing. We then share the experience of the child standing upright and facing the boat. If we fold the other side of the bay upright also, we get a model of the scene and we suddenly realize the interesting concept of the two skies, one at the bottom and the other at the top of the paper. Now both skies are folded up. This type of representation might be what we would do if we were asked to make a diagram of both sides of a room. On this side there are four windows and so we draw them, and then for the other side of the room we diagram the wall on the bottom of the page. Actually this is a perfectly valid concept: the child wants to draw both sides of the bay simultaneously because both sides are important. Basically, the subjective experience of this child is that of being in the center of the scene, seeing one shore to the left and the other to the right. This experience shows very clearly that it is an advantage to have children work on the floor or on low tables, so that the drawing or painting can be approached from all directions. In Figure 80, "I Say Hello to My Friend on the Other Side of the Street," this principle of folding over is used to show the opposite sides of the street. This was drawn by a nine year old partially blind boy.

Figure 80. *"I Say Hello to My Friend on the Other Side of the Street." These children frequently called to each other at the street crossing. Here the base lines are at the edges of the paper, in contrast with their location in the previous illustration.*

THE ACHIEVEMENT OF A
FORM CONCEPT

Occasionally a child who customarily uses the base line will drop the lines altogether. An experience can be so strong that it overpowers the feeling of being connected with the ground. The painting in Figure 81, "On the Seesaw," is a typical example of such a drawing. The sensation of this kinesthetic experience has determined the spatial concept. The boy shows himself way up near the sky and sun. His emotions are visibly expressed by the exaggerated size of his body as well as by his facial expression; the mouth is wide open. "My older sister lifted me up so high," he says. Although this indicates that his older sister is at least heavy enough to lift him up high, because of his own subjective experience he has exaggerated his own size and made his sister seem much smaller.

Figure 81. *"On the Seesaw," painted by a nine year old boy. The kinesthetic experience of going up and down determined this unusual spatial concept.*

Figure 82. *"Playing Checkers," painted by a seven year old boy. The checkerboard has been tipped up because it is important to see the top view when playing.*

Because the sister is sitting opposite on the seesaw, the boy has painted her seemingly upside down. In reality this is his subjective view and it can be better understood if we fold each child up so that they appear to be sitting on the ends of the seesaw itself.

Another important aspect of subjective space experiences results in drawing with a mixture of plan and elevation. The painting "Playing Checkers" in Figure 82, by a seven year old boy, shows the checkerboard apparently up on its edge. Because the child is involved with playing checkers, he has to show the full checkerboard. The table, however, would not be a table if it did not have legs. So the child has drawn a table with legs, and when necessary, he has folded over the top of the table to show its significance, thus mixing plan and elevation in one drawing.

Another drawing that shows the same type of experience is "Amusement Island" (see Figure 83). The child visited an island on which were all types of amusements, people playing cards, hot-dog stands, and so forth. There were boats for rent, and in such a boat the child took a ride around the island. The drawing shows a top view of the island, because it is important to show that water surrounds the land. Since the child rode

Figure 83. *"Amusement Island," drawn by an eight year old boy. The boy had gone around the amusement island in a rowboat.*

around the island in a boat, it is important that this too be portrayed. Each of the events is shown as a separate activity and the child has put them together as he experienced them. It is a listing of events, with each table folded over or boat tipped so that we can see what went on as the child must have experienced it. Here it seems as if three edges of the paper have become three separate base lines. Similarly, it is not unusual to see all four sides of a house portrayed at one time, nor to see all four wheels drawn on an automobile. It is quite clear that what a child includes in his paintings is a direct reflection of his subjective experiences. There is obviously nothing wrong with these representations. The sensitive adult can gain great insight and understanding about the child's relationship to his world by becoming more involved in the meaning of his creative expression.

SPACE AND TIME REPRESENTATIONS

By *space and time representations* we mean the inclusion in one drawing of different time sequences or of spatially distinct impressions. Just as a child has his own way of showing two- and three-dimensional objects, sometimes by using plan and elevation at the same time, so he has his own way of showing events that occur in different time sequences. Apparently, children have different reasons for developing these space and time representations, and an understanding of them is important because they can provide a rich source for motivation.

One method of space-time representation arises out of the urge for communication. A child likes to listen to and tell stories. This is one reason why we find different episodes represented by different pictures in one sequence of drawings. The pictures may be separate, like those in a comic book, although they may not be divided by a line. Journeys, trips, travel episodes, or other events that require a sequence of time belong in this type of representation. In such topics usually the most important events are described. Separate pictures show a complete event, so the topic of the series is usually the same.

Another manner of space-time representation occurs when distinct actions that have taken place at various times are represented within one drawing. This springs not from the desire to communicate something but from the importance of the action itself. This emotional involvement diminishes the child's consciousness of time to such an extent that he may not be aware of representing different time phases in one drawing. He is concerned only with expressing within one drawing what he considers most characteristic about the action, in much the same way as alternations between plan and elevation are used to express what is most characteristic about an object. In Figure 84 we see a boy in his house, supposedly upstairs getting ready for school. One drawer in the dresser must have special meaning, for it has been drawn darker. Notice the stairs going

Figure 84. *In "Getting Ready for School," what appears to be a bent ladder is the stairway connecting the bedroom with the dining room, so that the upstairs and downstairs appear to be on the same level.*

Figure 85. a. *This is a child's schema for "A Man." No particular experience is portrayed.* **b.** *"Searching for the Lost Pencil." Notice how the schema has been changed to show how the child looked for and found the pencil.*

C R E A T I V E   A N D   M E N T A L
G R O W T H

down to the dining room; they are drawn as he experiences them and not in the usual adult side-view representation. The breakfast bowls are on the table downstairs and have been folded up so that we can look into them. Turning back to Figure 73 and comparing the human schema, we can easily see that these drawings were made by the same boy, although actually several weeks apart. (An ironic note is the rubber stamp of a dog under the drawing of the boy himself. Apparently these stamps were available in the classroom for the less "artistic" youngsters to use.)

In space and time representations the picture is often confined to a single sequence of action or movements. Placing the various aspects next to one another in one space is merely a method of portraying the distinctive qualities of a particular experience. For a typical example of this type of expression refer to Figure 85b, the drawing entitled "Searching for the Lost Pencil." We are referring now only to the content of this drawing, which expresses different time sequences within one space. The figure on the left both is looking for and has found the pencil. The child uses the next figure to express putting the pencil into his pocket with one hand, while the other hand shows clearly that it no longer has any function. In other words, by means of two figures he has represented four different time phases. In a sense he could have given one figure four arms, as has been done in medieval manuscripts, but this would have contradicted his concept of a man. He was emotionally so tied up with the content that it overpowered his feeling for reality. The experience he himself had with all the phases—searching for the pencil, finding the pencil, picking it up, and putting it in his pocket—has made him draw all these aspects.

X-RAY PICTURES

A child may use another interesting nonvisual way of representation to show different views that could not possibly be seen at the same time. He depicts the inside and outside of a building or other enclosure simultaneously whenever the inside is of greater importance. In the same way as the child depicts plan and elevation at the same time while apparently unaware of the impossibility of such a visual concept, he mixes up the inside and outside concepts within his drawing. Sometimes the child may become so involved with the inside that he will completely forget that there is an outside altogether. Frequently, however, part of the inside and part of the outside are shown together as if the outside were transparent.

In Figure 86 the illustration "Coal Mine" shows an X-ray representation in which both inside and outside are shown. The child has realized

Figure 86. *This is a picture of a coal mine painted by a nine year old girl. She has shown both the inside and outside features of the mine in one representation.*

the significance of the mine shaft and tunnels, and becomes absorbed in the interior of the mine and how the coal is produced. It is interesting to note that the mountain surface is treated like a bent base line, with the house and trees placed perpendicular to it. It is not surprising to find that the child is the daughter of a coal miner living in a company house near the mine.

The pictorial representations of children follow laws of their own that have nothing to do with "naturalistic" laws. An awareness of the variety and an understanding of the meanings of these types of space schema give us a greater sensitivity to the inner thought processes of children. In some cases the subjective space representations may look confusing or incomprehensible. Although a child should never be forced to justify or interpret a painting, most children are more than eager to discuss their involvement in the experience that motivated the picture. A sympathetic and understanding adult can learn a great deal about the meaningfulness of these activities by showing an interest in how and what a child thinks.

SIGNIFICANCE OF VARIATIONS IN THE SCHEMA

If we accept the schema as the concept of man and environment that the child has mastered, then every deviation from it has special importance according to its origin and its meaning. Through considerations of variations of the schema we can gain insights into the child's experience. Three principal forms of deviation can be noticed in children's drawings: (1) exaggeration of important parts; (2) neglect or omission of unimportant or suppressed parts; and (3) change of symbols for significant parts. Exaggeration and neglect refer to size only, whereas the change of symbols refers to their shapes. Needless to say, all these characteristics refer to the way in which adults see them. Children are not conscious of these exaggerations, for as Barkan says, "Children do not overstate; rather they create size relationships which are 'real' to them" (Barkan, 1955). The origin of such deviations lies either in autoplastic experiences (that is, the feelings of the bodily self or muscular sensations), in the relative importance of specific parts, or in the emotional significance the particular part has for the child.

Figure 85 displays many types of deviations in a single drawing. Here we see a schematic representation of a man that the child drew when simply asked to draw a man. Thus, in this drawing no intentional experiences are represented; rather, it is the form concept of a man at which the child has arrived and which he repeats again and again whenever he is asked to draw a man. In comparing this schema with the drawing "Searching for the Lost Pencil" (Figure 85b), we see the deviations and the experiences that these deviations express. In this picture the arms and the hands express the theme. The searching and groping about for the pencil is expressed by the different emphasis and exaggeration of the arm, and by changes in the shape of the symbol for hand. The enormously lengthened groping arm in the first figure shows how the representation has been modified by the experience of reaching. "With this hand I have just found the pencil." The arms show a double line, indicating their special functional importance. Compare this with the schema. Notice, too, the enormously exaggerated pencil, showing the emotional importance it had for the child when he found it.

"With this hand I put it in my pocket," the child says, and points to one of the arms of the second figure which, in fact, represents the same person as the first one. The arm putting the pencil into the pocket is now far less emphasized and is represented by a single line only; the second arm of the figure, no longer having a function, has shriveled to a mere stump. The pencil has been reduced in size now that it has been found.

An experience of bodily sensations is also shown. The left figure in the drawing is supposed to be bent forward, and this is expressed by means of shorter legs, a lowered head, and an elongated neck. When the head is bent forward, blood accumulates in it, and this may be expressed in the drawing by exaggeration. The figure on the right is standing upright while putting the pencil in his pocket, and since the sensation of bending

163

down is no longer important, the head and the neck diminish in size and the figure looks more like the schema. We may also speculate that the introduction of a base line in the second drawing might be caused because of the awareness that the pencil is on the floor and therefore a representation of the floor becomes important.

We have here an example of a very natural form of expression at this age. Although the child has a definite schema for a person, this schema is transformed in the act of creation. Furthermore, it shows that disproportions nearly always result from some definite intention or experience, though this does not mean that the experience is necessarily conscious. We therefore have no right to speak of "false proportions," since such a judgment is determined by an adult visual attitude, the attitude of objectively representing the environment. Because the child is not aware of making exaggerations or omitting parts, correcting such expression would only serve to change a true and sincere feeling to an imposed rigid form. Measuring and comparing the size of body parts is obviously meaningless to the child. He is intimately bound up with his own experiences, and he portrays his world subjectively.

The Meaning of Color

The child discovers naturally that there is a relationship between color and object. It is no longer a random choice or emotional relationship that determines which color he selects for objects in his painting. In representing space the child draws his environment more objectively, and he has developed definite space relationships. In color too the child has discovered a similar definite relationship. Just as he will repeat again and again his schema for a man, or for space, he also repeats the same colors for the same objects.

The establishment of a definite color for an object and its constant repetition is a direct reflection of the continuing development of the child's thinking processes. The child has begun to develop the capacity to categorize, to group things into classes and to make generalizations. "What color is the sky?" "The sky is blue." "What color is grass?" "The grass is green." To the visually discriminating adult the answers might be quite different, depending upon whether it is a hazy day or a stormy sky, or whether the grass is dry and brittle or fresh from a spring rain. To the child, however, just to be able to realize that the color in his painting is the same as the object which he is painting is an important discovery and a satisfying experience. He has begun to find some logical order in the world and is establishing concrete relationships with things around him.

Although there are common colors used by most children for particular objects, each child develops his own color relationships. The origin of the individual's color schema is probably to be found in a visual or emotional concept of color. Apparently, the first meaningful relationship that the child has with an object can determine his color schema. If the child's first impressions were of a muddy back yard, and through repetition this experience has become firmly established, then all ground will be brown, regardless of whether there is grass over it or not. This established color schema will not change unless the child becomes personally involved in an experience in which a change in color becomes important. Therefore, in the same way as we have seen deviations in space or form concepts, changes in the color schema will give us insight into the meaningful experiences of the child.

In looking at Plate 5, "I Am Standing in My Back Yard," we can see that the child has established definite color-object relationships. Notice that the eyes, lips, and hair, and also the grass, tree, and sky have been painted in very direct bold colors that seem to indicate that the child "knows" the color of these objects. Plate 6, "Lightning and Rain," is drawn with crayon. Notice that the sky retains its blue color although it is raining. Criticism of the use of color in these two pictures would only be upsetting to the children. Also the happy accident when colors accidentally run into one another, which may stimulate an adult, can be very frustrating to a child. Not only is he unable to capitalize on these accidental happenings, but he does not have the need or observational powers to relate these interesting color patterns to patterns one might see in the sky. For the child such accidental happenings are just mistakes. The color schema is an indication, therefore, of the developing ability for abstract thought and shows that he can generalize to other situations from his own experiences. This is an important step in the developmental process.

The Meaning of Design

From our discussion we realize that a child of this age has no concern for any formal aspects of art. Art for him is chiefly a means of self-expression; he is not aware of the beauty in what he does, nor does he spontaneously decorate an object. However, adults can see many design

Figure 87. *Children paint in a direct, spontaneous manner. Sometimes their paintings can look beautiful to adults; however, it is not the child's concern to make pretty pictures.*

qualities in what a child of this age paints or draws. The teaching of "fundamentals of design" during this period would be an artificial adult imposition and could destroy the spontaneous creativity. Or, as D'Amico says, one "factor responsible for weakening the child's native sense of design is the nature of teaching design, the imposing of fixed formulas on the child, now in general practice" (D'Amico, 1953).

How does this native or innate sense of design show itself? Often adults take a great deal of interest in this natural sense of the child, although this was not true a century ago. Today it is obvious that a new freshness and directness in expression has become important in the adult art world, and the same freshness and directness can be seen in children's drawings during this schematic stage. One of the important attributes of design is rhythm, and this rhythm is often to be seen in children's paintings in their repetition of form. Looking over drawings or paintings by children of this age will quickly show that the way children deal with space contributes greatly to this "design." This is a natural part of the child's development. He paints spontaneously and the repetition of form or schemata is done unconsciously, whereas an adult artist uses repetition and manipulates forms on a conscious level. The teaching of formal aspects of proportion would be detrimental to the spontaneity and freedom typical of children's drawings, because they would interfere with the innate urge for expression. Formal elements like balance and rhythm, if used as a guide or as a motivation, miss the purpose. Although an adult may get satisfaction in teaching design qualities so as to develop beautiful drawings, it is quite apparent that this could be most harmful.

The Development of the Primary School Child

We have said that the drawing reflects the child's total being; the emergence of a definite schema has many implications and can give an understanding adult some valuable insights into the child's development. The child no longer represents objects in relation to himself but now begins to represent objects in some logical relationship one to another. A younger child of five will draw a house or a tree or a toy in juxtaposition without any objective order. Now, however, the child includes himself in his concept in the same way that he includes the tree, the house, or the whole environment. This experience—"I am on the street, the house is on the street, John is on the street"—is a decisive factor in the psychological development of the child. His egocentric attitude changes and this is reflected not only in his drawings but also in his total development. The child seeks to find order in his environment and to develop formulas for proper behavior (Piaget, 1959). These may make no sense to an adult but can often become very important in a child's life. Most of us can remember some of the laws governing our behavior at this age, such as avoiding stepping on the cracks in the sidewalk for fear of dire consequences, or performing some private ritual if two children said the same thing at the same time, or touching every desk in the row before sitting down to insure good luck. These laws and rules for behavior make a schema of sorts in another area of the child's development.

The development of the schema also signifies a change to a more co-operative attitude (Wall, 1959). The differences between the preschematic and schematic stages can easily be recognized by observing children in a kindergarten and then comparing their behavior with that of children in second grade. Kindergarten children play and work together only when urged to do so. One child will be going in one direction imitating a train, another child will be sitting self-concerned in a chair, whereas a third will be playing in the sand, scarcely noticing the others. Their conversation will also be ego-involved. Although they apparently are talking to one another, they seldom listen to, nor seem to expect a reply from, those near them. Their talk is usually tied up with their own play and seems to be more concerned with explaining what is going on to themselves rather than to others. This is clearly indicated, as we have seen, in the spatial concept of children during this age. However, when the schema develops and we detect a definite order in space, the child begins to relate to others and see himself as part of the environment.

Before the development of the schema is not a period for cooperative games. An awareness of others and of others' feelings will not be understood. It may well be that a tremendous amount of time is wasted at the kindergarten level in trying to maintain order and quiet, since true learning apparently takes place whenever a child is expressing himself, whether others are listening or not. At this egocentric age it is most important to converse with oneself and with one's own expression, whereas during the schematic stage the ability to share and understand others' feelings is beginning to develop.

The introduction of the base line in the schema has other important implications for the understanding of children. Since a child can now see logical relationships between objects in his environment, it is possible to begin to think of a meaningful reading program. In reading, for instance, this same correlation is necessary in relating letters to one another in order to form a word symbol (Sibley, 1957). Pushing a child into a reading program before he is ready may build negative attitudes toward

reading; these are difficult to erase and cannot be counterbalanced by any advantage derived from making a child conform to an arbitrary time schedule. His thought processes at this time are also less ego-involved than before, and he is therefore ready to accept and be curious about the meanings of objects and words outside himself.

The child's particular schema is uniquely his. We can readily tell the drawings of one child from those of another just by looking at the schematic representations. One child may have a very meager schema while another child may have a rich concept of his environment. Observing these differences can give us a deeper understanding of a child's sensitivity to, and awareness of, his environment. As we have said before, the type of representation that a child achieves depends largely upon psychological, biological, and environmental factors, and the stimulation the child has received. It is possible, then, to assume that a child with a

Figure 88. *"In the Bathroom." Notice the awareness of details in this drawing; even the tiles and water pipes are included. This child has a rich concept of his environment.*

rich schema will be one who has developed a greater active awareness and a greater interaction with his surroundings. Hopefully, this is an area in which art education can play an important role; we will discuss this at greater length later in this chapter.

Schematic Drawings As a Reflection of Growth

Within any classroom we find a large range of individual differences. It is not unusual in the area of intellectual development to have a third-grade class composed of children whose intelligence quotient may range from 75 to 125. This means essentially that the mental age of these children will range from the six year level to the ten year level. We will also find a wide range of physical differences. In looking at the drawings by children in this same third grade, we can also expect to find a comparable range of individual differences. A few drawings and paintings, in fact, may be more typical of a ten year old. We have come to expect the child who is more developed intellectually to be in general more developed physically, and because art is a reflection of a child's total development we can expect his artistic achievements to follow the same general pattern.

One of the indications of the child's growing intellect is his understanding of the world that surrounds him. Objects may be meaningful or meaningless to the child, depending upon his emotional relationship to them and his intellectual comprehension of them. Whether or not the world has become meaningful to the child partially depends upon the degree to which he has formulated his concepts. It is to be expected, then, that the child will express in his drawings a definite symbol for the things he repeatedly represents. If we look at the drawing of the children playing checkers in Figure 82, we can see where the child repeated his schema of a man for both figures; however, the sizes as well as the motions of the figures differ. Notice that the nose and the eyes are expressed with the same symbol, just a dot. Yet obviously these parts have different functional characteristics.

The inquiring spirit often goes deeply into details. The active knowledge of the child reveals his understanding of and interest in the world about him, and this is what is expressed in his drawings. The degree to which a child tends to differentiate his schema, that is, the extent to which he is dissatisfied with generalizations and wants to find more detailed characteristics, is a clear expression of his inquiring spirit. Our checker playing youngster shows little awareness of these details. His eyes have no eyebrows, lids, or any other details, nor are the nose or mouth indicated by more than a mere generalization. The only concept that shows some detail is the concept for hand. It consists of the palm and five fingers.

Of course, our checker player may not have been very involved in this particular picture; several drawings would be useful to help us understand him better. However, the field of art can contribute a great deal to a child's growth by stimulating an awareness of the things around him. "Do you have to watch the moves carefully in checkers? Are you hoping your partner will not notice that he can jump you? Do you keep track of how many men you have left?" The clarifications of concepts and the stimulation of an awareness toward details can be a big step toward developing a greater awareness of eyes. Children are a product both of their heredity and of their environment, which means that we should strive to make their environment as rich and stimulating as possible in order to develop each child to his fullest capacities. Figure 89 was drawn by a boy after a trip to a firehouse. He not only remembered the rubber boots and pole but became very involved with the fire truck, and was particularly interested in the hose and ladder. Such overlapping is unusual for this age. Certainly art can contribute much to a child's intellectual eagerness by developing his active knowledge.

The area of emotional growth can often be neglected in a classroom. A child who has hurt his finger usually gets immediate attention from the teacher and often from a nurse or even a physician. A child with hurt feelings, however, usually has no one to whom to turn for help in patching up his wounds. It has been well established, however, that a child's emotions, feelings, and attitudes can affect his learning situation. Art can certainly contribute a great deal to the area of emotional growth. The opportunity to express in socially acceptable fashion the feelings of anger, fear, and even hatred not only produces a release of tensions but also allows the child to discover that constructive use can be made of one's emotional involvement.

When a schema is used in a rigid fashion, it may actually be an escape from facing one's own feelings and emotions. The flexible use of the schema is an important requisite for true self-expression. The very nature of the schema, the child's concept used over and over again whenever he needs it, makes it dangerously likely to become a stereotype that is repeated without any personal involvement. Flexibility is therefore the most important attribute of emotional growth to which special attention should be given during this period. Usually many changes and deviations in the schema can be observed, especially if the child is free to express

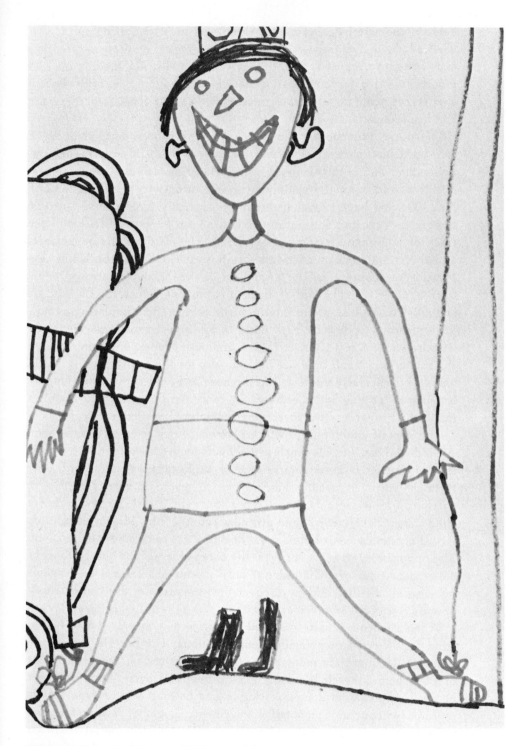

Figure 89. *"At the Firehouse." The boy felt as if he were a fireman. At the left is the back of the truck with its hose and ladder.*

CREATIVE AND MENTAL
GROWTH

his own reactions without fear of being censored. When the schema is used too rigidly, a child may hide behind these stereotypes; such hiding can readily be observed by noticing day-by-day changes or lack of changes in the schema itself. Another form of flexibility in response can be seen in the variation in the sizes of the represented objects. By such variations the child may indicate the emotional significance that various objects have to him. Exaggerations, neglect, or omissions, which indicate a child's relationship to his environment, are not only typical of this age but indicative of a child's healthy emotional reactions.

If a child becomes bound up with one part of a drawing by losing all ties with the rest of it, his response is no longer emotionally normal. He then continues to draw the one part of the figure to such an extent that the main part appears only as an appendage. Children who frequently draw such pathological exaggerations may be emotionally maladjusted. Continued and extremely distorted exaggerations are quite rare, however. A child who habitually uses the process of folding over considers himself the center. Such ego-involved reaction to the environment is not to be confused with the occasional use of folding over, which is typical of this age.

Art not only provides an opportunity for the release of emotions but it can also provide the child with an opportunity to use these emotions constructively. Schools have to limit the degree of emotional outbursts that can be accepted within the society of a classroom. Outbursts of anger, frustration, envy, and sheer joy are usually not tolerated. Even so, the usual classroom goes far beyond this and strives to make an emotionless environment in which only the intellectual pursuits are worthy of consideration. Art then can provide a place for emotional growth, and should encourage a greater emotional involvement in a healthy tension-free environment.

The social growth of children can also be seen in their creative productions. The presence of the schema itself indicates that the child no longer thinks of himself as the center of his environment. Most important, he has become less ego-involved and more aware of himself in an objective way. The child's putting himself on a base line signifies that he is beginning to view himself in relation to others.

The self-identificaton of a child with his own experiences in his creative work is one of the prerequisites for the establishment of a desire for some contacts outside the self. It is necessary to identify one's own actions and to feel responsible for, and to have some control over, these actions before one can develop a greater group consciousness. For example, in Figure 82 our checker playing friend wanted to show us how he plays checkers by folding over his checkerboard. He also went beyond the immediate self by properly establishing contact with the rest of his environment. Note also that the table, chairs, and children are all in relation to the base line. Other parts of his environment are also noted. The awareness of things around the self, which have no immediate relationship to the central experience, shows a high level of social growth. It seems that in this particular drawing the child was not personally aware of which room he was in or of the particular characteristics of the lamp or the window, which he did include.

Related here is the child's development in perceptual growth. The mere portrayal of a symbolic form for an object connotes little that indicates the development of a perceptual awareness. Since we know that perception includes many of the ways in which a child acquaints himself with his environment, the development of growth in perception is of prime importance in the field of art. The awareness of textures, sounds, smells, tastes, and visual shapes and forms can all be shown in a variety of ways in drawings. Developing a sensitive perceptual awareness becomes crucial when we realize that it is the interaction between a child and his environment that can establish the amount or kind of learning that takes place.

We have seen that color follows the same schematic patterns as form and space at this age. A child who has not yet established color-object relationships throughout his drawings has not developed perceptually as much as the child who is already aware that objects in the distance tend to become smaller. This does not mean that under the guise of developing perceptual growth, teachers should stress "proper" colors for objects or teach rules of perspective; rather, any motivation that attempts to focus upon perceptual growth should concentrate upon developing a more meaningful relationship between the child and what he is portraying. The products should be looked upon as a record of a child's growth rather than something to correct.

To some extent even physical growth can be seen in the productions of children. A child who is physically active is much more likely to give his figures movement and action than a child who lacks physical energies. As we know, continuous exaggeration of the same body parts may indicate some defect. The reader may be interested to know that the child who drew our friends playing checkers was hard of hearing. He continuously exaggerated or at least emphasized the ears, as we can see in Figure 82. Certainly we can see the continuing development of coordination by the greater control children exhibit in the use of their materials during this age. Providing a range of sizes in brushes allows the child to progress at his own rate of growth.

Aesthetic growth does not start at any particular age. Whenever objects or forms are seen in harmonious relationship to each other, and where we have an integration of thinking, feeling, and perceiving, we have devel-

CREATIVE AND MENTAL
GROWTH

oped an aesthetic awareness either consciously or unconsciously. The lack of aesthetic growth can be seen in pictorial representations that are disorganized either in thought and feeling or in the lack of awareness of any harmonious organization. We have already discussed the fact that rhythm, one of the basic elements of design, consists mainly of repetition, a natural type of expression during this schematic stage. Some children, especially those whose aesthetic growth is more developed, utilize this repetition in an unconscious way for decorative purposes. The bold and direct use of color, so typical of this age, adds to this decorative quality. However, we must remember that this is a natural outgrowth of the development of a child. No dogma regarding rhythm, balance, or harmony will ever have anything but a negative effect upon a child's natural growth pattern. It is the effect of art experiences and processes upon the individual, and not the final product, that is the true meaning of aesthetic growth.

If a child casually starts drawing somewhere and either does not have enough space to place everything he wants to draw, or discovers he has nothing to add and too much blank space left, he obviously lacks a sensitive awareness of the relationship between his paper and what he is expressing. To develop those senses, we need to involve the whole child. "Imagine that your paper is a treasure map of a large island. You will need to have an X marked where the treasure is. What else will you need on this map? Harbor? Boats? Trees? Mountains? Swamps? Lakes? Streams? Graveyard? Stockade?" Here the emotional and perceptual relationship to the use of the total paper may have become more sensitive. Certainly a motivation that makes the child more sensitively aware of his personal relationship with those things around him—particularly in terms of form, size, and texture—will help provide a product that is more developed along these lines. It must be stressed, however, that there are no set rules that can be applied to any individual. What is harmoniously right for one child may not be right for another. Just as we have large differences in the design characteristics of modern artists, we should also expect and encourage large differences in children's work.

Art Motivation

The kind and type of motivation a teacher should use at the different age levels grows out of the need of the children during each particular stage of development. We have seen that, during the schematic stage,

THE ACHIEVEMENT OF A
FORM CONCEPT

Figure 90. *Any art experience should provide the opportunity for a flexible use of materials and subject matter. These boys are busy making large paper masks.*

the child has formed a definite concept of man, space, color, and objects in all areas of art expression and in his psychological development as a whole.

The task of the teacher is to give the child an opportunity to use these concepts, not as rigid form symbols but as living experiences. Our motivation must create an atmosphere in which the child's consciousness of being a part of the environment is stimulated. In the same way we need to stimulate a greater awareness of the actions and functions of the human figure. Our motivations could be summarized by the words *we* (stimulating the consciousness of "I" and somebody else), *action* (meaning what we are doing), and *where* (referring to the actual description of the place, restricted to the characteristics only and not to depth or distance).

Knowing that children fuse time and space, it will be of advantage to use time and space stimuli. The motivation for these time and space representations should be concerned with subjective experiences such as hikes, trips, or personal experiences that include different time sequences. Later, stimulations should be added that refer to objective reports, such as "How the Firemen Prepare for a Fire," or "How I Come to

Plate 7. *"Mother is Picking Tulips," drawn by a seven year old child. The exaggerated size of the tulips remaining to be picked emphasizes their relative importance. The flowers in the hand are a different shape from the ones in the ground, which are representative of a stereotyped tulip form often taught in grade schools.*

Plate 8. *"We Are Playing on the Playground," drawn by an eight-year-old girl. There is a schema for running and a separate one for standing. The children standing in a circle are represented according to the child's experience of a circle, rather than perceived visually. This picture is unusual because it departs from the base-line concept.*

School," or "Our Trip to the Bakery." There are many topics appropriate for X-ray representations. Both the inside and the outside should be stressed in any motivation in this area.

Of greatest importance, however, is the need to create an exciting atmosphere that is flexible and open to any suggestions from the child. Rigidity is the death of any creative method. Any motivation should make the child more sensitively aware of himself and of his environment, should develop and stimulate an intense desire to paint a meaningful picture, and should encourage the child to be flexible in his approach to both materials and subject matter. Every motivation should have an introduction, a point of culmination, and a concluding summary statement. So, when we introduce a topic such as "We Are Playing on the School Ground," we would begin with a general introduction.

"When do you play? Didn't I just see you playing outside a short time ago? When do you usually play on the school grounds? When? During recess; I see. Where do you play? Do you use the whole playground? What do you play? Do you just stand out there and look at each other? Oh, you play tag! Yes, I have played tag, too. How do you play this game? You have to run! Do you run fast? Do you keep yourself nice and straight and tall? You mean you can't run fast that way? You have to bend forward when you run; why do you bend forward? If you run fast you would fall on your back if you didn't lean forward? Johnny, show me how you run fast! Yes, you really do have to lean forward! If you leaned too far, what would happen? You would fall on your knee! Oh, some of the gravel even got stuck in your knee once—that made it all bloody; yes, I know it hurts. Sometimes your body wants to go faster than your legs can. If you didn't bend forward at all, you would fall backward and hurt your head. . . . I guess it is better to hurt your knee than your head! How about your legs? Do you have both legs in front at the same time? No, that's like a rabbit! You are right, we cannot jump like rabbits and go very fast. Could both legs be on the ground at the same time? What happens when you run? Oh, one leg is in the air. Isn't that funny! One leg is in the air, did you ever think of that?" (In stimulating a greater awareness of the child's own actions you have also developed a flexibility within his schema for a man. The child can actually sense his legs and feet on the ground, so he has become personally involved in the motivation.) "Does everyone know how to play tag? We have all played tag! Let's paint how we play on the school grounds."

It is important in any motivation such as this to be sure that each child is personally involved. However, there should be a wide range of topics so that the child has the opportunity to identify with his own particular interests. At this age we begin to find differences in the subjects drawn by boys and girls. Boys begin to show an interest in mechanical

Figure 91. *Girls and boys often show different interests in their drawings. Here one sees an awareness of, but not an understanding of, the mechanical features of this tractor. These details are important to boys at this stage of development.*

and vehicle representation (see Figure 91) while girls tend to develop interests in houses and animals. Each child should feel that the motivation was planned just for him.

Subject Matter

The following suggested topics are presented only as a means of showing the direction our thinking should take when motivating children at this level. By no means should these topics replace an exciting and intense motivation; rather, they are suggested as areas in which this motivation may develop. The more emotionally interested and involved the child becomes in any experience, the better will be the development of his work. The following subject areas are divided into groups to point out some of the types of stimulation that are meaningful and educationally valuable to children at this developmental level.

This first group is designed to make the child's form concepts functional. Action and the awareness of action will stress a flexible use of the schema. The *we, action,* and *where* should all be an essential part of these topics.

Playing with My Friends on the School Ground

Jumping Over a Rope Held by My Friends

Pulling Myself High on the Playground Rings

Playing Ball with My Friends

Going to Church with Mother and Dad

We Are Climbing a Mountain

Doing an Errand for Mother

Helping Plant a Garden

We Are Sledding Down a Hill

We Are Skating on the Ice

Climbing a Tree

Saying Goodbye As I Go to School

The following group of topics provides an opportunity for using profile and front view.

Holding onto the Rope While Swinging

Playing Checkers with My Friend

Talking with My Mother and Father

Eating Breakfast Across the Table from My Brother

Watching a Parade Go By

We Are Learning to Swim in the Pool

The following group provides stimulation for a variety of space-time representations.

How I Come to School

We Eat in the School Cafeteria

Our Trip to the Police Department

When We Went to Visit the Farm

We Helped Bake Bread

The following may give some suggestions for X-ray pictures. Again we need to remember that stimulations for topics of this nature should be characterized by the *we*, *action*, and *where*.

My Parents and I Stay in a Hotel

We Visit Different Floors of a Factory

My Stay in the Hospital

We Visit a Cow-Barn and See the Hay Stored

My Father and I Go Shopping in the Hardware Store

We Watch a Chipmunk Store Food for the Winter

Just as we are interested in developing a flexible, functional use of the schema in terms of form, we are also interested in developing a flexible approach to color. Although it is obvious that some of these topic areas overlap, the following list may give some suggestions for particular reference to color concepts. It is interesting to see how effective a motivation is by comparing the use of color after a particular motivation with the use of color before such motivation.

We Find Bright Colors in the Fall

We Like to Play in the Rain

The Workmen Are Painting Our House

The New Grass in the Yard Is Beginning to Grow

We Got Our New Shoes Covered with Mud

Another area of importance to consider for subject matter is the private world of the child. This includes topics that have emotional significance to him, such as fantasy and dreams. When a child paints what is of deep concern to him, or reveals certain desires and conflicts, it should be remembered that any subject matter is acceptable. Although the teacher may show interest in the representations, under no conditions should any moral judgment be made about the content of these pictures.

The Time I Was Most Afraid

Once I Had a Horrible Dream

If I Could Do Anything I Wanted to Do for One Day

I Make Believe I Am an Animal

If I Were Teacher

One other area of subject matter that should be considered is the topic of the particular material itself. The principal reason for concentrating on the material is to insure that the child uses materials in a flexible fashion and has an opportunity to investigate their possibilities. Occasionally some children will use this nonrepresentational theme as a means of retreating from a creative expressive experience. This lack of involvement can be seen when children too often hide behind the phrase "I am just making a design."

Painting in Light and Dark Colors

Making a Collage

Making Tall Things with Holes out of Clay

Making Things from Boxes and Colored Paper

Using Crayons in Different Ways

A Rough and Smooth Picture

Art Materials

The selection of an art material, its relevance to a particular group of children and their needs at a particular time, and its preparation and handling are all important considerations. Any art material should facilitate the self-expression of children and not be a stumbling block. When children have become eager to create after a meaningful motivation, the art materials should be ready for their use. How frustrating to get all excited about painting "How I Broke My Leg While Sledding" and then have to sit still waiting for paints! Often the material can be prepared and distributed with the help of the children, and then the motivation can take place in another part of the room.

Three things are important in developing methods of working with materials. First, the teacher should know that each child must develop his own techniques, and that every "help" from the teacher in showing the child a "correct" technique will only mean restricting the child's individual approach. There are many ways of working with art materials; and, as mentioned above, time should be taken to explore many procedural possibilities. No child should be stopped in the middle of his expression to show him the "proper" way to hold a brush, use a crayon, or fill his paper. The teacher's job is to introduce the appropriate material at a time when a child is most ready to use it.

Figure 92. *Painting a papier-mâché animal is a form of expression different from painting a picture. Each art material has its own characteristics which call for different kinds of expression.*

Secondly, every material must make its own contribution. If a task can be done in a different art material with a better effect, the wrong material has been used. Therefore it is important that the teacher know the qualities of the material being used so that the best material will be used for any particular expression.

Finally, the teacher should not force too many materials on the children. In some books on art education we find that many materials are introduced and used from the very beginning of childhood. At a time when the child is overwhelmed by his own creativity, when he is full of intuitive power, too many different media may not only be wasteful but can often prove distracting as well.

The child at the age level from seven to nine years is not concerned with the representation of depth. What is most characteristic of this level is that the child has found a form, space, and color concept, which through repetition develops into his schema. At times these repetitions develop a designlike quality. The child should be able to repeat the same colors for the same objects whenever he wishes to do so. An art material that does not afford him the opportunity of experiencing mastery or self-assurance is not a good medium for this developmental stage. The consistency and texture of poster paint or tempera serve this purpose best, but crayon or colored chalk can also be used successfully.

There is no reason whatsoever for introducing water color at this stage. Water color is transparent, runs, and at time results in happy accidents. The transparency of water color serves best to paint atmosphere and landscape, but does not lend itself to repetition or to painting the designlike qualities so typical of this age. Since the child in his painting is more concerned with expressing his own ideas than with visual stimuli, these happy accidents can turn into sad disappointments. The child is striving for order and attempting to categorize his knowledge into a working form. This feeling of mastery is important for development and we must not sacrifice these gains for some happy accidents, regardless of their beauty to adults. We shall see that at older age levels, when the urge for repetition is not important, water color will serve to inspire the child. It is quite apparent, then, that an art material should be selected because it is closely connected with the child's development, and should not be introduced merely for the purpose of changing a material.

Larger paper can be used at this age, to give the child more freedom than smaller sheets provide. Since he has developed better coordination, and his arms have grown longer, the larger sheets may fit his needs better. Also, brushes made of hair can now be used along with bristle, because children have developed a greater awareness of detail.

Clay is not just another material. Since it is three-dimensional, it stimulates another kind of thinking. A material is wisely used only if it fulfills the purpose for which it is intended. Thus, nothing should be done in clay if it could better be painted, and nothing should be painted if it could be done better in clay; likewise nothing should be done in clay or paint if it could better be done with wood. It is important that the material selected suit the type of expression.

The real nature of clay is its plasticity. Because of this plasticity, clay can be used most advantageously with children of this age, for the very

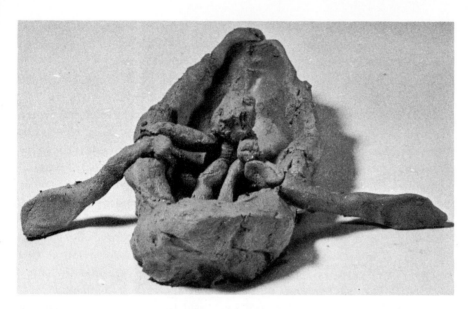

Figure 93. *"I Am Rowing the Boat." Clay can provide the opportunity for developing spatial concepts and understandings. It was not important that this product could not be fired.*

Figure 94. *In the synthetic method of modeling (left), single pieces are put together. In the analytic method of modeling (right), single parts are pulled out from the whole form.*

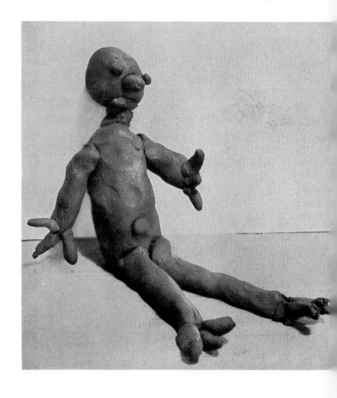

nature of the material will necessitate the flexible use of concepts. Whereas a drawing demands a simultaneous concept of one event (with the exception of the space-time representations), the process of modeling with clay permits a constant and continual changing of form. Figures can be added or taken away or changed in their position and shape. Therefore, action can be included in any motivation and should be related directly to the child's experience. Attention should not be focused on the environment because a comparison of the three-dimensional qualities of clay with space in nature could result in an attempt at small scale model making, which is not a creative activity but simply the development of a technical skill and has no place at this age level. However, the child may include objects of the immediate environment spontaneously. An example of this might be a child who models a picnic scene, making visitors come and sit down, moving the figures and bending them in the sitting position, and actually moving an arm up to the position of eating.

Two different methods of working with clay can be observed. One is that of pulling out from the whole and the other is that of putting single representative symbols together into a whole. In Figure 94 we have examples showing these two different modes of expression. Since both methods reveal different kinds of thinking, it would be disturbing to a

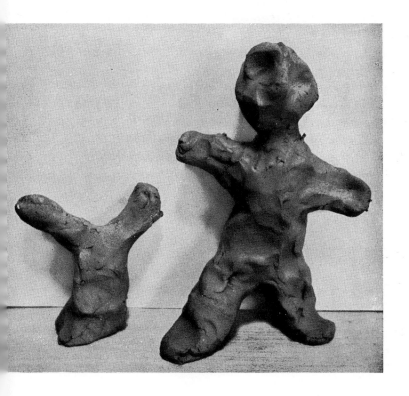

child to be diverted from his own method of thinking. Pulling the clay out from the whole means to have a concept of the total, however vague, from which details will be developed. This method of pulling out the single details from the whole is called the *analytic method*. Since this type of thinking is psychologically the same as that applied when observing or seeing things, we can assume that the thinking underlying this method is basically visual, although at this stage this type of thinking is not on a conscious level.

The other method of expression described as putting single representative symbols together into a whole means that the child is building up a synthesis out of partial impressions. Because the child arrives at a synthesis by putting single details together, we call this method the *synthetic method*. Since this type of thinking does not refer to observation, we assume that this type of thinking derives from nonvisual experiences. These nonvisual experiences can be of many different origins. They can refer to body experiences as well as to the activation of passive knowledge. Pulling out or putting together is not merely a superficial means of achieving a form, but is deeply rooted in the child's thinking.

You may at some time hear that it is wise to discourage modeling by the synthetic method of putting details together, because such modeling cannot be fired in the kiln. It is true that such pieces cannot be fired easily because of the danger of air bubbles and because the parts may separate in the firing process, but it is an adult concept that clay products made by children should be fired.

There are, of course, a number of materials in addition to those mentioned above that can meet the needs of this age group. Colored paper, collage materials, paste and scissors, many natural materials such as twigs or pebbles, and even a large soft pencil can be used to advantage. Care should be taken to insure that the child has an opportunity for a depth of art experience and that new materials are not introduced just to stimulate the teacher. Ideally, art materials should provide the opportunity for both a variety of experience and a depth of expression.

Summary of Growth Characteristics of the Schematic Stage

To some extent the products of this schematic stage appear more rigid than the drawings and paintings of younger children. However, we realize that the child is structuring his thinking processes in such a way that he can begin to organize and see relationships in his environment. This is not a step backward. The child is also beginning to structure his drawings and paintings to allow himself some basis for change and re-organization. Creative thinking is not disorganized thinking; rather, it is the ability to redefine and reorganize in a flexible manner those forms and elements with which we are familiar. Abstract thinking is based entirely upon symbols, and during this stage we can see the child's first steps toward this development.

It is essential that a child be given constant encouragement to explore and investigate new ways and methods. Occasionally children will try to copy each other, particularly if one child has just received praise and another wishes that he could have this praise too. Putting a positive emphasis upon differences and praising nonconformity and experimentation will encourage creative thinking. A child's *own* creative effort should be accepted regardless of how meager the product appears. Ideally, each child should be eager to create, with the teacher's role being primarily that of encouraging depth of expression and a meaningful experience. The child who clings too closely to stereotypes, or repeats too often a particular schema, or is constantly looking for suggestions, is the one who needs the attention and special guidance of the teacher to bolster his own self-confidence and to provide him with positive experiences in self-expression. At this age the opportunity to establish the self as an acceptable being who thinks for himself and is able to express these thoughts, whatever they are, becomes most important. Because the child is searching for a pattern or structure within the environment, his concept of himself as developed at this time may be an important factor in his relationships with learning abilities and with people. To develop a positive image of oneself, to encourage confidence in one's own means of expression, to provide the opportunity for constructive divergent thinking, should certainly be basic aims of the art program.

RELATED ACTIVITIES

1. Collect drawings of a man done by a second grade class. Find how many different symbols are used for nose, mouth, body, arms, and so forth. What percentage of these children are using geometric lines for their expression? Compare with drawings done by a third grade, to see if the percentages change.

2. Find one child's schema for man. See how this is repeated over a period of several weeks. After a strong motivation centered upon some physical activity, notice the deviations in his schema. A week later, has he reverted to his usual schema?

3. In observing the behavior of children of this age, outside the classroom, can you detect any social schemata? Are there fixed rules for games? Are there set patterns for certain activities? Are there set songs or chants for such games as jump-rope? Is there any evidence of adults' pressure for these patterns, or do they come from the children themselves?

4. How many children in a first grade use the base line in their representations? Compare the percentage with a second grade class.

5. Collect examples of X-ray drawings, folding over, and space-time representations. Why were these subjective representations important to the child's expression? How would adults portray the same event? Which is the most adequate portrayal?

6. In examining children's drawings and paintings, show how the use of color parallels the establishment of a schema in form. What are some of the differences found in color schemata for common objects?

7. Keep a list of the different reasons for exaggerations, omissions, or neglect of parts as shown in drawings. Illustrate each, from examples of children's work.

The Dawning Realism: The Gang Age, 9-12 Years

7

The Importance of the Gang Age

One of the outstanding characteristics of this age of development is the child's discovery that he is a member of society, a society of his peers. It is during this time that children lay the groundwork for the ability to work in groups and to cooperate in adult life. The discoveries of having similar interests, of sharing secrets, of the pleasure of doing things together, are all fundamental. There is a growing awareness that one can do more in a group than alone, and that the group is more powerful than a single person. This age is the time for group friendships and peer groups or gangs. The word *gang* has taken on some negative

189

Figure 95.

connotations within today's society, but we as adults may have some very happy memories of the gang of kids we went around with when young. This age shows an increasing development of social independence from adult domination, a learning about social structures in a personal way. This is a fundamental part of the developmental process and an important step in social interaction.

Because of the different interests of boys and girls in our society, and because of physical differences in development, the groups or gangs are commonly of the same sex. Boys ignore girls, and girls despise boys. It is a time when boys go camping, belong to groups that have rules of their own, take great interest in group sports, build elaborate hideouts from boxes or stray pieces of lumber, and not infrequently lead wars against girls. Girls, on the other hand, begin to wear fancy dresses, enjoy parties, sit with their own group, watch a love movie, invent their own secret codes or languages, and not infrequently lead wars against boys of their own age, although often secretly admiring an older junior high school boy.

These important feelings of an awakened social independence are often in direct conflict with the desires of parents or adults who do not want to give up the close supervision and guidance of their children. It is mostly for this reason that adults consider this stage of development as an undesirable one that often interferes with their own lives. Needless to say, teachers who are unaware of the important implications of group activities often find themselves the uncomfortable target of secret groups. Instead of giving support to this awakening feeling for group cooperation and the discovery of social independence, both parents and teachers often counteract it by prolonging close dependency with authoritarian means. Instead of showing their sympathetic and warm understanding of their children's desire for group life, they often oppose it, not realizing that by such actions they only drive their children into secrecy. This may be one reason why cooperation with adults reaches an apparent low point, and it is interesting to note that "delinquency usually has its beginnings at this age" (Stone and Church, 1968). The attitudes of adults may be responsible for some of the factors involved in delinquency.

A youngster of this age is becoming increasingly aware of his real world, a world that is filled with emotions, but emotions that are hidden from adults; a real world with friends, plans, and memories; a real world that belongs only to him. There is sometimes confusion in the use of the term *realism*. Often it is confused with the term *naturalism*. However, these terms can be self-explanatory so long as we remember that naturalism refers directly to nature and realism refers to what is real. Nature can be looked upon by many people. Their backgrounds, reactions, or emotions do not affect what is there. Nature may be snow on the ground, a hot summer day, or any part of the environment—it is this way whether we look at it or not. What is real, however, is firmly rooted within us. We can be inspired by the beauty in nature, be disgusted with the selfishness of man, or be full of hope for the future—and all of these are very real.

A work of art is not the representation of an object itself; rather, it is the representation of the experience we have with the particular object. A mere photographic imitation of his environment is not expressive of a child's individual relationship to what he perceives. The question is not whether the child should draw in a photographic way or be forced to rely upon imaginative patterns, but whether the art experience provides the opportunity for a child to identify with his own experience and encourages him in his own personal, sensitive artistic creation.

Characteristics of Drawings During the Gang Age

For the child this age may be the most dramatic and healthy period of discoveries, as can be clearly seen in his creative work. The schema is no longer adequate to represent the human figure during the gang age. The concept of the human figure as expressed during the earlier schematic stage was a generalized expression of man. Now the child is eager to express characteristics of sex, to show boys with trousers and girls with dresses; the schematic generalization cannot suffice. Greater aware-

Figure 96. *This is an age for discovering the excitement in one's environment. However, boys prefer being with boys and, as we can see, girls remain with girls.*

ness develops at this age; the modes of expression of the preceding stage are no longer suitable to express this increasing awareness.

In earlier stages of drawing the separate parts of these drawings were not self-explanatory, but were composed of geometric shapes and geometric lines. A part removed from the whole lost its meaning. Now, however, geometric lines no longer suffice as the child moves to a form of expression more closely related to nature. But the child is still far from a visual representation. For example, girls in their drawings do not yet draw their dresses with folds or wrinkles. The hemline itself is usually drawn straight across. The drawing is not an outcome of the child's visual observation, but rather his characterization of girls as girls or boys as boys. We find that the child gains a feeling for details, but often loses a feeling for action. Often a greater stiffness can be seen in the representations of the human figure in drawings by children of this age. Every body part has its meaning and retains this meaning even when separated from the whole.

Now that the child is developing greater visual awareness, he no longer uses exaggerations, omissions, or other deviations in expressing his emotions. Although at the age of nine most children still exaggerate the size of the human figure, studies have shown that this exaggeration tends to disappear during this stage of development (Lowenfeld, 1952). The child begins to substitute other means of expression to show emphasis, such as an accumulation of details on those parts that are emotionally significant to him.

The greater awareness and concern for detail at this stage of development can even extend to making a left hand quite different from the right. This concern for proper detail can occasionally make the total look distorted. Sometimes this exaggerated concern will even make a child exclaim that he has "goofed" if he has not drawn the proper number of buttons on his shirt. This dawning awarenes of the visual appearance of objects has little to do with true naturalistic tendencies, as can be readily seen in these drawings and paintings, where there is no attempt at showing the light or shade, the effect of motion, or any folds or wrinkles. Rather, the child is characterizing his environment. His drawings have taken on a certain stiffness and formality.

The X-ray drawing and drawings using folding over are now criticized by the children themselves as being unnatural. This type of representation is primarily subjective, and children who are becoming more aware of nature no longer look upon such a mode of organization as being appropriate. Girls of this age often focus a great deal of interest upon drawing horses. (See Figure 97.) Now that the anxiety about animals has disappeared, children will project their own feelings into this animal form. The horse becomes a symbol of running, dashing freedom that is

Figure 97. *Girls of this age frequently like to draw horses. These are free and unfettered, and rarely do we see horses portrayed as work animals.*

Figure 98. *Here we can see a boy who obviously enjoys driving this interesting car. A beginning awareness of overlapping can be seen in the steps starting under the car, but the house and the building with windows are both raised so that they can be seen.*

part of the joy of growing up. Boys identify more with cars, and it is not unusual for boys with questionable mathematical ability to be able to spout statistics about the horsepower and displacement of the latest engine design. Sometimes it even seems as if the boy *becomes* the car, making shifting noises as he draws, just as the girl can seem to *be* the horse. The emotional and psychological concerns of children of this age demand constructive outlets, and at any age the feelings and concerns of an individual are the basis of true art expression.

THE MEANING OF COLOR

There is a great unity in the way in which children change their expression. The child moves from a rigid color-object relationship to a characterization of color. Now he distinguishes between a bluish-red sweater and a yellowish-red sweater. This greater awareness of color differences cannot be called a true visual perception. This is because he does not indicate the changing effects of colors in light and shade, or the effect of atmosphere upon color. Some children will find that the sky has a different blue from the blue of the river or the lake, and some will find that the tree is a different green from the green of the grass. If a child in this stage of development still uses rigid color-object relationships, he is slow to develop in his color relationships. This is because the child has not yet refined his visual sensitivity sufficiently to see the differences that distinguish a green shrub from a green lawn. We shall discuss the methods of developing a greater sensitivity to those things around us, because refined perception can add a great richness to our lives.

The closer a child comes to a visual relationship between color and object, the more teachers are tempted to misuse this dawning sense for naturalistic colors by teaching how to use and apply color. There is no place in the elementary school for the teaching of color theories by means of color wheels or other such aids. Such teaching would only disturb the child's spontaneity and would make him insecure in his own developing sense of color relationships. A child can be made more color-conscious by emphasizing his own reactions to color and making meaningful the interaction between child and color.

The child enjoys colors and is now capable of being much more sensitive toward differences and similarities; his eager explorations through fall leaves, or his sudden realization of the constantly changing sky colors should certainly be encouraged. Any discussion of color, therefore, should focus upon experience and not upon the "proper" use of color in a particular painting.

Figure 99. *This drawing of a farm shows a meager development of visual concepts, but has an interesting space interpretation. Two base lines are used, the upper with barn and trees and the lower with a tree and horses. The space between has been filled in as for grass.*

THE MEANING OF SPACE

Just as his greater awareness of the self and of the environment leads a child to realize that geometric lines and forms are inadequate expression for the human figure, his representation of space reveals a change from the symbolic expression of the base-line concept to a more naturalistic representation. As a result of this growing visual awareness the child discovers that the space between base lines becomes meaningful, and the plane is discovered.

The change from a single base line to the discovery of the plane is usually a fairly rapid one. The stage of transition can be seen in drawings that include several base lines; we find the space between these base lines being filled in. An example of this appears in Figure 99. We can only speculate on how the child himself physically discovers the plane: maybe through his increased physical activity and developing curiosity.

One can picture a first grader walking to school, carefully following his prescribed route. Compare this with a fourth grader who acts as if the sidewalk were there to ignore; he is much more interested in walking on the wrong side of the hedge, kicking a can in the gutter, or going around in back of some of the houses to see if something interesting is happening. At any rate, the base line begins to disappear, the trees and houses no longer stand only on the edge of this line. Although for some children the base line representation remains in frequent use, the space below the base line now takes on the meaning of ground.

We also find that the sky line is no longer drawn across the top of the page. It now extends all the way down to what at the beginning may be a base line but which gradually assumes the significance of the horizon. The child has not yet become aware, however, of the meaning of the horizon. He has not yet developed conscious visual perception of depth, although he has taken the first steps toward such an awareness. With the sky all the way down, the child soon realizes that a tree growing from the ground will partially cover the sky. Hence he becomes conscious of overlapping, and another step toward a more naturalistic representation has been perceived, as can be seen in the buildings behind the car in Figure 98. That it is possible for objects to overlap can be an exciting discovery; this awareness can be utilized by the sensitive teacher. That one object can cover another is important, because it implies an awareness of the existence of the other object. We have not seen the development of such an awareness in earlier stages.

THE MEANING OF DESIGN

As children now discover the meaningfulness of their environment and begin to relate this to themselves, it becomes most important for education to give them a feeling for what is sincere in our environment and what is insincere. One of the main functions of design can be the establishment of harmonious relationships. At this age it is vital that we stimulate children's thinking and provide them with opportunities for discoveries relating to the natural beauty of materials that are found unspoiled within our environment. This means developing a feeling for differences in rocks, pebbles, shells, barks, moss—all the wealth we can find in nature. Children of this age are normally collecting a variety of objects anyway, from bits of string to toads, as any mother of a nine year old can testify (see Figure 100).

Collecting a pile of pebbles can be very exciting. Discussing the different shapes and different colors, noticing how the water has worn down some edges, or seeing how the light tries to shine through some varieties

Figure 100. *Toads, beetles, rocks, and other natural objects are fascinating and inspiring to children of this age. This is particularly true of boys, who sometimes make collections of such objects.*

Figure 101. *Holes and textures were the prime concern in this collage.*

but not others—all of this can be real discovery and can awaken perceptual sensitivity. Such explorations require a relaxed atmosphere, for such learning cannot be rushed.

We need not be limited to discovering the beauty of natural materials in woods and streams alone. Even scrap material can have beauty hidden in it. Rusty iron, or wrinkled paper, or even mold and mildew can be pleasing to look at if we are able to redefine our values and not think of them as discarded and rejected parts of our sometimes over-sterile environment.

The sincerity of beauty as found in nature should be stressed, because this is a natural extension of the child's own direction at this age. Occasionally children will enjoy putting these collections into some form, such as putting the pebbles into a little sand in a box and pouring plaster over the back of them to make a mosaic, or arranging scrap material in a collage (see Figure 101). Becoming sensitive to the qualities of a material is of great importance, and children improvise on their own account combinations of materials that need not necessarily serve a useful purpose. Getting acquainted with the different functions and qualities of materials is the main aim.

From our discussion it may seem as if undue emphasis is being placed upon a knowledge and understanding of materials, while the area of design may be bypassed. However, there should be no separation between the material and its function, or between crafts and design. Rather, from the very beginning, the inspiration for working with materials should come directly from the structure and nature of the material itself. The results of such relationships between a child and the materials will be crucial in later years, enabling the child intuitively to adapt to any design the qualities that are inherent in the materials. In our greatest cultures, workmanship has been inseparable from skill and design. Today we are again beginning to see signs of a closer relationship between the craftsman, the material, and the function or design.

In the drawings and paintings by children in this stage of development we begin to see a conscious awareness of decoration. Girls more and more frequently decorate the dresses in their pictures. Boys become more aware of the plaid of their flannel shirts. This developing awareness of pattern and decoration does not provide an excuse for the formal teaching of design. We certainly would not start to teach the formal elements of grammar to a two year old child who has just discovered that he can make his needs known through speech, nor would we teach the formal problems of balance, rhythm, or half-drop repeats to a child who is beginning to discover these patterns within his environment. A project such as designing a decorative border for a tea towel has little meaning, and it is entirely unsuitable to plan a design carefully on paper for possible transfer to some other material with which the child is not involved. However, simple potato, eraser, or spool prints may convey some understanding of repetition as part of the principles of design. This is feasible only when the material and the design itself both have a function in the life of the child. Such repeating patterns, although they look primitive to adults, will give the child an understanding of the nature of repetitions; the folds in a fabric will show how the pattern can become dynamic through the nature of the material. To identify with the needs of the materials and to learn their behavior is important not only educationally but also ethically, because it will promote a feeling for sincerity and truth in design.

The Development of the Gang-Age Child

During this stage a child begins to develop a greater awareness of, and sensitivity to, his environment. He has come to wonder why things work the way they do, and about his own being. He may now raise questions about areas that not very long ago he looked upon as unquestionable. The child is becoming increasingly critical of others and of himself, and some children will begin to hide their drawings from an inquisitive adult or else make some disparaging remark about their efforts. Children of this age also develop a sense of justice and may object violently to actions that "aren't fair." There is also an increasing concern with sex differences; although publicly the opposite sex is treated with a great deal of disdain, privately there are awakening feelings of curiosity and affection. A child of ten has gained a fair amount of information about the working of the world, both natural and social, but to a large extent this tends to be isolated, concrete learning. Much of the information that has been drilled into him in the classroom therefore tends to be meaningless. The fact that the Pilgrims landed in 1620 is readily repeated in a test, but whether 1620 was before or after the last ice age is not clear. Some of the concepts children develop by this time continue with them through adult life. This is even true of their drawing characteristics. Studies have shown that there is surprising similarity between drawings by children during this stage and the drawings by adults who have had no formal art training.

At this age children have not yet developed full control over their emotions, and often we find that a seemingly minor incident will be of extreme importance to a youngster. This intensity of emotion can be utilized within the art program. The emotional relationships a child

Figure 102. *Boys and girls do not always need to be in separate activities. Here a mutual interest in making a large group painting has provided the opportunity for sharing ideas.*

develops with various segments of his environment can often be expressed either directly or symbolically. Topics centering around religious themes, individual justice, or the expression of love or hate may involve a youngster completely. In such cases exaggeration or overemphasis of particular parts within a composition will be noted. Color in such cases can also be used symbolically, as in painting a face green. Such distortion should be looked upon as acceptable, and support should be given to the free use of exaggeration and distortion for emotional effect.

Gang-Age Drawings As a Reflection of Growth

One of the outstanding characteristics of this age is the child's discovery of his social independence. He has learned that he can have actions and thoughts that are quite independent of adults. He has developed a feeling for himself as a member of a group. He has also become more aware of the details of his environment. His drawings no longer contain a schema for people, because his concept of people has altered so that the schema is no longer adequate. How much he has departed from schematic representation and how much he feels the need to characterize particular objects, figures, and his environment is indicative of his intellectual growth. It can be easily understood that a child of low mentality neither becomes aware of his changing environment nor discovers those characteristics that will allow him to individualize objects or figures.

The ability to break away from the schema and to recognize particular details connected with the self and with the environment is one of the characteristics of this age. We have also seen that children between the ages of nine and twelve are much more observant of their environment, and that their interest in discovering the details of nature can be seen in the variety of collections made by boys and girls. To a great extent, however, these children do not remove themselves from their own observations. That is, their drawings and paintings show quite clearly that they see things through their own experiences, and assume that this "reality" is the way things really are. Children can sometimes be critical of the drawings of others and even of their own drawings if these do not live up to their own interpretation of what is real. We can see that naturalism is not the ultimate goal at this age, because there is usually no attempt at showing light and shade, atmospheric effects, or even color reflections or folds in cloth. The child, then, has left behind him the stage of schemata and laws for behavior; instead he has developed a curiosity about himself and those things around him, but he has not yet achieved an objective, naturalistic viewpoint. It should be emphasized at this point that there is no value judgment implied in discussing the various stages of children's development. Our concern here is simply to understand these differences and to become more sensitive to the great variety of artistic expression.

If we look at Plate 10, "Standing in the Rain," we can relate our discussion to a particular drawing. This picture was done by an eleven year old girl, using crayons. The schema has practically disappeared except for some facial features. Notice, for example, the repeated symbol for the nose in the three central figures and the sharp nose form in the rest of the figures. One of the distinguishing characteristics of this stage is the fact that parts of a drawing can now be subtracted from the total without losing their meaning. No longer do geometric forms suffice. It can be noticed in "Standing in the Rain" that the feet or facial features would remain as recognizable parts even though they were removed from the context of the drawing. It is also very apparent that the child has departed from her base-line representation and has a distinct feeling for the plane. The inclusion of such details as puddles, houses with windows,

Figure 103. *"Man with Umbrella," painted by a ten year old boy. For some children the base line and the exaggeration of meaningful parts, such as the enlargement of the hand holding the umbrella, continue at this age.*

raincoats with buttons and belts, boots of various colors, and umbrellas of various patterns clearly shows that this child is very much aware of her environment. It can be easily understood, then, that a child of lower mentality would draw quite a different picture. Notice for comparison the drawing, "Man with Umbrella," in Figure 103, where the awareness of detail is much less.

The question may be raised whether intelligence alone might cause such differences in representation. In comparing "Standing in the Rain" with "Man with Umbrella," might not lack of motivation be a real consideration? A closer look at these drawings can give us a better understanding and some insight into thinking processes. Lack of motivation may indeed cause great differences in drawings, but here we are dealing with functional intelligence, with how one actually acts and performs within the environment. In some cases a potentially brilliant person may never be motivated to utilize this potential. One of the important roles of the teachers is to motivate and excite children to utilize their potential to its fullest capacity. It might be a little more exact to say that these two children have differences in their functional intelligence that may be caused by several unknowns. For the teacher, however, it is quite clear that promoting in the child a greater sensitivity to his changing environment and awareness of his own thinking, feeling, and perceiving will help to develop him to his fullest potential.

Within the framework of art experiences we have the opportunity to provide for the development of emotional growth. Within our society, all too often, children's emotions and feelings are squelched. This is particularly true of boys, who at an early age are told not to be sissies. Even within a group of age-mates a boy usually has to conceal his true feelings in order to remain "manly." To be able to express emotional content and to develop in emotional growth, children need to identify with their own experiences in their art. Children who constantly depend upon stereotypes or who are unable to paint their own relationships with their environment are not able to express their true feelings.

Children at this stage usually refrain from using as much exaggeration as they did earlier. We find that there is a more naturalistic proportion. One of the characteristics of emotional interest in a particular part of a drawing or a painting, as we have seen, is the accumulation of details in this particular part. This fact can be easily understood, for the child naturally uses more affection and spends more time to characterize a part that is of emotional significance to him.

Social growth, during this period, is one of the outstanding factors of development, yet when something interferes with this new feeling of social belonging the child may withdraw and remain an outsider. Whether or not a child identifies himself with a group can be recognized by two factors from his creative work: the content of the work, and his participation in group work. The child who drew "Standing in the Rain" (Plate 10), is aware of people and has made the children different sizes. However, every figure is looking straight ahead and seems to have but little relationship with the others. The figures appear more like a group of individuals who happen to be standing next to each other. To some extent, however, the topic may have been responsible for this lack of a common feeling of participation. The illustration indicates that the child has identified strongly with the scene and with the people involved, but has not shown much interaction within the group. This child is obviously socially conscious of the environment, however. Not only is a particular setting portrayed, but there are differences in clothes, an awareness of everyone's being in the rain, and in turn the rain, boots, and puddles indicate an awareness of the child's own relationship to his environment.

The ability of children to participate in group activities can readily be seen when children work together on murals of such topics as "A Dairy Farm." Children of this age usually have the urge to work in group activities, but it may be the child who withdraws from such activities who

Figure 104. *These boys are working on a mural directly on the wall. As can be seen, they are interested in undersea exploration. Such a mural provides the opportunity to participate in a group activity.*

needs this social experience most. To a great extent democracy is based upon social action. A child who avoids the group and who is unable to relate to his own experiences in his drawings may need some support from the teacher in order to develop greater social growth. Experiences such as being in charge of a section of a mural may be of value. Certainly the individual's contribution to the group should be recognized, and a sensitive teacher can insure that each child is able to participate.

It is readily apparent that changes in drawing and painting will come about naturally when a child has experienced greater interaction in group activities. Pointing out that his figures do not relate one to another would only make the child unsure of his own creative abilities, and would in any case be contrary to the basic premises of art education. It is only through the child himself and his interaction with the environment and with people that significant changes will take place in creative productions.

The child who drew Plate 10 ranks high in perceptual growth. The child's growing visual awareness and her awakening feelings for nature are part of her perceptual growth. One of the first indications of a child's visual awareness is expressed by the inclusion of the horizon line and the painting of the sky to meet this line. Here we can see that the child has become very much aware of depth, even though no sky is indicated. Another aspect of visual perception is expressed by the child's awareness of overlappings, and here we see not only overlapping of people but overlapping of objects. There is also a visual awareness of differences in color, although, as we might expect during this age, there is no particular awareness of light and shade. The hemline continues to remain straight, at least in this particular illustration. The child has an advanced awareness of detail, which can be observed in the raincoats and in the background houses. Certainly the encouragement of perceptual sensitivity is a vital part of any art experience.

There are also indications of aesthetic growth in this picture. Notice the conscious awareness of design in the umbrellas. Aesthetic growth can

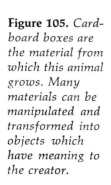

Figure 105. *Cardboard boxes are the material from which this animal grows. Many materials can be manipulated and transformed into objects which have meaning to the creator.*

also be seen in the way children relate the material to the subject matter; that is, how sensitive they are to the qualities of the material with which they are working, and to what extent their treatment of the subject matter reflects this awareness. Children of this age are now much more aware of the nature of the clay, paint, or crayon with which they are working. Using a material to its fullest extent and utilizing its intrinsic qualities is a characteristic of aesthetic sensitivity. Children who work with clay as if it were a flat drawing material are not aware of its distinctive qualities. Apparently, our artist who drew "Standing in the Rain" was very much aware of the possibilities crayon could afford.

One of the most important areas of growth to which art can contribute is that of creative growth. During this stage of development there is a great deal of pressure put upon children to conform not only to the wishes of adults, but also to the demands of the group. To function creatively, however, one must first be able to function as an individual. This means that imitation and conformity to patterns outside the self must be discouraged. The encouragement of the individual child's own approach to working out problems is vital in this area. To what extent a child is creative at this age can be seen by the desire he shows for experimentation, exploration, and invention. A child who is rigid or does not utilize material in new ways needs to be encouraged in his flexibility. Encouraging new and different ways to use materials and rewarding the interesting stipple or the effect of one color being placed over another will be positive steps in the direction of supporting creative growth.

Art Motivation

Adults often have pleasant memories of childhood; however, most of these memories are of happenings and situations outside school. Probably each of us has particular memories of the time when we were either nine, ten, or eleven. One adult remembering back to this stage had the following to say:

If I remember back at my childhood—now, you see, if I remember back at this stage, it must have made a very distinct impression on me, but I remember very distinctly how we converted a small, little, oh, island into something, into a wonderland. When I was a child we were in a gang—a wonderful gang—and we would sit on a footbridge over a small stream, I am quite sure it was not larger than a few feet, but when we went over this bridge it appeared to us like, oh, miles long you know, going over the bridge and entering our land which no one knew. This was fascinating. We made a building there at the highest point—there was a little hill, and we made our own money, of course, we collected the money, you know, for entrance into this island. I can still remember that we had pockets full of paper money which we ourselves printed. And we had there, we found bones of a dead animal and made a little sign saying, "These are the bones discovered of an animal two thousands years ago," and we really looked at it as we put it there in a certain order, and you know, this was something magic to us. And another place was the Snake Point where we had spread out a dead snake which we found, and when we went there we really got goose pimples. This was the Snake Point, let's go to the Snake Point, and then, you know, we collected gravel and built little paths, and these were then real paths, you know. We had a hideout when it rained, so this island was really something magic.

Imagine if we could promote in school these same intense experiences. All too often school is looked upon as being a place to "behave," a place to suffer through. But there is no reason why school should not be a stimulating, exciting place, where the natural drives of children are not only accepted but developed into meaningful stimulating education.

Motivation during this period must stress the newly discovered social independence in order to give the child a feeling of self-esteem. An art experience must give him an opportunity to express his growing awareness of sex, to develop a greater awareness of self, and to satisfy a new curiosity about the environment. It must also inspire the child to use the newly found methods of group cooperation as beneficial means of achieving results.

To inspire cooperation, two means can be used successfully. The first or *subjective* method of cooperation deals with representations of individual experiences of cooperation, or the representations of scenes in which cooperation is important. It is vital, however, for the teacher to know that much depends upon the way such motivation is presented to the group. The atmosphere the teacher develops during the motivation contributes greatly to its success. Such topics as "Helping the Flood Victims" or "Cleaning Up After the Storm" can be presented very dramatically. Whenever a child can identify with a large undertaking in which he feels himself part of the group effort, such a topic will inspire cooperation. It still continues to be important that each motivation be stimulating and develop a greater awareness of the possibilities in the subject matter. Such motivation should include a discussion and a point of culmination. "Whose house is under water? Suppose you were living there and we could watch how the water rises and rises! How would we feel?" The youngsters need to identify with the flood victims. They should also identify with those people who are responsible for social welfare. Such activi-

Plate 9. *"We Are Exploring the Surface of Venus," a four by eight foot mural painted by a group of ten year old boys. In a project such as this, where imaginative subject matter is used, diverse ideas are welcomed by the group and cooperation is encouraged. No one boy could have done the mural by himself.*

Plate 10. *"Standing in the Rain," drawn by an eleven year old girl. Color, use of space, and wealth of detail combine to give an aesthetically pleasing whole. Here we see a growing visual awareness coupled with a child's directness and freshness.*

Figure 106. *"A City Picture," drawn by a nine year old boy. The boy feels himself in the role of the traffic-directing policeman, who is symbolic of order in our society.*

ties as drawing the firemen during the big fire or the policeman during the evening rush hour can also effectively stimulate greater social coopera-tion (see Figure 106).

The second or *objective* method of cooperation deals more directly with group work itself; a whole group works on one project (see Figure 107). Here also the type of motivation is vital for its success. The group

Figure 107. *Here a group of youngsters are involved in making a mural. Much planning and discussion goes into this activity, but the finished picture is much larger than one child could have done alone.*

work can be quite simple in its planning, such as having each child make a fierce animal of clay and then assembling these animals into a large zoo. Straws or sticks can serve as bars, and the children will enjoy making signs for the various parts of the zoo. Group work can become quite elaborate, with a class dividing up into several working units.

Another example might be making a mural of a city. "What makes a city? Yes, houses and stores and factories. But we cannot have them all mixed up together! How would you like to live right next to a factory? Yes, we need to have some zoning laws. We will certainly need the residential district. How many children would like to work on the residential section of our city? There are so many different kinds of buildings that people live in! Now we have the industrial area for our factories. How many would like to work on this section? And, yes, the shopping area, too. But there are more than just stores in the shopping section! What other districts do we have? Oh, yes, playground and recreation area, fine! Does everyone know what section he is going to be working on? You had better pick a leader to help your group decide what kind of buildings you are going to need. You say we still need a school district? Oh, I think the residential area committee should worry about that. Why, John and Joseph, you are not on any committee! Would you like to plan the background for our city? Should we have a stream or river near the city? Do you think we should have some mountains, fields, or forest land around?"

Probably a material such as colored paper would be quite suitable for this topic. A large background paper or board would be essential. It should not be expected that a cooperative enterprise like this will be a smooth, quiet operation. Democratic action may not be easily learned, but it is an essential part of our way of life.

When the various committees of the city have completed their districts, the city can be assembled. A lack of trees may be very apparent, or some small houses may be needed, and maybe nobody has remembered to make cars and trucks for the streets. In such a way all the children can become involved in the activities. It is probably best to staple or tack the various buildings in place so that these buildings can be readily moved from one spot to another. There may be a sudden cry of dismay as Johnny finds that someone has placed a church right over his house. This provides a fine opportunity for some explanation of the meaning of overlapping, especially at the time when overlapping becomes meaningful. "Did you ever go to a movie and find a nice seat where you could see the screen, and right in front of you a lady with a big hat sits down and now you can see nothing? Is that good? Would it be all right if a little boy sat in front of you? It wouldn't matter if a little boy sat in front because you could still see and people could still see you. Overlapping is fine, but one should not completely cover the other. Maybe the small house can go in front of the church since the church could still be seen. And look, a tree can go in front of the house." The child has developed a fair amount of understanding when he can accept a minor role for one of his buildings, but maybe he can feel better when his tree goes in front of someone else's building. Every individual, every child in the class, should think, "I could not have accomplished by myself what the whole group has done." This is the heart of cooperation.

As we can see, the teacher's role is a subordinate one in this activity. His main role is to act as a catalyst. It is a far harder task to stimulate and encourage children to learn, produce, and explore on their own. An easier method of producing products would be to authoritatively assign projects and have the "best" method for achieving results already worked out beforehand. But to provide a rich, meaningful experience for children, such authoritarian methods must be discarded. It is much more important to increase the interest of children in the materials of expression, it is much more important to give a sense of discovery, it is much more important to give the child an opportunity to determine his own relationships with the world than to worry about how "artistic" a particular product looks.

Care should be taken in any art motivation to insure that the individual has ample opportunity to develop his own means of expression. As we have seen, there is a need for group activities, but these group activities should never be accompanied by pressure for conformity to the norm.

Figure 108. *This picture of heavy machinery was obviously drawn by a boy who took a great deal of interest in the mechanical details of the equipment.*

Both boys and girls at this age can develop an interest in particular, individualistic subject matter. Boys may like to spend a considerable length of time drawing guns or airplanes, whereas girls may spend a comparable time drawing horses or fanciful figures. Whatever the particular interest of these youngsters, this interest can be capitalized upon in the art program by expanding the frame of reference. A project—making many different types of airplanes, jets, transport planes, and helicopters, and fitting all of these into a larger background of airstrips, tankers, and people—can provide an excellent art experience. Other individual interests can be utilized in comparable fashion.

Subject Matter

Subject matter throughout the grades is determined by the subjective relationship of man to his environment. As the child changes, so does his expression. The following suggestions for subject matter are based upon the particular characteristics of this developmental level. These topics are only meant to be suggestions; it is assumed that they will always be adjusted and subordinated to the particular classroom situation and to the particular group of children involved. The important thing is that the teacher become involved and excited about the content of art expression. The following topics, then, are not to be considered as assignments, but as areas of interest which can be pursued with enthusiasm.

To stimulate subjective cooperation and to encourage children to identify with group activities the following topics are suggested.

Picking Up After the Storm
Helping After the Flood
Gathering Wood for Our Campfire
Building a Clubhouse with My Friends

It is also important to stimulate cooperation through the identification of a child with the forces of social preservation and maintenance. Such topics as the following might be appropriate.

Installing a New Telephone

A Policeman in Five o'Clock Traffic

Repairing the Broken Water Main

A Nurse Taking Care of the Sick

There are of course many ways in which a group can work objectively together for group cooperation. We have discussed a few possibilities, but there are many more. There should be opportunity for small groups of children to work together on such a project, and the final product should be large enough and complex enough so that each child can contribute in his own way and so that no one child could possibly do the whole project alone. The following are some suggestions for group projects.

We Are Making a Circus

The County Fair

Making a Farm

Exploring the Surface of Venus (see Plate 9)

We have discussed the disappearance of the base line at this age, and ample opportunity should be given children to explore the possibilities of using the plane. Since there is an increasing awareness of differences in sex and a greater attention to detail, the children should be allowed to explore and express subject matter that will provide for these tendencies. It should be stressed that all subject matter should have meaning for the child and not be removed from his own experiences. Suitable topics for this age might include:

Sitting Around a Table for Supper

Planting a Garden in the Spring

Watching the Parade Come Down the Street

Skating on the Pond in the Woods

Playing Baseball on the School Grounds

One of the characteristics of this age is the beginning awareness of overlapping. We have discussed some of the possibilities in this area, and it is to be expected that discussions will arise normally from the painting procedures. However, some specific topics to stimulate thinking in this area might include:

Looking out the Window of the School Bus

Sitting in the Movie Theater

Looking at Clothes in the Store Window

Singing for the School Assembly

There is another large area of subject matter in art that is related more to the development of skills and the increased familiarity with the nature of materials. These experiences with different materials may not have a specific subject or topic to represent, but the purpose and reason behind each of the activities should be made quite clear to the youngsters. Because children of this age are becoming more outspoken about themselves and about adults, these children should have a knowledge and understanding of the purposes of any project. A number of craft activities can be included under this heading, although care should be taken to insure that the direction and planning of them rest with the children involved. This would mean that activities such as those that are preplanned by the teacher or those that are cute or tricky would be discarded. Some suggestions for projects in this general area follow.

Geometric Potato Printing on Textiles

Making a Collage for Our Fingers to Feel

Making a Funny Animal in Papier-Mâché (see Figure 109)

Making Some Prints for a Christmas Card

Putting Together an Object from Wood

Making a Mosaic from Pebbles and Plaster

Some Imaginative Animals in Clay

Using Shiny Paper for Decorations

There is one very important subject matter area in art that should never be overlooked, and this is the subject matter that is within each child. In some cases this subject matter may be very apparent, such as a boy's love for working with tools; sometimes, however, it can be hidden beneath the surface, as in a quiet girl's feelings of rejection. There should be ample opportunity for these extremes to be expressed. Not only should the joy and pleasure of creating be given free rein, but deeper emotional

Figure 109. *A make-believe animal made out of papier-mâché can take advantage of the material. Mistakes or accidental folding of the paper can be flexibly adapted to the form.*

feelings and subconscious drives should also be given a chance to be expressed. Some materials lend themselves to such expression of the inner self better than others. Finger paint provides a direct release for such feelings; working in clay can provide the opportunity for frustrations to be eased. Ideally, every child should express himself freely, but in some cases the understanding support of a sensitive teacher is necessary to guide strong feelings and emotions into artistically constructive channels.

Art Materials

The child has advanced beyond the use of geometric forms and base-line representations in their literal meaning. With the discovery of the plane he feels the need of filling in spaces, as, for example, in the representation of the sky, which is now usually painted down to the horizon. Although crayons can be used on their sides to fill large areas,

Figure 110. *Mixing their own paints gives these girls an opportunity to enjoy and explore the possibilities of color.*

a better material for this purpose is poster or tempera paint. Since the child now has greater control over the paint, it is no longer as necessary to have the paint mixed to a thick consistency. In fact, the child himself can add water to the paints to make them the consistency that he himself likes, and he can also be responsible for refilling his own paint container.

We have found that children during this stage of development are more concerned with detail than formerly. Therefore, some children will want to use a hair brush in addition to the bristle brush. Although children of this age differentiate their color-object relationships, using different greens for grass and trees, it is not necessary to increase the number of colors the child has available. Actually, having a limited number of paints encourages a child to creatively mix his colors himself (see Figure 110). Good crayons also mix, but this is more true with poster paint. If you give children a limited scale of colors you encourage them to invent their colors if they feel the desire, and if they do not feel the desire for greater color differentiation, it is useless to give them a larger color scale anyway. Actively engaging in mixing colors for a particular reason is much more desirable than providing a variety of hues that the child passively accepts.

A material is good only if it contributes to the child's needs and helps him to express what is in his mind. Although there are unlimited materials available for the use of children, care should be taken that those chosen lend themselves to expression and do not restrict children's originality. If a material is by its very nature restrictive or inhibiting it should be discarded. Some strange creations have resulted from some misguided "arty" programs. Such things as marshmallows on toothpicks, wilted phonograph records, decorated light bulbs, or lamps made from old ginger-ale bottles can make a mockery of an art program.

Colored paper is a basic material at this age. It provides a natural means of overlapping and is an appropriate material for the early stages

Figure 111. *This fierce creature made from clay was designed as a special fantasy pet to scare away intruders at night.*

of cooperation through projects. Another essential material is pottery clay, which can be used for many three-dimensional projects. This clay can be easily stored in plastic bags and, of course, it can be used again and again. There are certain advantages to using materials that are considered adult art materials, and clay is certainly one of these. However, sometimes clay is used as a craft material to make such things as plaques and ash trays. Unless these objects meet a real need in the life of children—and not very many children between nine and twelve smoke cigarettes—these projects will be mere busy-work. Pressing various textures into clay, or exploring the possibility of space and form, such as holes in clay, or repeating a pattern of lines in a clay batt may have some utilitarian value if the clay pieces are fired. However, the teacher must not put the emphasis upon the preservation of the final product. If the child can participate in the total process—from seeing the clay in its natural state to watching it come fired from the kiln—this can be a very worthwhile experience. Occasionally, however, teachers take the clay pieces away and have them fired. Then the finished product has no relationship to the child who made it; the color, texture, and consistency have been so altered that he can no longer identify his object. Under such conditions it is better to leave the clay piece unfired. Clay that has been modeled or made to represent some object, person, or animal is usually not fired anyway. This is merely because the experience has been expressed in the process itself, and the procedure of firing can often cause these pieces to break apart. Most of the synthetically modeled pieces (those put together from single details) would not be able to stand firing. It is not worthwhile to sacrifice the child's individual thinking to conform to mere procedure.

Finger paint is a material that we have not considered to any degree before this stage. Now, however, it can be used for expression without the concern that children will be too involved with its textural consistencies. Needless to say, there should also be a good supply of other basic art materials. These include scissors, a stapler, paste, cellophane tape, and some woodworking tools.

For craft work many materials can be used, such as wood, papier-mâché, wire, cloth, and a scrap container with a wide range of straws, buttons, boxes, colored cellophane, and anything else that looks interesting. Children themselves will collect barks, rocks, pieces of wood, feathers, or whatever happens to attract them. Although some care should be taken to insure the safety of the children from such things as broken glass or sharp points, undue concern for sanitation and cleanliness may stand in the way of a child's developing skill in hammering or cutting, or of his digging up a particularly pleasing pebble.

It is quite possible to stimulate a greater sensitivity toward common materials within the usual classroom setting. For example, a common material like paper has many possibilities. "What can paper do? How does it feel? Is it smooth or rough? Can you fold it or crease it? How does it look when it is crumpled? Notice how it tears. Can you make it turn or bend so that it looks happy? Can you make it feel sad?" Other materials can be treated in somewhat the same way, with the emphasis being upon the process of manipulation and exploring the material and not upon achieving a nice-looking finished product. There is no reason why all children should be equally occupied and interested in the same materials. Boys at this age often develop great interest in working with wood. If simple tools are available a great deal of interest can be generated in discovering the qualities of wood, and the physical exertion of hammering and sawing and nailing often gives positive release to bottled-up energies (see Figure 112).

A word should be said here about exposing insincerity in the use of art materials. We constantly see around us examples of sham and falsehood in the use of materials. There is so much in the way of natural beauty for children of this age to discover, that exposing the false flowers, the imitation stone floors, and the false chimneys, for what they are

Figure 112. *Not only does the opportunity to work in wood provide the chance to use bottled-up energies, but wood also provides a new opportunity for discovering and exploring an adult art material.*

should be a part of these children's awareness. To a great extent children accept the things around them as appropriate, and unconsciously we may go on living in an insincere environment. If we wish to live in a more truthful society, it is not too soon to stress the sincerity of design.

Now that the child has developed an interest in the possibilities of working with a variety of materials, he can be a "pushover" for a range of noncreative craft projects to be found on the market. Such items as precut leather tooling kits, easy-to-glue-together plastic objects, or mosaic kits that "anybody can put together" can be a real menace to his normal curiosity and development. The teacher should point out that making a boat from scrap wood can be a much more enjoyable activity than trying to fit together some adult's preconceived plastic model. If a child could learn to get satisfaction from working with a range of common materials, and if misguided parents would stop praising products instead of children, the precut, already-thought-out "easy projects" companies would be out of business.

Summary of the Gang Age

In summarizing this stage it seems obvious that art can contribute to total development. One of the greatest needs of children during this period is to find themselves, to realize their own power, and to develop their own relationships within their own group. Second is the need for each child to discover his own sincere relationship to his environment, and to the objects and materials that make up this environment, as we have discussed them. There are no short cuts to the development of perceptual abilities or creative growth. Although the range of individual differences can be very great, the end product should be viewed only as an indication of individual development. Standards of value should never come from the teacher, nor should group influences be so strong as to dictate a particular kind or type of product. We have seen how growth affects the products and also affects the aesthetic awareness of children; any standards outside the child himself become false.

During the earlier schematic stage we observed that children had a need to repeat the same symbol again and again. Now, however, the repetition of form should gradually disappear, and there should be a development of new forms or shapes that are not constantly repeated. Working in unfamiliar materials can often have a positive effect upon drawings and paintings. Children who have worked in collage materials may become much more aware of a variety of textures and forms and be able to transfer this awareness into a painting medium. Art should certainly give support for individual expression and creative thinking.

As we have gained a greater understanding of this peer-group age, we can readily see how the teaching of particular techniques in art may stand in the way of children's exploring and experimenting for themselves. As adults we can help a great deal in the physical development of children by providing them with the proper nutrients and the place and encouragement for the development of the necessary physical skills; in the same way we as adults should provide the essential ingredients for children's artistic development—but we cannot do this developing for them.

RELATED ACTIVITIES

1. Collect the drawings of a fourth grade class and tabulate how many children depend upon base-line concept. How many use more than one base line? Have any children begun to use the space below the base line as a plane?

2. Save the drawings of a third grade child over a period of several months. Trace the development of symbols from a representation using geometric forms to a representation more closely related to nature. Compare with drawings from a fifth grade child during the same period.

3. Observe several group activities within a school setting at several grade levels. Which activities were the most productive? Which were most satisfactory from the child's point of view? Analyze the reasons why some activities were more successful than others.

4. Make a list of materials used in a fourth grade art program. Revise this list according to the appropriateness of these art materials for expression at these age levels. Compare this list with what is appropriate at the kindergarten level.

5. Make a list of examples of children's growing awareness of design and textural pattern in their drawings. Pay particular attention to clothing and objects important to the artist. Are any differences observable between the sexes? How does the extent of awareness compare with academic ability?

6. Keep a record of which children begin to make the sky come down to the base line. What is the first realization of overlapping beyond this initial step? Are these the same children who are also more socially developed?

The Importance of Art
in the Secondary School

8

ART OUGHT TO PLAY a very important role in the lives of students in the secondary school. Within the framework of our public school system, however, art usually plays a subordinate role, whereas within our society it is playing an increasingly large one. Art is more than pictures on a museum wall, more than the making of paintings or sculpture, more than the creation of our environment by building up structures, or planning and landscaping open spaces. These are the tangible evidences of art within our society, and those people who call themselves artists are the ones who design, build, paint, and cast. But art can also mean an attitude toward living, a means of formulating our feelings and emotions and giving them tangible expression. It is a means by which our sensitivities to experiences are heightened and refined. In a broad sense, art is both

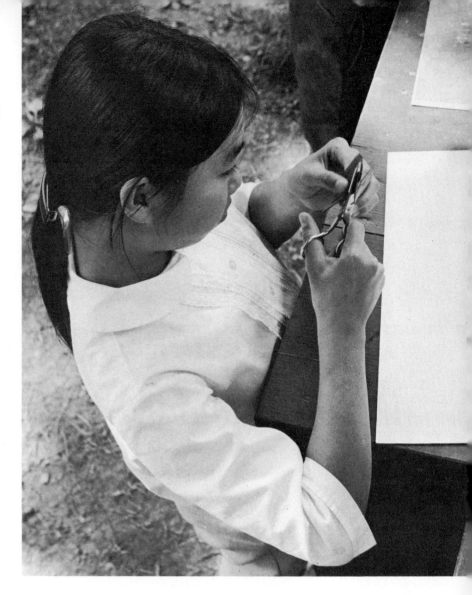

Figure 113. *The development of a sensitivity toward art is at the same time the development of a sensitivity toward one's environment.*

external and internal. The sensitive awareness of the things around us develops through a system of attitudes and experiences into new forms.

Even with such a broad point of view, it is quickly apparent that most school experiences are unrelated to art. The art classes currently offered in most public schools tend to emphasize the production of art rather than the development of artistic attitudes. This is not to say that the production of art is bad in itself, but an undue emphasis upon producing paintings or pieces of sculpture may be detrimental to the process of thinking, feeling, and perceiving in an artistic manner. It is the *process* of art that is important, not the products themselves.

There is an increasing awareness today of the need for developing not only sensitivities to our environment but sensitivities to the needs and feelings of others. This whole area is one which in the past has been ignored by our public school system. The usual secondary school curriculum is divided into small segments of subject matter, and these segments are usually justified on the basis of vocational or educational preparation. However, in our rapidly changing society, there are emerging professions and specific job opportunities that were not dreamed of twenty years ago, and youngsters in our junior and senior high schools may be preparing for jobs that have not yet been defined. There is also an increasing awareness of the fact that the study of science alone cannot provide the means by which we can deal with values and attitudes. In our changing society those values and attitudes established by older generations are not values and attitudes that can be easily assumed by youngsters in the junior and senior high schools. The means of expression that are socially acceptable and at the same time available for youngsters of this age to use, are strictly limited. Art may be the only field within the framework of our school system where the development of feelings and emotions is given proper recognition.

It comes as something of a shock, then, to find that, according to a survey, only half of the secondary schools offered art at all, and that only 15 per cent of students enrolled in these schools took a year of art beyond ninth grade (Davis, 1963). Occasionally there is a required course in the humanities for all high school students, which is an attempt at combining art with other subjects to make a supposedly meaningful whole for the students. Intellectually, this may have some value, for the student needs to understand art as a reflection of the culture of the times and recognize its relationships with the changes in our society; but the establishment of values and attitudes cannot be imposed upon the student from without. Personal involvement is essential to a feeling for art.

The Psychological Change from Elementary to Secondary School

Children in the elementary school paint and draw without inhibition. This can be seen especially at the nursery school and kindergarten levels. However, by the time a child arrives at fourth, fifth, and especially sixth grade, we find that he is becoming increasingly aware of his own product. Spontaneous and uninhibited expression disappears and by seventh grade he has developed a critical awareness. This critical awareness is not limited

THE IMPORTANCE OF ART
IN THE SECONDARY SCHOOL

to art products, for the youngster is now agonizingly conscious of himself and his own limitations within the society of peers. It is at this age that a youngster begins to realize the unhappy position in which he finds himself: he is now an aware, thinking individual but is not yet in a position to take any particular action to change his state of being. These youngsters are hostile toward their parents, disillusioned with school, and at times discouraged with themselves. It is not surprising, therefore, to find that they are also critical of their own art products.

Now that the child has lost his uninhibited approach to drawing and painting, he has become very conscious of his actions. This is indeed a critical period in his development. He has not developed a conscious objective approach to his actions, yet he is at the same time insecure with his childish approach to art. This is one reason why so many individuals stop their creative work when they are through with the required courses of art in the junior high school. It is only for those students who have developed a profound interest in the subject, or have found in it a mechanism by which they can satisfy some of their needs, that art can take on greater meaning. There are, of course, earlier indications of this change coming about. The sixth grade child usually covers up his drawings when an adult comes by. The seventh grader is quite reluctant to show anything or have any sort of outside evaluation made of his product. By comparison, the kindergarten child will eagerly show and explain his products to any and all interested adults. One of the important tasks of art education during the secondary school, and particularly during the junior high school, is to provide means by which the child will continue in his use of art and will sustain his confidence in his own means of expression.

For the purpose of investigating the change in imaginative concepts in the school years, the topic "Playing Tag on the Schoolground" was assigned to three different groups: to a number of elementary school children of the first three grades; to boys and girls of the upper elementary school; and to students in the secondary school. There were approximately three hundred subjects in each group. The topic was presented to the youngsters with no requirement that they draw it, and they were allowed to select other topics within their interest if they so desired. Ninety-five per cent of the lower elementary school children made some attempt to represent this experience, whereas only 35 per cent of the secondary school students tried to depict this game. The drawings were analyzed on two variables: the ways of expressing the experience of catching and being caught, and the spatial relationships representing the schoolground.

The elementary school children of the first three grades generally made no attempt at naturalistic representation. This was true both in the representation of the human figure and in the representation of the schoolground. Environment was almost entirely missing in the youngest age group tested. In Figure 114, done by a boy aged six and a half, we can see a typical representation. Here the boy has used an oval for the body and a circle for the head. Arms and legs are expressed differently in the two figures; whereas the arms of the captive are entirely missing, those of the captor are greatly overemphasized. Notice particularly the exaggeration of the grasping hand. It is interesting to note that apparently only one hand is needed for tag. The legs of the captor are longer than those of his playmate, which may give some indication of the faster running ability of one child. Notice also that the schoolground is indicated by a base line only. It can be said that the child's method of perceiving space is determined primarily from his own being and not from a visual experience. The child's world of images is bound up with the self, with his own feelings and emotions, and is not involved with a naturalistic representation.

Figure 114. *"Playing Tag on the Schoolground," painted by a six and a half year old boy. Notice the exaggeration of the arm that is doing the catching and the omitted arms of the captive. The environment is expressed only by a base line.*

THE IMPORTANCE OF ART
IN THE SECONDARY SCHOOL

Figure 115. *"Playing Tag on the Schoolground," painted by a nine year old girl. Here we see exaggeration of important parts. The environment is expressed by two base lines on which the children and school are placed.*

In looking at the second drawing, Figure 115, we see a more elaborate drawing by a nine year old girl from the upper elementary school. This too is typical, and shows quite clearly that the girl is aware of naturalistic details and her own relationship to her environment. The girls are

Figure 116. *"Playing Tag on the Schoolground," drawn by an adolescent. This picture is an attempt at naturalistic representation. Space is shown through the use of visual perspective.*

wearing dresses; there is even an attempt to show the hair blowing in the breeze; the schoolground is clearly indicated, surrounded by trees and a fence. The upper section of the picture serves as a base line for the school and swings. The lower section has a base line with the girls and what appears to be a slide resting on it. There are the beginnings of the realization of depth with what seems to be the addition of boxes tying the upper and lower sections together. One arm of the chasing girl is exaggerated, but otherwise the figures are quite stiff. Although there is a greater awareness of nature, the drawing itself is not an attempt at visual accuracy.

When we turn to the drawings of the secondary school students, as in Figure 116, we see an attempt at naturalistic representation. The figures attempt to be as naturalistic as possible, are fairly well proportioned, with arms and legs bent, and parts of the environment are drawn in a sketchy but well-proportioned manner.

These three drawings show quite clearly how the method of representing the same subject changes from an egocentric representation of the self to a representation that attempts to reproduce a more photographic likeness of the event. The secondary school student is no longer bound up with the self. For him, the success or failure of the sketch would probably be determined by its close representation to nature, although this method of comparing one's own product to naturalistic surroundings is not true for all secondary school students. Another study dealing with highly creative and highly intelligent high school students (Getzels and Jackson, 1962) also used the title "Playing Tag in the Schoolyard" as a theme for drawings. They found that about 70 per cent of their sample drew pictures that carefully represented the schoolground. The others were more subjective. The portrayal of the visual environment may be confusing to at least some secondary school students; however, we will discuss this in more detail later. But the appearance of the picture or construction now has become much more important to the student.

The Importance of Self-identification

To some extent, the period of development covered by the secondary school could be considered a time when a youngster finds himself. The child straight out of sixth grade has left behind him close attachments to his parents. Up to now, however, the child has been controlled, guided, and commanded by the older generation. At the other end of our secondary school system the adult emerges, ready to take his place in society. The six years or so between these two stages can be characterized by a search for the self. "Who am I? What am I going to do? What do I be-

Figure 117. *Secondary school students often catch the bus at eight o'clock in the morning and do not return home until four or later in the afternoon. The day is spent with their own age-mates and usually within the confines of the school grounds.*

lieve?" These are all problems to be worked out during this period. Yet the school curriculum is usually planned so as to provide little opportunity for contemplation, and little time for the youngster to face himself. Somehow, this time for thinking is considered dangerous and the old axiom of a busy person being a happy one is forcibly applied to most of our secondary school population.

The art program in the secondary school ought to provide the means for this important self-identification. The adolescent is constantly bombarded by a world of advertisements stressing the importance of the proper hairspray, toothpaste, or deodorant, all of which can lead to success as measured by gaiety and attention from the opposite sex. Rigid conformity to peer-group standards is a must; the wearing of the "proper" length of skirt, or length of hair, or tightness of pants shows quite clearly that the individual is under tremendous pressure to belong. In fact, the adolescent can be quite ruthless in his criticism of his peers who are unwilling or unable to conform to the latest hair styles or dress fashions. His criticism, of course, is often leveled at parents and teachers.

Unfortunately, art in the secondary school is usually aimed chiefly at producing technically acceptable products. Little attention is focused upon the needs and desires of the secondary school student himself. This is somewhat preposterous when we realize that most students who elect art in the secondary school are not going to become artists. In fact, the limited learning that takes place within these elective art courses usually needs to be unlearned if the student does continue on to a professional art school (Brittain, 1961). Most elective art courses ignore the problems of the students, yet it is from the needs, desires, and frustrations of adult artists that great art is made. The focus of these programs should clearly be on the process of making art and not on the art itself.

To identify with oneself, to identify with others, to identify with a product and be able to say "This is mine," to be able to set problems and goals for oneself and to be responsible for the direction and method of expression—all these are important considerations in developing an art program for the secondary schools. The life of the junior or senior high school student is not to be ignored. It is the need upon which the program should be built.

It is quite clear that a variety of art activities can take place that provide this important means for self-identification. Certainly painting, sculpturing, making prints, potting, and making murals can all be executed with the youngster's own means of expression and own subject matter. Later chapters will deal more specifically with how this can be accomplished. However, it is also possible to identify with the work and art products of others. Here it is important not to analyze and look at the art work itself in abstract or objective terms, but rather to identify with

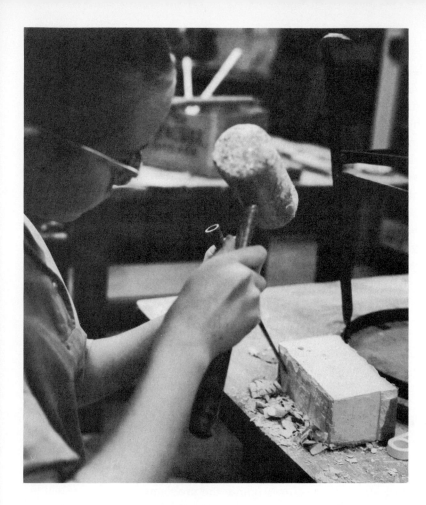

Figure 118. *Art can take many forms, but the youngster's own expression should be considered the most important element of any product. This boy is beginning to chisel a block of plaster*

the creator and with the problems and emotional relationships that he has had in completing his work of art. Each person as an individual reacts and responds to objects on different levels. To ignore the responses and concerns of the individual students could cause a frustrating experience. The important consideration is to make the individual sensitive to the values, attitudes, and judgments in an appreciative experience. The imposition of set standards or learning rules for discussing art may be irrelevant to the student. Certainly political or social history may be a factor in the development of a particular work of art, but this is secondary to how this work is viewed by the individual.

To be more specific, the study of a mobile should not be limited to an appreciation of the work of Alexander Calder. Rather, nature itself can provide the understanding for this type of art in observing how a paper flutters when the breeze strikes it, or how the leaves of a tree create constant new patterns as the light changes, or how maple seeds or thistles glide as the wind carries them. An understanding of the mobile in this context becomes much more meaningful than looking at the mobile only as an abstract art form. Identifying with the artist as he views his environment and tries to translate some of the forms and shapes into a tangible product makes the appreciation of art part of the experience of the viewer.

The importance of identifying with oneself at a moment in time should not be minimized. Painting or drawing is usually the most expressive type of art, but posters and montage provide an opportunity to deal with the social problems of our time. Where we are going and the problems of getting there are very real issues to the senior high school student. For girls, the problems of sex and marriage are frighteningly close, and for the boys the prospects of a job or induction into the armed services become of increasing concern. For both, the voting age is getting closer, and the will to do something about the present condition of our country is a powerful driving force. Art has not limited itself to the portrayal of the beautiful in the past, and the art of youngsters in the secondary school does not have to be beautiful today. It is much more important to provide an environment in which expression can be encouraged than to be concerned about the development of a feeling of beauty in these students.

It is interesting and rather surprising to note that youngsters who have run into problems with the law and been put into institutions under the label of "delinquents" have apparently not been able to express themselves creatively. In a study by Burgart (1968) it was found that a group of delinquent boys ranked lowest on a creativity test, compared with other groups of school children and some nonschool groups. Another study comparing creative thinking between delinquent boys and nondelinquent boys (You Yuh Kuo, 1967) found that sixteen and seventeen year old boys reading at the fourth grade level tended to be nondelinquent if they scored high in measures of creative thinking compared with delinquent boys who scored low on the same measures. Apparently having the opportunity to express oneself in creative fashion provides some means of reacting to the social environment in ways that are acceptable to that society. Possibly those who find they cannot create, who have found no satisfaction in building or producing, may react in negative ways. Unable to contribute in a positive manner, they destroy or deface what others have built. There may be more danger in having a passive view of life than in being aggressive about one's role. T. C. N. Gibbens (1968) reported that submissive, helpless, and unrealistic boys having an inadequate response to life were more apt to be reconvicted to jail sentence than those boys who rated as being aggressive, extroverted, and dynamic. It is clear that the problem is not one limited to delinquent boys. Everyone, particularly those who are confined to our school institutions, needs to have a means of self-expression, and this should be especially encouraged for those who seem disinterested and submissive. Art can play many roles, but the channeling of energies into productive means and the opportunity for self-identification should certainly be stressed at the secondary school level.

The Development of Two Creative Types

Two types of art expression can now be distinguished. These have gradually evolved, and at about the age of twelve or so it is possible to see examples of these two types of expression. One is called the *visual* type, and the other is usually referred to as *haptic* (from the Greek word *haptos*, meaning "laying hold of"). These types are theoretically at opposite ends of a continuum and refer to the mode of perceptual organization and the conceptual categorization of the external environment. The visually minded person is one who acquaints himself with his environment primarily through the eyes and feels like a spectator. The person with haptic tendencies, on the other hand, is concerned primarily with his own body sensations and subjective experiences, which he feels emotionally. Most people fall between the two extremes. The very visually minded individual would be disturbed and inhibited if he were to be limited to haptic impressions, that is, if he were asked not to use sight but to orient himself only by the means of touch, bodily feelings, muscular sensations, and kinesthetic functions. An extremely haptic individual, although normally sighted, uses his eyes only when compelled to do so; otherwise, he relies upon his sense of touch and body self as his main means of becoming acquainted with and reacting to his environment.

The initial work in discovering these two separate means of acquainting oneself with the environment was done by Lowenfeld (1939), while working with the partially blind. He found that some partially blind individuals would use the limited sight they had to examine objects, or when they expressed themselves in clay modeling. At the same time, other partially blind individuals would not use their eyes, but were content to remain with the sense of touch. This led to his study of normal people, and here he found similar tendencies. Further work was done in measuring these qualities (Lowenfeld, 1945, 1966). Using 1,128 subjects, Lowenfeld found that 47 per cent had clear visual tendencies, whereas 23 per cent could be scored haptic, and 30 per cent received a score somewhere in between. In other words, approximately half of the individuals tested reacted visually, whereas not quite a fourth reacted haptically.

Using an electroencephalogram, W. Grey Walter (1963), in a study of alpha rhythms—the brain waves or electrical pulsations that are recorded with the mind at rest—discovered that in one group of persons these rhythms persist even when the mind is active and alert. He administered a test to six hundred individuals that enabled him to distinguish between a visualizer (the M type), the nonvisualizer with a persistent alpha activity (the P type), and a mixed type (the R type). Individuals with persistent alpha rhythms that were hard to block with mental effort tended to have kinesthetic and tactile perceptions rather than to have visual imagery. This group of persons had continuing alpha rhythms even when the eyes were open and the mind active. However, the visual type retains mental pictures of his environment and, according to Walter, thinks primarily in terms of visual images.

In a study by Drewes (1958) using a variety of testing devices, Rorschach responses from a group that he called visualizers tended to be whole and three-dimensional forms, while the nonvisualizers in his population produced more kinesthetic movements and shading responses. Some work by Flick (1960) indicated that this haptic expression can be found not only in the field of art, but also in literature and other areas.

A thorough discussion of the haptic system was set forth by Gibson (1966). He documented the vast range of perception that people have open to them in addition to the eyes. The skin feels, the touching of hairs carries a message, heat and pressure can be understood, and the size and shape of objects can be realized. Gibson's work indicated that objects can be identified and selected without their even being seen.

There may be some relationship between the haptic-visual theory and a theory dealing with different modes of perception: Field-Independence versus Field-Dependence (Witkin, 1962). However, a study of paintings by some sixth and eighth graders conducted by Rouse (1965) found no correlation between these theories. In an experiment with children's reading ability, Templeman (1962) found that there was a relationship between a first grader's creative type and the ease with which he learns; those children who were considered haptic had more difficulty in learning to read. Kagan, Moss, and Sigel (1963), reporting upon several studies on cognitive style, found results similar to aspects of haptic-visual types in what they termed the analytic and nonanalytic responses of children.

This documentation of the haptic-visual theory is less important than its implications for art in the secondary school. Realizing that extremes

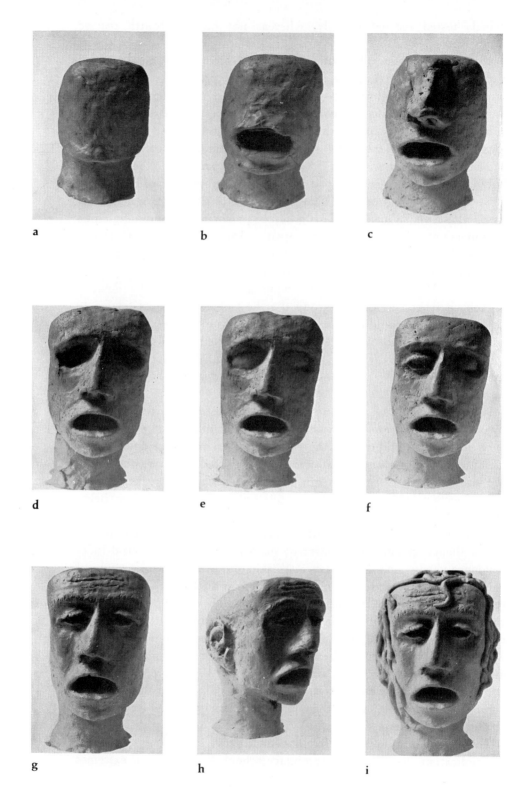

a   b   c

d   e   f

g   h   i

Figure 119. *"Pain," sculpture by a sixteen year old blind girl who is visually minded.* **a.** *The general outline is made.* **b.** *The cavity of the mouth is formed.* **c.** *The nose is added.* **d.** *Eye sockets are hollowed out.* **e.** *Eyeballs are put in.* **f.** *Lids are pulled over.* **g.** *Wrinkles are formed.* **h.** *Ears are added.* **i.** *Hair is added.* **Below: j.** *In the finished product, all features are incorporated into a unified surface.*

j

 a

 b

 c

 d

 e

 f

g

Figure 120. *"Pain," sculpture by a sixteen year old blind boy who is haptically minded.* **a.** *The chin is constructed.* **b.** *The teeth and tongue are put in.* **c.** *The mouth is closed, hiding inside features.* **d.** *The nose is added, eye sockets are made.* **e.** *Eye balls are put in from inside, head is closed.* **f.** *Ears, muscles, and hair are added.* **g.** *The head is finished.* **Right: h.** *All features remain isolated as partial impressions on final product.*

h

THE IMPORTANCE OF ART
IN THE SECONDARY SCHOOL

of either type are rare, it is important to understand that some children may be inhibited by references solely to visual stimulation. This is particularly important to keep in mind for those teachers who themselves may be strongly visually minded.

The visual type is the observer, and he usually approaches things from their appearance. One important factor in visual observation is the ability initially to see the whole without an awareness of the details. Apparently, the visual type first sees a general shape of a tree, then the single leaves, the twigs, the branches, the trunk, and finally everything incorporated into the whole tree. Starting with the general outline, partial visual impressions are integrated into a whole image. The visually minded individual can analyze the characteristics of shape and structure of an object and be concerned with the changing effects of these shapes as they are influenced by light, shadow, color, atmosphere, and distance. How something looks is of prime importance, and even tactile sensations are translated into visual form. For him, the complex and ever-changing appearances of shapes and form are exciting and pleasurable experiences.

The haptic type utilizes muscular sensations, kinesthetic experiences, touch impressions, and all the experiences of the self to establish his relationship to the outside world. The sizes and shapes are determined by their importance to the individual. His thinking relates to the details that are of emotional significance (Zawacki, 1956). The haptic person enjoys textures and feels objects pleasurably with the hands. There is no attempt at trying to translate these textures into a visual image. The art of the haptic is more subjective. The artist himself becomes a part of the picture, and in his pictorial representations, subjective values determine the color and form of objects.

It is important to remember that our teaching should encourage the expression of students regardless of their mode of representation. There is no need to reward one type of representation over another, because our culture provides the opportunity for honest expression of all types. Unfortunately, the teaching of art is usually thought of in visual terms. However, even color is impossible to teach as a purely visual phenomenon. Although color can often be thought of in terms of hue, lightness or darkness, and strength or intensity, there may also be many variations within an object itself, as reflected light or changes in contour affect the color. Color can also be described as bright, cheerful, and warm, or cold, forbidding, and hostile. Even the representation of concrete objects will differ depending upon the way in which an object is viewed and the response of the individual to these objects. Both haptic and visual stimulation should be provided and both kinds of art should be rewarded.

As an example of the differences in expression see Figure 121. Here

Plate 11. *"Barns," painted in watercolor by a preadolescent girl. Her direct expression shows her developing aesthetic awareness. Such decorative and pleasing preadolescent art should be valued for its own sake. It should not have to conform to adult standards, to inflexible rules of perspective and proportion, or to arbitrary principles of design.*

Plate 12. "*The Circus,*" *block-printed by junior high school girls. Printing presents a challenge for the young adolescent who is capable of mastering complex procedures. Here a variety of levels of conceptual development are united into a colorful whole, an expression of group cooperation. Overlapping is tolerated and space is not rigidly organized, contributing to the feeling of excitement of the circus.*

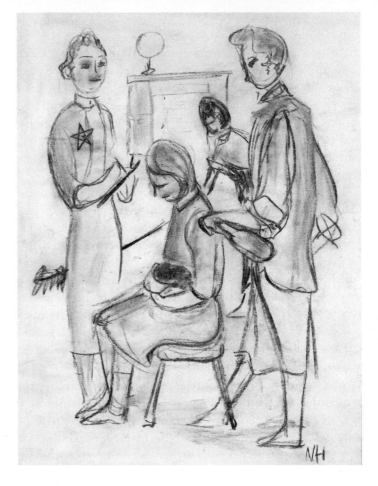

Figure 121. *"A Scene at the Police Station," drawn by a visually minded adolescent. Correct proportions, lights and shadows, and three-dimensional quality are important to the artist.*

Figure 122. *"A Scene at the Police Station," drawn by a haptically minded adolescent. The elements of this composition are determined subjectively; proportions, lights and darks, and space are of emotional importance.*

there is a concern for correct proportions and measurements, and the changing effects of light and shadows are necessarily a part of the visual image. These are qualities of representation that can be discovered with the eyes. In turning to Figure 122, we see a more haptic type of representation. Here the human figure is used as a means of expressing emotions and feelings. Because different parts of the body have various functions and importance, the proportion given these parts assumes emotional significance.

The history of art is filled with examples of art of both the haptic and visual types. Michelangelo's "David" is a type of expression very different from a piece of sculpture from the South Pacific islands. Both, however, are true art expression and sincere forms of art. In the past classic Greek sculpture was highly admired. The beauty of the visible form was considered a high achievement and the religious art expression of the medieval period was thought quite crude in comparison. However, the forces that determined the religious expression were symbolic of deeply personal experiences; viewed with this in mind the distortions and exaggerations of the medieval art take on an intriguing beauty in themselves, quite different from the classic purity.

The experiences of the adolescent youngster can often provide intense motivation for visual awareness. The blazing flames of the sky at sunset, or the reflections of a shimmering image in a puddle, or dark silhouettes in the evening can be inspiring. At the same time, these youngsters can be deeply touched by the human qualities of life and become involved in the struggle of mankind; the sky becomes only a reflection of this struggle, while the puddle reflects merely poverty, and the shadows are symbolic of man's false façade. It is important to provide the range of stimulation that will make those individuals who are at either end of the haptic-visual continuum acutely aware of the problems of artistic expression; and this type of motivation will be equally meaningful to the individuals who are able to produce from both haptic and visual experiences.

The visual-haptic theory is important to understand, for it underlies much development in art. Young children's art can be generally classified as haptic in nature, for the experiences portrayed are those that originate primarily with the self, and include what might be considered touch-space. The increasing visual awareness of children can be seen in their drawings and paintings, as we discussed earlier. For some the emphasis on visual representation can become a burden with which they are not able to deal, and art for the haptically minded individual may in some cases be a frustrating experience. The rewards in the elementary school may have gone to those children who were the most visually aware of their environment. The teacher in the secondary school may be confronted with children who have rejected the world of visual art and decided, therefore, that they cannot draw or paint. The haptic art that can be elicited from such children whose expression has previously been thwarted is often emotionally charged and full of released expression. The sensitive teacher is the key to such growth.

Methods of Working in Art

Just as no two students are the same, their ways of working in art will also be different. This may greatly complicate the teacher's role, because he is dealing with the many diverse ways in which youngsters approach an art experience. This can readily be seen in the way some youngsters tackle projects with enthusiasm, while others will begin the same project with hesitation. In some cases these attitudes toward materials or toward certain art activities may be a reflection of how a youngster feels that day; in others, these may be the manifestation of a long-term attitude.

In studies by Biettel (1966) and by Beittel and Burkhart (1963) two methods or strategies of learning in art were differentiated. These were called the *spontaneous* and the *divergent*. The spontaneous students began with a big whole that was devoid of detail, experimented with form, and took advantage of accidents. Their products looked quite free and tended to be nonvisual in nature. The divergent students usually began with fine drawings of details and added single elements together, developing an organization as they did so. Although this study was done with college students, these types can also be seen in the secondary school. There may be some relationship here to the visual-haptic theory, but Beittel has been more concerned with analyzing the way students draw than with the development of their modes of thinking. However, it is obvious that these are related.

In studying these two different strategies of working in art, Beittel provided a situation where students could see photographs that were made of their work in progress. The opportunity for students to look at these and clarify their own thinking in turn provided an opportunity for self-motivation. The goals of the student were an important part of this learning situation. The study indicated that self-discovered criteria were more effective and motivating to these students than were some predetermined criteria. But the researcher also played an important part in these studies: the student had someone to talk to. Apparently, it was important to have some means by which the thoughts and directions that students saw for themselves could be clarified; and the role of the teacher, or in this case the researcher, was merely to listen.

Although these two methods of working in art are quite opposite from one another, they also appear to be flexible (Beittel, 1966). At least some students could assume the methods or strategy of the opposite type, for when told to paint with the opposite strategy their work changed. Surprisingly, this shift in method did not mean that their paintings dropped in quality. There may even by an advantage, then, in pointing out to students other methods or ways of working once they have clarified some thoughts and directions on their own.

Teachers need to be aware of their own methods of painting or working with art materials. There is no reason to believe that the spontaneous method of working is any more appropriate than is the divergent method. But there might be some danger in a teacher imposing his own method of working in art upon his students. Drawing in one method continually could put the student in somewhat of a rut, however, so that he might indeed benefit from the realization that there are other approaches. As an example of this let us take a student who is working diligently and with good control over his drawings. He may have excellent detail and add parts to his composition to make a whole. When drawing buildings he may draw large and small buildings, with fine detailing around the windows, add smokestacks and sidewalks, and be mostly concerned with line quality. A discussion of where he is going and what he is trying to do can probably clarify some of his thoughts. However, if he becomes dissatisfied with this method of drawing, the suggestion that he draw something large and forceful, with rough edges, with a great deal of freedom and movement, using many ways of smudging and shading, may provide him with other approaches to art which he can incorporate into his own method. Of course, the opposite procedure may work well with a spontaneous student. The concern of the teacher, then, is to enrich the possibilities of working in art and to provide the student with an opportunity to evaluate his own direction.

Several theories have been advanced to explain how learning takes place in art. June McFee (1961) feels there are four steps to the process. Her first is readiness, which includes the diverse backgrounds of the students; the second is the psychological environment or conditions surrounding the instruction; the third she calls information handling, where the students think and make decisions; and the fourth is delineation, or the actual production. Arnheim (1954) feels that artistic production is not based upon intellectual abstraction, but upon a broader cognition, and that the form that is represented cannot be derived only from the object perceived. There are other theories of how learning takes place in the arts (Dewey, 1958; Eng, 1931; Munro, 1956; Read, 1958). How these

Figure 123. Depth of personal experience is of prime importance in art activity. The meaningfulness of an art program can be measured only in terms of the individual.

theories differ is less important than the fact that differences in theory exist. For the teacher in the secondary school it becomes imperative that each student be considered unique and that his way of learning be considered. Environmental conditions or situations can be altered so that the student feels his art is worthwhile. In a true art experience the artist displays his inner self, and how he sees, thinks, and feels is laid bare. One of the goals of any secondary school art teacher should be to provide an environment where these thoughts and this expression, however it is produced, can be treated with sensitivity and respect.

Creativity in the Secondary School Art Program

In recent years there has been an increase in the interest and concern that educators have shown in the field of creativity. Many innovations have been made in the teaching of the usual academic subjects to provide for the creative responses of students. One method has been to provide problems that students must work through in order to arrive at axioms or postulates in mathematics, rather than having this information memorized in advance. In history, questions such as "What might have happened if the battle had been lost?" or "What would you have done if you were President?" are becoming much more common. In art, there has always been the feeling that creativity is an essential part of the experience, but unless care is taken to insure that students develop a creative attitude, and that the environmental conditions are such that they will foster creative growth, there is no assurance that art experiences in themselves will develop creativity.

The change from a natural, spontaneous manner of working with art materials, which we saw in young children, to one of a critical awareness of one's own actions calls for a well-developed plan for encouraging creativity. With younger children we could encourage and foster the enthusiasm and freedom that seem to be a part of life. In the secondary school, however, the development of creative thinking must be a planned part of the art program. Flexibility, fluency, originality, and the ability to think independently and imaginatively must not be left to chance. It is most crucial to develop creative thinking patterns at this age, for the attitudes and values that these youngsters develop now will continue with them through adult life.

The art teacher must therefore plan for experiences that develop creative thinking abilities. It is not enough just to have students produce, even if these productions can be called art. It is important to develop the ability to think creatively, to learn how to create. For some students this may be a difficult experience, because many of them have achieved success by following the formulas or patterns of others. This may be true even of the highly intelligent youngster (Getzels and Jackson, 1962). There is a certain amount of risk involved in setting out on new and uncharted paths. This risk is not limited to the students; the art teacher himself takes many risks in encouraging students to think for themselves. It is certainly a great deal simpler for the art teacher in the secondary school to follow a set syllabus and to develop an art program around easily graded projects. However, the excitement of discovery and the growth of the student in the process of exploration can be most stimulating.

Creativity is not fostered in an unstructured, chaotic atmosphere. However, a certain degree of ambiguity and diversity, or what might appear to be lack of organization, may be a better environment within which the individual can develop his own structure than an environment that is already predetermined and made neat and orderly by someone else's standards. The creative person has a greater tolerance of ambiguity (Barron, 1963); and a sterile working environment, both psychological and physical, lacks stimulation.

The usual classroom, and this often includes art classes, has a well-defined course of study outlined. The youngster is quite aware of this fact and his usual comment is "What am I supposed to do?" Obviously he does not expect to be included in the planning of the activity. Any opportunity that comes up which provides the chance for him to escape or deviate from this predestined path is welcomed. The problem goes even farther, because the next logical question is "How am I supposed to do it?" This question is customarily followed by "Is this the way you wanted it?" For some students it may be somewhat uncomfortable to shoulder the burden of helping make decisions rather than relying solely on the teacher. This may be particularly true at the junior high school level, where there is an indication that creativity hits a low point (Kincaid, 1964).

The usual concern voiced on the part of teachers is the tremendous pressure that peer groups have upon the individual in the secondary school. There is good reason for this concern. Studies have shown that individuals are very susceptible to pressures from their peers to conform. Some college students, when asked to pick out the longest line from a series of lines of different lengths, went against what their senses told them and agreed with the group that had already selected one of the

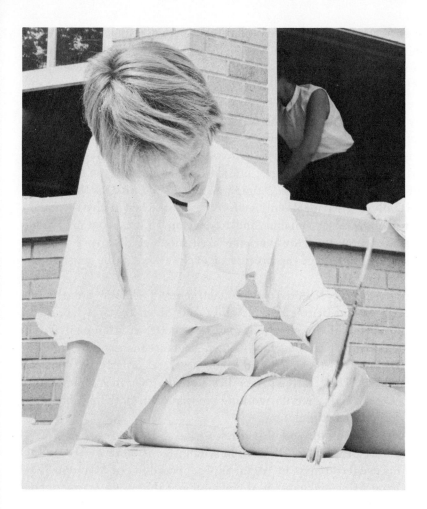

Figure 124. *Sometimes it is important to support the individual who wants to paint or draw by himself. Art expression should be free of pressures for conformity.*

shorter lines (Asch, 1952). Apparently, most people are seriously affected and influenced by the decisions and judgments of others. Testing this in other ways, Crutchfield (1963) found similar results. It only takes a minute to observe youngsters in the junior high school to note the conformity and rules of dress and behavior that they impose upon themselves. Similar pressures will be found in the art room and will have an influence on what is produced.

On the other hand, the group can provide a great deal of stimulation and support for innovative thinking. The brainstorming technique perfected by Parnes (1964) has as its objective the goal of freeing the thinking of individuals, with the support of the group. Each individual within a working group is asked to express as many ideas as possible spontaneously, and no negative or critical evaluation is allowed. This technique apparently works well in industry. A different system, which is called synectics, involves a group in trying to join together different and apparently irrelevant elements (W. J. J. Gordon, 1961). In these instances the group is used as a means for furthering creative thinking. The pressures of the group can be used positively if the atmosphere is such that creativity is rewarded, and the new, novel, or unusual response is recognized. An important element in this is the deferment of action, which gives the opportunity to play around with divergent thoughts before evaluating the best method or most appropriate subject matter or the obvious material to use.

Although there are numerous tests for creativity, these have little value in an art room. How a student performs, the way in which he feels free to express himself, the flexible way in which he uses materials, the amount and number of things he can produce, his unusual approaches to drawing or painting, and the number of original or unique solutions that he provides to artistic problems offer an excellent indication of creativity, which can only be approximated by standardized tests.

It would probably be more valuable to know who is the least creative person in the art room, for this is the individual who needs the most support in his creative endeavors. In some cases this may be the highly intelligent youngster who has set overly high standards for himself. In some cases it may be an extremely sensitive individual who is afraid of the unknown, who needs the support of an encouraging adult.

It must be emphasized that the art teacher should never lose track of the fact that the development of creativity is one of the basic reasons for art's existence in the secondary school. Creativity can be improved at any level; the most effective method starts with the unreserved acceptance of a student as a worthy individual with thoughts and ideas of his own. We must deal with the student simultaneously from an intellectual and an emotional point of view by providing a stimulating environment for him within the classroom.

The Art Teacher in the Secondary School

Unquestionably the art teacher has a favorable position in the schools. In part it may be because art has an aura of being somehow different from other subjects, which permits the art teacher in turn more license. So we find that teachers of art are often able to run a different type of classroom without the wrath of the administration falling on their heads.

Figure 125. *The art teacher in the secondary school has a teaching role with many advantages. The biggest one is that youngsters invariably enjoy art experiences and usually look upon the art class as one of the good parts of the day.*

In part this may be because it is difficult to evaluate progress in the arts, and in part because art teachers are intrinsically more creative individuals anyway. That is, art has a fascination for people who are willing and eager to express their thoughts and feelings in an imaginative way. It could also be argued that art provides the training for creativity in itself. Either way, the art teacher is usually looked upon as somehow different, and may therefore be in a more enviable position that the usual academic teacher.

The art teacher has other advantages. Youngsters *like* art. There is a delight in teaching a subject which has a natural attraction for youngsters. Although the art teacher must spend hours in preparation and planning, he does not have the dull hours of correcting essays or papers that plague other teachers at the secondary level. One would expect therefore that the art teacher's job should be a delightful one.

Although the art teacher may view himself as fortunate, the youngsters in his classes view him in a rather different perspective. In an investigation into the character of early adolescent art, Brittain (1968,a) found that the teacher is seen by the junior high school student as a potential threat. Most art teachers would like to consider themselves closer to youngsters than the average academic instructor, and this may come as quite a surprise. However, Brittain's study showed that the student clearly rejected the teacher as a fit person to evaluate his work or to set standards for his performance. Apparently, the youngster himself decided whether he was successful on the basis of his own feelings about what he had done rather than on the teacher's evaluation. This study also indicated that the junior high school youngster rejected the teacher not only as an evaluator, but as a source of ideas on what is important to do in art. When placed in the situation of having to perform art tasks assigned by the teacher, the student's own expression was thwarted. The only positive role that students saw for the teacher was that of providing new materials.

This is rather humiliating. Perhaps, the traditional-style art teacher these youngsters must have known was concerned primarily with the handing out of materials. Obviously this method is still used in some elementary schools, and sometimes one can find programs even in the junior high school that seem to be oriented primarily toward using one material after another. There may be good reasons, in fact, why the youngsters should treat the teacher as a guardian of materials, rather than as a person able to help them with their aesthetic development and expressive needs.

These findings are borne out in other studies. A group of high school students was asked whose disapproval would be hardest to take: that of their parents, their teachers, or their friends. Although there were slight differences between boys and girls, high school youngsters seemed chiefly concerned about parents and friends disapproving of their actions, for only 3 per cent of these teen-agers thought that the teacher's approval was important (Coleman, 1961). Part of the problem may be that adults do not attribute the same values to behavior and performance that youngsters do. A study by Cunningham (1951) indicated that eighth grade youngsters had different values for certain experiences than did their parents. Whereas the parents thought it important for youngsters to work at home without pay, these eighth graders thought working for pay was much more important. However, the eighth graders thought that talking with adults who were engaged in various types of work was quite important, although parents did not value this highly for their youngsters. High on the list of values for these eighth graders was the opportunity to work or play in a group of four or five people, while the adults ranked this close to the bottom of the list. This finding gives support for the organization of the classroom into small workable units.

Although the teacher may be viewed as a threat and his values may be different from those of the secondary school student, the teacher's perception of students is very important. It has been clearly shown that individuals who are expected to perform creatively, and who are aware of this expectation, do much better than a group of people not so prepared (Hyman, 1964). The teacher's attitude becomes a crucial one in the classroom. A study by Rosenthal and Jacobson (1968) indicated that the teacher can also be influenced by how he expects the student to behave. Some 20 per cent of the children from a certain elementary school were randomly selected and the names of these youngsters were reported to their teachers as showing unusual potential. Eight months later these "unusual" children showed great gains in intellectual performance on standard tests compared to the rest of the youngsters. The fact that the teacher expected the best paved the way for this to happen. Maybe the most exciting and creative art class happens because the art teacher expects it to happen.

The usual teacher has many tasks before him in an art room full of students. These include a concern for classroom structure, the dissemination of materials, the need to save time for proper clean-up, and the presentation of some new material or method; so it becomes somewhat surprising to find that he also has time to talk to students. However,

Figure 126. *"My French Teacher," "My English Teacher." Secondary school students need to have the opportunity to express their feelings about their environment in socially acceptable ways. Although this may not be viewed with pleasure by the teachers concerned, this type of art activity is important for any student who has ever failed a test.*

students may rarely have time to talk to him. A study by Clements (1964) found that teachers rarely paused for student answers to their questions. In an average fifty minute art class in which fifty-nine questions were asked, a total of only five seconds of pausing occurred. Clements looked upon the shortness of pupils' answers and the lack of time allowed for them to answer as casting real doubt on the value that art teachers attached to their students' opinions. Closely related to this is a study by Jones (1964), which showed that art students who replied to the teacher's questions in long statements had definite gains in the aesthetic quality of their products. It may be important in the teaching role to listen as well as to talk.

The art teacher in the secondary school has an extremely important position. It is through him that the direction and atmosphere for learning takes place. He must have a genuine faith in students and be willing to accept their values as well as his own. He must provide an atmosphere where creativity can be fostered and where external evaluation is absent. He cannot be a threat to students. Certainly the freedom of the individual student in the classroom must in some cases be limited by the physical environment and by the limits of behavior that society imposes. However, the symbolic expression of these feelings need not be limited; the opportunity to put concerns, real or imagined, into constructive art forms should never be minimized. At the time when there is an increasing concern for individual freedom and a discontent with existing social conditions, we must find ways to use the power of the mind creatively and to unlock the potential of every secondary school youngster.

RELATED ACTIVITIES

1. Compare the drawings of an eighth grade with those done by a fifth grade class. Point out the changes that show the development of a critical awareness toward creative expression.

2. Make a list of the characteristics of the child who tends to be haptic. What would be his preference for subject matter, his manner of representation, his use of color, his use of proportion? Plan a lesson that would emphasize nonvisual responses.

3. Make a list of the characteristics of a child who has a preference for visual stimuli and plan a lesson, as above, emphasizing the visual elements.

4. Discuss the changing relationship between the child and his environment as seen in his representations of space. Point out how the use of space changes and how these changes reflect changes in development as the child grows.

5. In a free and open group discussion among school art students, observe to what extent the group gives support to novel and creative suggestions, and to what extent the group rejects original ideas. Would this vary with different groups?

6. Observe an eighth grade class working on an art project. Keep a record of the number and type of questions or comments made by the students. Keep a record of the teacher's comments and questions. Can you draw any inferences?

The Age of Reasoning: The Pseudo-Naturalistic Stage, 12-14 Years

9

The Importance of the Pseudo-Naturalistic Stage

This stage of development marks the end of art as a spontaneous activity and the beginning of a period of reasoning when children become increasingly critical of their own products. For some this means a change from unconsciously drawing what is known, to consciously relying upon what is seen. These attempts at naturalism assume great significance when we realize that this indicates the shift to adult modes of expression.

This period is one of the most exciting and yet one of the most trying

Figure 127. *Although the youngster in junior high school has become more critically aware of his own product, he has developed new interests and the desire to express his own ideas.*

in the entire field of art. It is an age of turmoil and excitement for the child, although the term child now no longer applies. This is a time when girls start to develop mature sex characteristics and boys are wondering if they will ever grow hair on their chins. It is a time when the youngster finds that he is not a child, but is also sure he is not an adult. This age is sometimes referred to as the period of pubescence or preadolescence. It is a period of great individual differences; this is most noticeable in physical changes, but it is also true in the mental, emotional, and social areas as well.

Although school systems vary from one part of the country to another, most youngsters of this age will be in the junior high school years, the seventh, eighth, and ninth grades. For most children this will be the last formal public school art they receive. This fact becomes very important, because we must realize that the attitudes and skills that are developed at this age will influence their reactions and feelings toward art in adult life.

The child from the elementary school has become much more critical and aware of himself as a junior high school student. This developing self-awareness is expressed through a self-conscious approach to his environment. He is concerned about how he looks, how he dresses, what he says, and particularly he is concerned about how he appears to others. To a great extent he is searching for himself. He wants to know who he is, what he believes in, what he can do, and what is important in life.

The significance of this stage might be better understood if we think of it as a transition from a period when the adult world was all-powerful to a world in which the young adolescent is beginning to assume an important role. After the child has gone through the gang age, he enters a stage in which he develops intellectually to the point where he can tackle almost any problem, yet in his reactions he is still a child. The difference between children and adults can be seen in the diversity of their imaginative activity. The young child may play hide-and-seek with abandon, he will pick up a pencil and move it up and down while imitating the noises of an airplane, he will laugh or cry when he is amused or hurt, without inhibitions. Such unawareness is characteristic of children. If an adult were to do the same things he would be considered insane. For an adult a pencil is a pencil, and a pencil is for writing. He has no time for games, and emotions must be kept under control. This change in the imaginative activity from unconscious to critical awareness can create conflicts in the child and concern on the part of the adult. This becomes particularly apparent when we realize that at this age some girls are as tall as they will ever be—often bigger than either parent or their teachers—and therefore are considered big enough to behave as adults.

One parent recalled this stage of development with his own child in the following words.

When Tommy, my son, was in this stage, of course he was a member of a gang, he had his fun, he had his group of children. He was always tall and a little bit out of proportion to the other children, but he didn't even recognize that, he didn't see it. He associated with younger children who were not as tall. He had his wooden gun, or his wooden stick—and enjoyed playing. But there came a time when I came home from my office—when I saw that when I approached the house he sort of tried to hide the gun, and I said, "Why don't you play with the children?" and he said, "Oh, I think—isn't it silly?" I said, "No, not silly at all, why don't you play with them? It is fun, isn't it?" And when I went into the house, of course he went on engaging in his pretend-to-be games. He felt again as though he were no longer being watched, and since the smaller children accepted him in the group—in the gang—well, he continued the game. But these interruptions became more frequent as he grew older, and I could see him with his wooden gun, sitting there and watching them playing pretend-to-be games, now and then participating or giving orders, but already standing outside. Until one day he put the wooden gun he had so carefully whittled into the basement, but still he could not part with it. Sometimes he went downstairs trying to improve it, but he no longer associated with the group, just watched them.

Just as the youngster has become more critically aware of his own actions, he has become more critically aware of his art products. During the gang age some children were quite reluctant about showing their products to adults. Now the focus is on the end product itself; a picture has value or is good, not because of the effort, interest, or involvement, that went into it, but because of the visual appearance of the product. This recognition of the growing significance to the student of the final product must be accepted by educators. The role of art in this stage of development should give support to the youngster's individuality, should provide a socially acceptable release for his emotions and tensions, and should ease the transition from the expression of a child to the type of expression expected of an adult.

The Representation of the Human Figure

We would naturally expect that changes in the representation of the human figure would follow the increased awareness and concern for changes that are beginning to take place in the bodies of the preadolescent. Since girls tend to develop earlier than boys, we usually find a greater interest in drawing the human figure among girls. As biological changes occur, there is more interest in drawing in notebooks, on scraps of paper, or on book covers. Usually the sexual characteristics of these drawings are greatly overexaggerated, reflecting the concern of these children over their physical development. Often these drawings are concealed from adults, and in some cases a sense of guilt or shame accompanies the drawings.

Children who tend to be visually minded will strive for greater naturalism in their drawings of the human figure. Before this age, youngsters usually employed clothes only for identification, that is, to show that this is a girl and this is a man. Now, however, there is an increased awareness of changing appearances when clothes fold or wrinkle, when lights and shadows change with the sitting body, when color changes under different atmospheric conditions. The mere statement that a dress is red does not imply a visual analysis any more than the statement that a boy wears pants. Both are merely factual recognition. A visual experience means that the changes of red are observed according to light and shadow and the influences of distance and reflected light are noticed, or that the pants change appearance while the boy is running, or that folds and worn spots are observed. This increased visual awareness of the human figure is limited primarily to those who derive pleasure from the changing appearances of objects around them. For those not so visually aware, and at times for all youngsters, great pleasure is taken in cartooning and

Figure 128. *The cartoon becomes a favorite means of expression for some children. Not only does this provide the opportunity for satirical comment, but it also provides an escape from naturalism.*

representing the human figure through satirical drawings. Boys seem particularly interested at this age in developing this ability and sometimes will enjoy making cartoons of teachers, parents, and those of their class-mates who hold enviable positions.

Probably one of the most difficult assignments a youngster can have at this pseudo-naturalistic stage is that of drawing himself. The difficulty of coming to terms with one's own identity can clearly be recognized, not

Figure 129. *It is sometimes diffi- cult for young- sters of this age to draw them- selves. An honest appraisal is often forsaken in favor of an idealistic representation.*

only in the drawings, but in the self-conscious and reluctant manner in which youngsters approach such a task. Although an examination of drawings done by preadolescent youngsters will look surprisingly like drawings done during earlier stages, there will be an increased awareness of detail with special attention to clothing, hair style, and facial features. The suggestion that individuals project their own personality into these drawings has been given support in psychological literature (Machover, 1949). If a youngster is concerned about his nose he may exaggerate this or leave it out entirely, although in drawing other people the nose may become a focal point for ridicule. The drawing of the self becomes, then, a reflection of one's own ability to face oneself; the youngster who has developed or learned certain formulas for drawing a figure, or a method for developing a symmetrical being, will produce a human figure drawing that is less expressive of the self and at the same time less artistically meaningful.

In a study of self-drawings of youngsters from twelve to fifteen years of age, it was found that they treated their drawings in derogatory terms (Brittain, 1968,b). These students were asked to put comments on the back of their drawings, indicating the parts they liked best or the parts with which they had the most difficulty. The drawings themselves ranged from what might be more typical of a fifth grade youngster to a quite sophisticated sketch in fair proportion. However, the comments on the back of these drawings were invariably negative, such as "It's terrible," "What a lousy drawing," "It looks nutty," "The head is stupid," and "What a gooney-looking nut." The arms and legs particularly were described in negative terms. It is interesting to note that there seemed to be little relationship between the comments and an objective appraisal of the drawing itself. This might raise the question of whether the development of certain skills in figure drawing is what is important, or whether the self is looked upon in negative terms, regardless of how it is drawn.

Usually at this stage of development, joints appear in the drawing of the human figure. There is also an increased awareness and often overemphasis on sexual characteristics, especially in the drawings of the human figure by girls, for these sexual changes can no longer be experienced in a passive way. There is no reason to look upon these exaggerations as anything but normal. In fact, the very opposite may be true; that is, a child who is beginning to develop sexually and who does not include these changes within drawings may be showing a fear of expressing these changes. Drawings should not be censored. Throughout history, art has been one area where intense concern and feelings could always be portrayed.

The Representation of Space

One of the important discoveries for the visually minded youngster is the apparent reduction in size of distant objects. Space can now be realized by some youngsters in its three-dimensional qualities. Since some youngsters discover the possibility of making drawings with this illusion of depth, many art teachers seize upon this as an indication that all children are ready to learn the mechanical rules of drawing in perspective. In fact, one can often find programs designed for seventh grade students that concentrate upon teaching perspective, starting with one-point perspective, two-point perspective, three-point perspective, with slanting roofs and stairs going off in a number of directions, with railroads disappearing into the distance and telephone lines marching across the page. Of course, for some youngsters at this age the rules to follow become merely mechanical and have no relationship to the world that they experience. Most children will be able to deal with the problems of representing space in depth, but the question remains whether time is best spent in trying to develop this competency in these youngsters.

Figure 130. *"Thinking," drawn by a thirteen year old boy. A need for visual perspective is beginning to be felt by this boy, who here achieves a representation of depth.*

The representation of depth must be discovered by the student. To take this discovery from him by "explaining" perspective would deprive him of an important experience. The teacher must capitalize on the child's own findings and start on the child's own level. "What makes the tree more distant in your drawing?" Let him become aware of his own discoveries: that he has drawn the tree smaller, because distant objects appear to be smaller to us; that he has included less detail, because we do not see as many details in distant objects; that he has given it a less intense color, because the air in between makes the color appear less bright. All this should be used as a frame of reference for later experiences that may be less simple. "I want the road going to the house in the background, but it looks funny" may be one remark a teacher hears. "Let's see whether the road is doing the same as the tree" would be a good starting point, using a previous experience for new discoveries. The child will soon find out for himself that the road as it goes into the distance should grow smaller or narrower in his drawing just as the tree does. It may also be less intense in color. Such discoveries should be supported by real experiences in nature. The teacher should not deprive the child of the excitement of his own discoveries, but instead pave the way by providing the right stimulus whenever the need for it arises.

Certainly for the child who is more inclined toward haptic responses, the experience of being taught perspective can be a frustrating one. For him, and perhaps to a lesser extent for others too, art may be more emotionally important. The illusion of visual depth as achieved through mechanical perspective is unique to our own culture. Possibly culture is not a good word to use here, for perspective seems to be more tied in with the teaching of art in public schools than with the field of professional art. At least the art of today ignores perspective as it is usually taught; the professional artist is much more concerned with the representation of his relationship to his social world than he is with attempting photographic likeness. For some youngsters the discovery of methods of portraying three-dimensional space on paper, guided by a sensitive teacher, can be an exciting experience; to other youngsters, possibly in the same class, perspective is irrelevant.

The Importance of Color and Design

It is easy to see that the young teen-ager has become very aware of design qualities within his sphere of influence. Although the teacher or worried parent may question the aesthetic taste of this youngster, there is no doubt that he has definite likes and dislikes in the selection of clothing, in the colors he wears, and in the jewelry or other accessories that he chooses. This increased awareness of design is sometimes used as an excuse to teach the formal elements of design, and one still hears of art classes spending time making plans for never-to-be-used wallpaper with half-drop repeats. The increasing awareness of color is sometimes used as an excuse to spend considerable effort in making color wheels or color charts. Both of these practices are gradually disappearing. The young teen-ager has an intuitive sense of color and design, and the formal teaching of these factors seems unrelated to his interests.

Much has been written about the psychology of color and its emotional effects on individuals. Such emotional reactions to color are to a large extent determined associatively, through the effect of past experiences. To one individual, horror might mean red and he might associate it with blood; to another it might be green, and he might associate it with mold or decay. No generalizations should be applied to teaching that deny the child's right to creative approaches to color. Emotional reactions to color are highly individualized, and the nonvisually minded child may use color in contradiction to nature. Color can be highly subjective in its meaning (Corcoran, 1953).

The notebooks of these youngsters may be filled with rather interesting and intricate designs. These are often related to lettering, such as designing one's name with fancy letters and seeing how these letters can fit into other patterns or can become quite elaborate in a manner echoing the medieval manuscript calligraphy. Sometimes these doodles are of body parts that can look quite grotesque or resemble preliminary sketches for a gargoyle. Sometimes they look more like psychedelic forms that might impress adult artists.

These youngsters also develop a great sympathy and understanding for design in nature. The design on a turtle's back, the scales on a fish, or the pattern of moss as it is growing out of a crack in the pavement can be exciting discoveries. These are elements of design that are constantly around youngsters and make excellent raw materials from which a genuine understanding of the function of design can spring. We found that in younger children there was an urge to collect many, sometimes unrelated objects. This urge for collecting objects is not limited to the elementary school; the young adolescent too can find a great deal of color and design in objects around him. These can be jars and bottles from the drugstore, which may be enjoyed because of their shape or tactile sense; they can be parts of nature such as worn wood, pebbles, or feathers; or they may be something that has been discarded by society, in the form of a piece of junk mellowed by rust. Putting some of these objects into a setting designed for a work of fine art seems to transform them into things of beauty.

Figure 131. *Notebooks and scraps of paper often reveal a child's interest and concern with himself and things around him. This form of spontaneous art expression should not be repressed.*

THE AGE OF
REASONING

Because most youngsters of this age will not be exposed to further art experiences, attention can and should be paid to industrial products. Although the question of aesthetics is raised once we begin to consider the merits of a variety of designs for everyday objects, the tastes of the teacher should not be forced upon the students. A great deal more understanding can be achieved through discussion than by merely having the students guess which kitchen knife the art teacher likes best. The functional reason for good design can be understood. Discussions may have to start with the merits of the best designed sports car, but the concern for and interest in design is much more important than the establishment of good taste from the point of view of the adult.

The problems of color and design can take on new meaning when critically examined by the young adolescent. Much harm may be done in our society by those who are unaware of the possibility of action. Active participation in group discussions will help prepare him to assume responsibility for his environment as an alert, perceptive adult.

Growth As Reflected in the Art of the Young Adolescent

It is easy to see that the work of young children is closely related to their developmental level. Their feelings and emotions and understandings of the world around them are clearly reflected in their art products. In the same way the products of the young adolescent reflect his reaction to his world, although maybe not as clearly. Just as we have great ranges in intellectual ability, physical development, and obvious differences in sex, we also have differences just as great in the art products of these youngsters. The range and variety of art work increases with each grade level. This can easily be seen in the junior high school. The dainty drawing of a movie star that is perfected by a timid girl is just as valid a means of expression as the elaborately decorated bicycle is for a boy.

Between the ages of twelve and fourteen we find many new problems arising for youngsters and many changes occurring, both in themselves and in their relationships to their peers and adults. Boys and girls alike are beginning to break numerous childhood ties to the family and are questioning adults' authority. We have mentioned their concern about personal appearance and the fact that there is a good deal of idealism and a romantic feeling about becoming an adult member of society, but there is also fear and insecurity about the beginning stages of leaving childhood. Girls are no longer making war on boys, but may have a handsome film star for an idol. Boys are attracted to the opposite sex, but are not ready to admit this. Instead they are busy collecting baseball statistics, developing their muscular powers, and seeking out boys who have comparable interests in such things as motorcycles, BB guns, or electronic equipment.

In some schools students are segregated by so-called ability levels. This may mean that some art classes consist of those who have achieved academic success and some art classes may be composed primarily of those who are lowest on the academic ladder. A study by Madeja (1967), using secondary school students, found that academic achievement correlated highly with grades in art. At the same time he found that nonverbal tests of creativity of the same students showed no relationship to their grades in art. Apparently, art teachers are looking for some of the same attributes that teachers in math and science are seeking.

The implications of this are somewhat frightening. Those students who have achieved respectability and are able to cope with the system are those who are rewarded in art too. At the same time, those who are not able to adapt to the school setting and are having problems achieving the type of success usually rewarded in schools, are also failing in art expression. Perhaps the art program in the secondary schools needs a thorough overhaul, for it is essential that *somewhere* in the system students should be able to express feelings and emotions that are important to them without the fear of failure. The creative child may not be well liked (Torrance, 1962) and this may be so even in the art room.

One college student was asked to write her recollections of her own experience in the junior high school she attended. This particular girl was not only a success in that she was able to go on to college; she was also considered well liked and well adjusted by her teachers. Included are only those parts which seem most pertinent to our discussion of the relationship of art to youngsters of this age.

Junior High

One Girl's View

Junior High is a period of my life I would definitely not want to live over again. It was sort of a changing point, the point where I stopped playing with dolls, started noticing boys, decided I want to be a writer, passed through puberty, first really became aware of such things as "popularity."

I wasn't too fond of life but it never occured to me that life could be changed so it was any different; I accepted things as they came. Adulthood was a magic, privileged life, to be looked forward to, but for now I was stuck being an early adolescent, forced to accept life. I was usually optimistic about things getting better, but I didn't think anything I did could change them. Perhaps I would have been happier if I had felt at one with a crowd all of whom shared a common misery of being in junior high, but I couldn't verbalize my discontent. Discontent wasn't something you talked about. And if something was wrong, it was *me* that was wrong, not the environment. At the time, I did not think myself unhappy.

Social relations were a very important part of junior high. This did not mean boys so much as the other girls. Boys were something seen from afar, rarely contacted. Girls, however, were all around. Boys were extremely terrifying objects. I could scarcely stand up when I was in the presence of one I liked. When I was in eighth grade, a boy, named George, said "Hi" to me in the hall. I had never particularly noticed him before, but I was overcome. I instantly developed a deep and binding crush on him. I don't think I could have stood it if he had started carrying on a conversation with me; I would have been completely overcome by it all, but much of my energy was spent in contemplating those "Hi"s.

Sex had very little to do with boys. It was a subject of its own, fascinating, secret, and frightening. I first heard dirty jokes at a slumber party in seventh grade. A slumber party was a Good Thing because being invited to one indicated being In. From dirty jokes, the way was open for bigger and better things. Any passing reference to sex in a book was hugely shocking and hugely thrilling. I used to lie in bed at night and make up dirty stories of my own. At the same time, I was terrified at the whole thought. Starting to menstruate, feeling that I was suddenly a woman, was a very strange feeling. I was embarrassed by it.

School had very little relevance to anything. It was there and I had to go, and so I went. Homework was something to be avoided, done quickly, gotten out of the way as quickly as possible so I could do something more interesting. If I wasn't doing well, I didn't work harder. To be caught with homework undone was a stomach-tightening feeling, and so I did it. The only saving grace in most of my classes was that Mary sat next to me and we could pass notes. To have fun in school was an inconceivable concept.

If someone had sat down with me and said, "Talk to me about some of the things that are really important to you," I wouldn't have understood. It was one of the facts of life that nobody but yourself really cared about what you really thought, especially grown-ups. Parents might be nice to you, but if you told them your inner thoughts, they would either laugh or beat you up. If you had problems and worries, you didn't broadcast them, didn't even write them in a diary, because they couldn't be admitted, even to yourself. You knew what you were supposed to say and do, and you did it, and you tried to feel what you were supposed to.

I didn't draw as much as I had in grade school. I spent most of my spare time either reading (which I did a great deal) or writing. However, I doodled a tremendous amount, all over my notes, usually overdeveloped girls wearing short skirts. A lot of the time they carried knives; they were full of self-confidence

Figure 132. *This drawing by a ninth grade girl becomes a social commentary on the junior high school population. To a great extent, it reflects the girl's emotions and impressions about her peers.*

and off to fight and win in the name of some unspecified desperate-but-worthy cause. Sometimes, in ninth grade, I would draw boys and girls walking together, but girls generally outnumbered boys in my doodles about 100 to 1. If I drew a regular picture, it generally had some sort of sexual overtones or else was drawn in some style of some subject which I thought would meet parental approval. Art class in school was sort of fun; it was the class period you could goof around and get A's without trying. Wallpaper design, three-point perspective, and lettering had no significance for me, but they helped break up the boredom of math and science.

I guess I was really pretty miserable in junior high. The school itself was pretty bad: fierce teachers who'd never try to understand a kid's thoughts; strictly enforced rules about needing a pass in the halls; stairway monitors who grabbed me; boys who called me "bitch" and hit me with their books; waiting in line for ages in the cafeteria for an unappetizing plate of food; looking at trees outside the window and wishing I could go out; having to stand up on the school bus; having to run up three flights of stairs from gym to science after a four-minute compulsory shower; having to stand in line for a toilet at lunchtime. I was trying to figure out who I was and where I was going and not having much luck, perhaps in part because I didn't realize that

that was what I was doing. I certainly lacked self-confidence; I used to get all upset and cry if I was criticized and couldn't stand being laughed at. I haven't thought about junior high in a long time, this is the first time I've brought out my memories in quite a while. I'd be just as happy to forget it.

Art Motivation

One of the central themes of the adolescent is the striving for an identity. He needs to come to terms with himself and be able to express the intense feelings that need a constructive outlet. He is very aware of being alive and is developing an increased awareness of himself as one who can build, construct, and create objects. This is no time for pre-scribed busy-work. The junior high school student is full of thoughts and directions. He resents having to perform art tasks set up by the teacher and denying his own expression. The prime role of the teacher during this period is to provide guidance and encouragement so that this expression can take on a meaningful form.

We have already discussed how the art teacher is considered somewhat irrelevant to the production of art. It is important that the art teacher quickly establish a role for himself in the art room different from the one that is customary for the usual teacher. If the atmosphere is going to be such that mutual trust and exchange of ideas with junior high school youngsters is possible, then the usual classroom procedures may not be adequate. Youngsters of this age enjoy and need the opportunity to share and exchange thoughts with a few of their peers (Brittain, 1968,a). Possibly the best physical arrangement for an art room would be to have tables arranged for several small groups of students so that activities could be discussed and evaluated by peers as well as by teachers. In addition, the opportunity for isolated work may be important for some students, or for all students at some times. An occasional mural project that requires cooperative effort provides a chance for a group to solve artistic problems.

Often an ineffective art program is planned around the use of one material after another. The first three weeks may be devoted to pencil sketching, the following two weeks may be spent doing copper etchings, the next three weeks may be spent working in colored chalk, and so forth. Such a program ignores the basic assumption that it is more impor-tant to have something to say in art than to worry about the development of skills in case something might someday be expressed. To put this

Figure 133. *For some youngsters, particularly boys, art needs to be a challenge in which they can be physically involved. These boys are carving blocks made of cement and vermiculite.*

more clearly, the need for materials must grow out of the need for expression. The teacher who hides behind the material approach may be afraid of facing the real expressive needs of the adolescent.

Any art motivation should stress the individual's own contribution. At this stage of development it is important to reinforce individualistic thinking. An art program that is primarily concerned with productions may entirely miss one of the basic reasons for the existence of art in the school program, which is the personal involvement of the individual and the opportunity for developing a depth of meaningful self-expression.

Probably one of the most powerful features of any motivation is its relevance to the students. Unless the activity has some meaning for them it becomes an exercise to be done for the teacher. To some extent boys have less of an interest in the usual art program than girls have. A practical problem, such as making a three-dimensional working structure, can often challenge boys, particularly if there is some doubt implied that they can really do this. Sometimes such a project can become so engrossing that it serves as the basis for expanding into many of the more recognized art areas.

The development of a critical attitude toward the world that surrounds him has made the young adolescent much more concerned about naturalism. The schema that we saw earlier in drawings has now disappeared. However, the youngster may feel reluctant to become involved in art experiences. In part, this may be because his past performances in art have been ignored or even ridiculed. In part it is because of his developing critical awareness; in part it may even be a reflection of the feeling that art is not an important activity.

It is vital that every youngster feel that his activities in art are his own expression. To a great extent the teacher's motivation is responsible not so much for the performance of art but for the desire to perform. If the youngster is not involved, excited, and completely swept up in the art activity, then the drawing or painting becomes a mere exercise for the school system.

At this age children have not yet developed full control over their emotions and we often find that a seemingly minor incident will be of extreme importance to a youngster. This intensity of feeling can often be utilized within the art program. The emotional relationships a child develops with various segments of his environment can often be expressed either directly or symbolically. Topics centering on religious themes, individual justice, or the expression of love or hate can often involve a youngster quite completely. In such cases exaggeration or overemphasis of particular parts within a composition can be seen. Such distortions should be given support, and the flexible use of color and the exaggeration of form can develop an emotional impact in the art product.

It is not diplomatic to say, "Put your innermost feelings down on paper about some adult whom you feel has treated you unjustly." Many children have been taught that it is not nice to have unpleasant thoughts about people, and in some cases these feelings may very well be directed at parents and teachers. It is usually best to let such feelings of aggression, and in some cases love, be expressed more unconsciously. Such subjects as "The Ugliest Person in the World" would provide the opportunity for the release of such feelings. "What would the ugliest person in the world look like? Would he have smooth or rough skin? Would he have a long or short nose? How about his ears? Would his teeth stick out? And his hair? What color would go well with him? Could the ugliest person in the world be a woman?"

Plate 13. *"My Barber," painted by a fourteen year old boy. This haptically minded child has used flat areas of color and has not attempted to show light and shade. This type of art can be very decorative.*

a

Plate 14. *"Trees," watercolor paintings done by adolescent girls, illustrating two different methods of approach to the same subject. The artist of* **a** *has utilized the flowing qualities of the material with no concern for photographic representation. On the other hand,* **b** *is built up out of carefully drawn details: leaves, branches, and flowers. Although an individual may identify himself more with either the subjective or naturalistic approach, it may be valuable to encourage experimentation with both methods.*

b

Figure 134. *"The Hairy One," drawn by a twelve year old girl. By giving vent to her imagination, she had the opportunity to release feelings of aggression.*

As we have already discussed, this stage of development is characterized, among other things, by a tendency toward two different types of expression. The extremely visually minded person and the extreme haptic are relatively rare; often both tendencies can be seen. The awareness of wrinkles and folds when clothes are in motion is usually an indication of visual awareness, whereas the use of distortion, the lack of depth in drawings, and the continued use of flat color may indicate a more haptic approach to one's environment. Any motivation should include the opportunity to allow for all types of expression. The limiting of opportunities for art expression to the individuals who are primarily visually minded, as is the usual case, may restrict or definitely hamper the expression of those youngsters who are not capable or not ready to portray their world in a method they do not understand.

Once again, it should be emphasized that the drawing or painting or other art product is not the objective or goal of any art motivation. Rather, it is the opportunity to develop within the youngster a greater awareness of himself and those things around him. Therefore it becomes evident that changes imposed on the art product may have no effect upon the youngster himself. For example, an increased awareness of textural differences and tactile sensations cannot be achieved by telling a youngster to include more tactile properties in his painting. Time is needed in which to develop an awareness of a variety of textures and to experience these on an intimate basis. To merely "correct" the painting itself does not provide the experience of textures; it might be much more effective to allow the picture to be completed in the way that is important to the youngster himself. Once this is done, the broadening of the youngster's experience in the changes and qualities of tactile impressions can be undertaken.

Involving children in art experience may take many different directions. The motivation itself should vary considerably, depending upon the conditions of the classroom, the interests of the students, and the objectives of the teachers, but it should also vary just for variation's sake. If the class is concerned with the expression of emotion, quite a different motivation would be necessary than if a problem in design or aesthetics were to be considered.

Youngsters of this age are becoming more aware of beauty, although this must be interpreted in their terms and not the teacher's. Time for thought and contemplation is required if children are to become more aware of and more sensitive to the design qualities of various art forms. Turning a picture 180 degrees and looking at it as though it were an abstraction, relieved of its content, can call attention to the distribution of the various forms and colors. Obviously a drawing of loneliness would be quite different in design quality from a drawing portraying excitement. The design of an object as simple as a spoon can arouse critical discussion by means of searching questions. "Why isn't a spoon made out of cloth, or paper, or glass?" "Would the addition of holes in the handle of a spoon, or bumpy roses embossed upon the spoon bowl help or hinder its function?" "Would the spoon work better if its bowl were turned sideways?" The purpose of these questions would be to stimulate thinking about the relationship between material and expression and to sensitize youngsters to the design elements in their environment. This is not a time for listing or memorizing rules to follow; rather, it should be an opportunity for developing an awareness to art as a quality of life.

A word needs to be said about motivating the youngster who has lost his self-confidence in art expression. He is the "I can't do it" child. It is relatively easy to motivate youngsters who are eager to draw and paint, but the child who refuses to budge may be the person who needs the experience the most. Often the problem can be easily solved by using a material that is not "sissy" or "arty." Clay, wood, or other three-dimensional materials are often a good way to start. A second approach is to start where the youngster himself is. This may be simply having him cut out racing cars and putting these into a mobile or collage, or, if the problem is deeper than this, having him put some of his thoughts on large cardboard, even by cutting out headlines from the newspaper so as to make his resentment an issue which can be dealt with openly. To try to coax a child, or to tell a youngster that he really can draw, or to make something just for the teacher this once, may do nothing but make this young adolescent even more sure that art is not for him. The motivation, however it is given, or however it is developed, should provide the youngster with a desire to create and not be aimed at getting projects done, or putting marks in a book, or keeping youngsters busy.

Subject Matter

Subject matter itself is much less important than the way it is integrated into the life of the students. Junior high school youngsters have little opportunity in the usual classroom to have any voice in the subject matter covered. Mathematics follows a pattern that is difficult to break; history, science, and English are usually outlined in advance of the students' involvement in the class itself. In art, however, there is ample opportunity for the art teacher to make the subject matter content truly a matter over which students have some control.

With the developing awareness of themselves as individuals with opinions, tastes, and voices of their own, it is important that students be involved in the planning in such a way that the projects become essentially theirs. In one study (Brittain, 1968,a) the junior high school students clearly saw themselves as the source of ideas for art. In fact, the students involved in this particular study voiced amazement that adults would actually be interested in what junior high school students thought. One of the important roles that the teacher can play is that of an earnest

a

Figure 135. *These girls are printing linoleum blocks with a circus theme for a Girl Scout project. The finished product can be seen in Plate 12.*

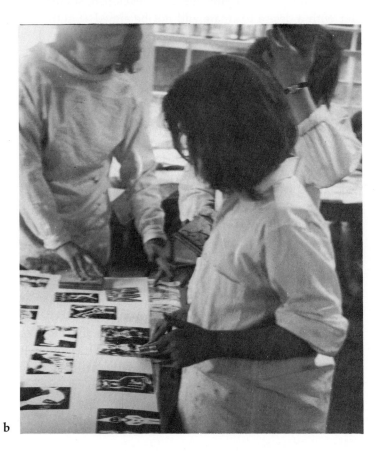

b

Creative and Mental
Growth

listener who can make these youngsters feel that their thoughts and ideas are worthy of consideration, and that they are not necessarily limited by having to look to the teacher for inspiration.

Occasionally topics are pushed upon the person responsible for an art program, topics that may actually be detrimental to the development of a meaningful art education program. Such topics as a poster for the local women's club bake sale, the mass production of table decorations for the annual teachers' meeting, or the making of a monogram for the gym team may all be worthwhile activities, so possibly the art teacher could do a few of these tasks some Saturday morning, but the art program has a much greater role than to fill its time with busy-work and service activities.

The expression of feelings and emotions should play an important part in the school art program. There is little opportunity for youngsters of this age to give vent to their feelings; sometimes they bubble to the surface and are expressed strongly outside school, and sometimes in school. The following suggestions should be used flexibly and any motivation should open up many possible ways of expression rather than converging on a particular method.

The Ugliest Person in the World

A Fierce Villain

All Alone on a Dark, Cold Night

A Good-looking Television Star

Feeling Full of Joy

The youngster of this age has an increased awareness of his own physical development. He is very conscious of himself and has developed a curiosity about the opposite sex. It is at this age that drawing from posed models may make an impact on youngsters such as no other subject matter can. Munro (1956) even went so far as to suggest that the adolescent be given the opportunity to observe and draw from the nude model. Certainly the hiding of the body seems more the concern of adults than of youngsters; there is no doubt that pictures of nude females are readily available to most junior high school boys, although this is usually in the boys' lavatory and not the art room. However, the best time to introduce the drawing of the nude might be in the elementary school so that the junior high school youngster would treat the body in a matter-of-fact manner. Drawing from the draped figure, or using each other as models, can be a most meaningful experience.

Modeling in clay from the posed figure provides another means of expression. A plastic three-dimensional form can be readily altered and allows for the expression of kinesthetic experience. The pose should be short for any type of representation, and the model should be used only as a stimulus.

During drawing or modeling, care should be taken to provide ample opportunity for the expression of haptic representations, and the pose should be treated in such a way that the student can identify with the model through personal experience. That is, the drawing of the model should not be a lesson on proportion, balance, anatomy, or a study in light and shade. Rather, it should be an opportunity to see the model as someone involved in life, with problems, with faults, and with whom the student can feel some empathy.

Waiting at the Corner for the Bus

Being Lost in the City

Doing Homework After School

Repairing the Street

Doing Chores at Home

Taking Part in the Game

Hiking with My Friends

There are certain activities within the junior high school itself that provide ample opportunity for expression. These can range all the way from annoyance at some seemingly arbitrary rule to participation in a forthcoming fair or dance. In our democratic society the opportunity

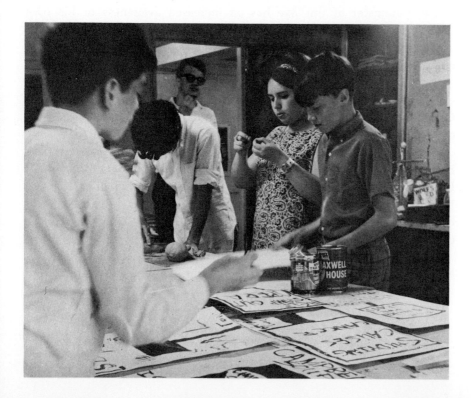

Figure 136. *These youngsters are involved in making protest posters. Sometimes these can be quite serious, but often they are humorous.*

should exist for constructive participation at all ages. This cannot be learned easily, but the opportunity to suggest changes in established procedures or to have a voice in meaningful decisions should always be encouraged. The prospect of making protest posters can be exciting in itself, and the concern for clarity of message and impact on the viewer can develop a real understanding of the problems that some of the artists in our society have to face. A serious school election, or events outside school such as a community action program, can provide the impetus for expression; however, nothing will turn youngsters away from art so fast as the suggestion that everyone make a poster to help raise funds for the local women's club benefit. A rule about dress regulations in the school, objections to passing in the hall, or reactions to shortening the lunch hour, would all make excellent topics.

The area of design is unlimited in its applications, and at this age the developing awareness of beauty and the concern for ornamentation become important. Again these areas must be relevant to the youngsters. Many shapes, patterns, and forms in shells, wood, moss, or other objects in nature can provide the stimulation for design experiences. Since the laws of symmetry are related to dogmatic periods of history, including periods of symbolism, they seem to be more and more out of place when individualism, emotions, and social changes dominate our lives. No imposed lessons in design can hope to match the design qualities that the youngster is led to discover for himself.

Mounting or Framing Pleasing Forms from Nature

Collages with Symbolic Meaning

Abstract Designs Using Paper, Wood, or Glass

Cloth Banners with Personal Insigne

Inventions from Industrial Scraps

Adapting forms from nature can also be quite interesting. The discovery of a logical order in an orange or an apple core can sometimes come as a surprise. Leaves or bark of trees, dripping water or ripples on a puddle, a skeleton of a fish or a frog's back can all become transformed. The camera makes an excellent means of studying such forms, but drawing them directly in greatly enlarged dimensions can provide insight into the amazing dynamic design qualities of our natural environment.

Subject matter becomes more than the assigned topic. It should be the impetus for exploration and creative experimentation in art. Unless the topic is meaningful and of real import to the young adolescent, producing the art form becomes a sterile act.

Art Materials

At this age art materials should play a secondary role in the art program. The material should be geared to the expressive needs of the students. The youngsters have become physically capable of dealing with almost any material, although plaster will still be spilled and paint will still drip, but the experience of working with these materials provides the best means of understanding them.

Care must be taken to insure that art is something special. The usual 12 by 18 inch size sheet of paper may no longer be the ideal size, and crayons may not be the best material to use for color. Both large materials and small materials can be intriguing at this age. The large materials provide the opportunity for real physical involvement and the problem of doing a painting that is three feet wide and five feet high can be a challenge in itself. At the same time, small muscle control provides the opportunity for detail in ink drawings.

Because of the increased ability to work with complex materials, craft projects are often introduced at this age. These provide excellent opportunities for a variety of artistic experiences and expression of a utilitarian nature. However, the continued use of craftlike material may encourage a narrowing of interests and a concealment of true expression rather than an opening up of new avenues to explore. This is not to say that youngsters should not have the opportunity to concentrate on one art material. Mattil and others (1961) showed that concentration in one area in depth provided the greatest gain in individual progress for ninth grade students over a one-year period. If a student constantly uses one material mechanically, producing without new discoveries, the material may become a substitute for expression.

Depth of expression can be achieved in many ways. One way would be to concentrate on one material, using it for a variety of subject matter; another approach in depth would be to concentrate on a particular subject matter and utilize a great number of materials in its development. For example, the human figure can be drawn, painted, modeled in clay, abstracted, dismembered, drawn in detail, and so forth. At the same time, tempera painting can be used as a means of expressing feelings about love or hate, of studying visual depth, or as a means of composing abstract color forms, or as a means of communication, or to illustrate a theme or mood.

New materials are now available for use in art classes, many of which were not readily available a few years ago. Although tempera paint is most commonly used, there is an increasing number of other paint materials that are suitable. Polymer, vinyl, and other water soluble paints are

Figure 137. *"Cow and Calf," modeled by a thirteen year old girl. Clay continues to be a good, expressive, three-dimensional material which here is used for an understanding of and feeling for animals.*

available. Plastics of a great variety are usable, as are new drawing instruments and inks. Some of these new materials, and some old ones too, are potential hazards in the classroom; the possibility of strong odors, fire hazards, and danger to the skin are important considerations. A review of these problems and hazards of art materials was carefully documented by Siedlecki (1968).

Probably the oldest three-dimensional material is clay. At this age, the potter's wheel can be a real challenge. As with many other projects, no preplanning can be done. Starting with a preconceived notion of the finished product when working on a potter's wheel is almost impossible for the beginning student, for much depends upon the consistency of the clay, the speed of the wheel, and the positioning of the hands and body. But clay can also be used as an excellent modeling material, and the casting of plaster from original models made from clay can be an exciting experience. Mixing cement with expanded mica, or plaster with sawdust, can provide a material that can be both built up and carved down.

Many of the art materials that have been discussed in earlier stages are also appropriate at this level. However, it is important to make sure that any materials used are also used by professional artists. That is, the child should be able to identify his work with those people who consider

Figure 138. *These puppets are made from paper bags and scrap materials. They can often be used for acting out dramatic situations when youngsters are reluctant to give voice to their own feelings.*

art a vocation rather than thinking of art in terms of children only. Exploring the qualities of charcoal and India ink with brush can stimulate an interest in the potential use of these materials. Exploring other possibilities, such as making papier-mâché moon-men, paper-bag puppets (see Figure 138), or plaster-and-wire space sculptures can involve the most reluctant youngster in art materials. When the child "is encouraged to invent or imagine unusual forms, such as strange machines, environments, and animals," his imagination can definitely be boosted (Kincaid, 1964). It should once more be emphasized that the main function of art materials is to provide a means for increased knowledge, understanding, and expression in the arts, and not to be an end in themselves.

A Summary of the Pseudo-Naturalistic Stage

This stage of development is one of very rapid changes. Girls discover the feminine role, and try desperately hard to be pretty and alluring. Boys' voices begin to change and most of them try to become very masculine. The young adolescent not only wants to be well liked by his peers, but also wants and needs the respect and attention of adults. The development of a critical attitude has made him aware of the world that surrounds him, sometimes painfully aware. His growing concern for naturalism is reflected in the drawings of objects and figures. Usually the schema that we have seen in earlier stages disappears; for some children the discrepancy between feeling themselves as adults and seeing their art product as childish brings a shock.

We have emphasized that creative growth is a vital part of the art program. This is especially true between the ages of twelve and fourteen. Here the child becomes much more critical of his own work; the pressure to conform to adult standards of behavior, or to the standards of the crowd, may work to stifle the creative urge. The art teacher plays a vital role in developing individuality in expression, in providing the opportunity to delve deeply into an area of interest, and in showing that the thoughts and ideas of youngsters of this age are welcome. The art room should have an atmosphere that is emotionally free and flexible, and provide the opportunity for an experimental and supportive attitude. It is important to stress that every project in which the child becomes involved should be accepted without any outside criterion or evaluation.

That is, the child who produces pleasing looking products and the youngster who is not doing the type of work that suits the teacher's aesthetic taste should be treated with equal respect. This in no way means that a *laissez-faire* attitude should prevail. The very opposite is true. The halfhearted attempt, the stereotype, and the presence of copying should all be clear indications to the teacher that the program is not a meaningful one. To stimulate the child's thinking, to have him come to grips with a problem that is meaningful, and to encourage a depth of expression are all much more important than making pretty end products.

We have discussed several aspects of growth that are exhibited by these young adolescents in their art. The art program can play a very real part in this total developmental process. Art is not merely a subject matter area; it is the expression of the total youngster. As children grow into adults the art program should constantly change to meet their needs. This particular age of development assumes greater importance when we realize that many youngsters have no further art experiences in the public schools after this time. It is unfortunate that our school systems are arranged in such a way that at the onset of adolescence a program designed to provide an opportunity for the expression of feelings, emotions, and sensitivities should be dropped for the majority of the secondary school population. Attitudes that children of this age develop from their art program in school will determine their future interest and participation in the arts. It is therefore of vital importance that teachers of this age group show a high degree of involvement and enthusiasm in the art experience itself.

RELATED ACTIVITIES

1. Compare a twelve year old girl's representation of females over several months. Are there any changes in drawings that reflect maturation? Compare these drawings with representations by girls a year younger.

2. Collect the drawings of a seventh grade. What proportion of the class are observing visually by drawing distant objects smaller? What proportion apparently are showing a nonvisual type of space representation?

3. Observe the working process while students are using clay. Which youngsters give a subjective interpretation of the topic rather than a visual? Are these the same ones who model synthetically?

4. Record examples of behavior that show the change from an unconscious approach to that of a critical awareness of the child's own actions. Are there any indications of the child's becoming critically aware of his own drawings?

5. Have children of this age become aware of joints when drawing figures? Are differences in size and age characterized? Collect examples of such drawings. Are there differences in the age at which these changes occur?

6. Observe a class for several sessions. Can you pick out some students who seem to be less involved in art activities? Does their work show this lack of involvement? How? Analyze some of the possible reasons for the hesitancy or fear of expression. Plan definite steps to take to improve the meaningfulness of the art experience.

The Period of Decision: Adolescent Art in the High School, 14-17 Years

10

The Importance of High School Art

Art has now become the product of conscious effort. For the student in high school, art has become something he can do, or leave alone. With young children art is primarily an expression of the self, done unconsciously. An eight year old will draw like an eight year old even if he has not had much opportunity to use art materials. The sixteen year old, on the other hand, will draw in the same way that he has been drawing for the past two or three years, unless he has had the opportunity or the desire to improve his artistic skills. This period becomes important, then, because it marks the beginning of purposeful learning in art. Art in the high school takes on a different atmosphere. It is now geared more toward

Figure 139. *At the high school level, art becomes purposeful learning. The development of skills and the interest in artistic procedures can become an exciting activity.*

the teaching of skills and the development of attitudes toward art that the student can freely accept or reject. For some, art is looked upon as something unrelated to the drive toward vocational goals, for others, art becomes that goal.

For most teen-agers, art is no longer a part of their lives. At least on the conscious level most sixteen and seventeen year old youngsters will not feel that art is essential to their needs. Art is constantly around them, it is dictating the clothes they wear, the buildings they live in, the packaging that induces them to buy, and the automobile they are saving for, but this is not part of what these youngsters consider art. For most high schoolers, art is something that was fun, but that belonged to the elementary school. Only one out of seven high school students elects art when it is available, although half the schools do not offer art at all (Davis,

1963). The larger secondary schools are more likely to offer art courses, but even here students are often advised not to take art courses because of the fear that the more able students will not be able to get into college unless their program is filled with the usual academic subjects. The fact that colleges do accept credits taken in high school in art is either not known or ignored (Michael, 1968). At any rate, art as an elective in the high school is taken by a very small percentage of students.

There is the possibility that art may no longer be considered an important part of learning; society seems to have accorded art courses a very minor place in the curriculum. The reason for this may be justified. Often the program of art is geared toward grooming students for an art career and giving some sort of recognition to those who are supposedly talented. For those teen-agers who feel they do not have the talent (and this obviously includes most of them), the possibility of flunking or getting a poor mark in art is not appealing. Even so, not all art classes are filled with talented youngsters, because there are always a few students whom the guidance counselor feels must take a few courses so as to graduate. For the most part, however, art has not been in the mainstream of interests for students in the high school. This is really sad when we consider that both for an individual need and for society's needs art can fulfill a real function.

The secondary school usually extends from seventh through twelfth grade. The young adolescent is very concerned about his gang, or crowd. He has found a new independence from adult domination, and is searching for identity. The older adolescent is still somewhat concerned about these things, but has become a great deal more aware of the adult world of responsibility. He is also beginning to be aware of the fact that he must soon be on his own and must fit into society in order to make a living. Love is no longer associated with fantasy and T.V. stars, but begins to be more closely tied to the nearest members of the opposite sex and the prospects of marriage. For boys, adult responsibilities may be only a year or two away, and it sometimes comes as a shock for girls to see one of their own sex, just a year ahead of them, becoming a wife and mother. This is a time for many decisions, and a great number of these decisions depend upon the teen-ager himself. Art can play a special role with young people, if the art program is responsive to their needs.

There is also a great need to bring art closer to the conscious awareness of students in the high school. These are the people who will be making decisions in the future about our society, and the necessity for making art a part of their thinking is paramount. Many philosophers and artists have lamented the condition of our visual world, but efforts to change the elements that comprise it will have little success unless the need for

Figure 140. *This is an interpretation of leaves and greenery. Although this is not a visual copy, it includes the essence of a forest. The adolescent is able to abstract from nature and enjoys making new forms.*

this change is made apparent to the citizens of tomorrow. In today's society there is very little opportunity for self-identification, very little opportunity to feel responsible for what one is doing, very little opportunity to master a portion of one's life. Increasingly, demands are coming from sources outside the self: the hours one keeps are decided by the job requirement, the clothes one wears are decided by designers and fashion magazines, the house one lives in has been built by someone else, the car that is driven was made miles away and is serviced by others, the food one eats is grown elsewhere and purchased in impersonal stores; and to build a fire outdoors or add on a room to one's house requires special permits from an impersonal official. As yet society has not fettered art. There is a great need to provide a touch of saneness and a contact with one's own thinking, and the high school art program is a valid place for this to happen.

The High School Student

For the past ten, eleven, or twelve years, the high school student has spent a considerable length of time in classrooms. Although there has been some experimentation in organization, he has typically spent six or more hours each day in classes with others his own age and with one teacher in charge. For some, the age of compulsory education cannot be over soon enough. With others, the end of high school means that they now have a choice in deciding their own futures. However, graduation from high school does not necessarily mean the end of society's restrictions for the student. There are a few years to wait before voting age; if he can now get a license to drive, he must pay an additional premium for his car insurance; in some states he cannot legally drink or buy alcoholic beverages; his credit is no good; and generally the teen-ager receives the message that even after high school he is not fully trusted in adult society.

Sex has begun to play an important role. There is no doubt that the awakening of sexual urges gives rise to some of the greatest concerns of this age. Girls are bombarded with advertisements about how to make themselves more femininely alluring by the use of hair rinses, deodorants, cosmetics, by squeezing or padding the body, or by various dress styles. For boys greater attention is often focused upon muscle building and attaining masculinity. This is a real problem for the youngster who develops later than his classmates. Added to all of this, of course, is the general feeling that somehow sex is taboo. It has been shown that in other cultures this uncomfortable period between puberty and marriage may be considerably shorter. Although some girls leave high school for marriage, especially in the lower socioeconomic levels, marriage for others can sometimes be delayed well beyond college. The high school student has not outgrown his concern about himself. The adolescent is concerned about his hair, the pimple on his nose, and the proper clothes to wear. In the same way that he is concerned about his appearance he is becoming much more concerned about how he is seen by others. The older and closer to graduation the student gets, the more he decides that he will have to live with himself as he is. The crowd is still important, especially to reinforce one's own feelings.

Everyone knows of the five year old who is anxious to be a fireman when he grows up, but rarely do we find a sixteen year old who is this definite about his vocational goals. At twelve or fourteen, the possibility of becoming an artist may have sounded very nice, particularly for boys who imagined themselves painting delightful nudes in some attic, but the possibility of making a real choice of a lifetime career is a frightening thought for the graduating senior. Often the choice is accidental. For the youngster whose family is less financially solvent, the part-time job may become a full-time occupation. For the more academically successful student dear old Dad's college may be the easiest route into the insurance business. Few youngsters are able to maintain their idealism beyond eleventh grade, and earlier romantic interests in art are soon put aside.

THE SECONDARY SCHOOL ENVIRONMENT

Adults have the opportunity in our free society to make decisions about where they will work, the kind of people they want to be with, or if they want to be a part of society at all. The economically disadvantaged adult male has less opportunity for this freedom, but even he has a right to speak up, and this right is protected by law. For the youngster there is no comparable freedom. In fact, the law is usually quite definite in requiring him to attend school for a specific number of years, and to take certain courses in high school; even the number of days of attendance is usually clearly specified, and if he is not there everybody gets excited. Society looks upon the public schools as being an extremely important part of the training of individuals to perpetuate society. Youngsters are admonished to graduate from high school, and if a youngster does reject the school system his chances for economic success are severely limited.

Although society may place a high value on an education, the young-

Figure 141. *Society places a high value on education, but the students find themselves taking mandatory courses within the confines of the school grounds, and they may consider high school something to survive rather than enjoy.*

ster in the secondary school may view this in quite a different light. Often the high school is looked upon as something to survive rather than as something to enjoy. The successful student is one who has learned to cope with the system, but he may not be the one who is getting the most out of the learning situation. It is fairly common for students not to study anything but that which will appear on examinations; usually the most important thing learned in a classroom is what the teacher expects rather than an understanding of the subject. It is a question of survival with the least amount of effort, and it is the rare teacher who is able to instill the classroom with an atmosphere of excitement for learning.

The usual high school program is made up of many isolated subjects that have a tradition from the past as solid academic requirements. Learning is fragmented, and the youngster has no choice but to attend one class after another according to the bell, which in itself may interrupt learning. Girls seem to get more satisfaction from school than boys, but for both, school tends to be a dull place where interest is found in the unexpected happening rather than in learning (Jackson, 1968).

Students view education primarily as the imposition of already established truths, with little or no concern paid to the personal needs or desires of the youngster himself. There is no course aimed at providing the high school student with knowledge about himself, his own struggle in society, or even about the dreams and wishes he may have for the future. The usual academic program for those who will attempt to go on to college has no real relationship to objects, people, or jobs. The alternate choice that students usually have is the vocational program, which is concerned primarily with providing job skills.

Too often, controversial subjects are considered dangerous; a teacher who encourages students to think about politics, sex, or marriage, who raises questions about the process of law, or who gets his class involved in local issues may very well find himself looking for a new position the following year. Schools tend to isolate youngsters from the real world, at a time when the energies and idealism of these youngsters can best be incorporated into society.

There are, of course, exceptions to this dismal picture. Often programs are attempted which utilize the energies of the adolescent in constructive ways, either through sports or community activities. Too often these school sponsored projects are considered in the same light as other school activities and thus are doomed to failure. Occasional attempts are made at bringing the arts into the curriculum of all students, either under the heading of courses in humanities or by requiring at least one semester in the arts for each student. However, just because a course has a name dealing with the area of art does not mean that this course provides opportunities for the high school student to get involved in a meaningful way with his society, nor does it mean that he is now able to express his feelings and emotions about himself or the world around him. All too often, the art courses offered in the high school are planned well in advance by some committee in the state capitol, and courses have a step-by-step progression that is clearly stated in the syllabus. There is a real need for an exciting, meaningful program in art for high school students.

To some extent the secondary school system may be caught in its own web. That is, if art is going to have any meaning for high school students we may have to find ways and means to provide an exciting program other than those followed by the rest of the school system. The usual routine of keeping track of the students as they come and go, worrying more about attendance than about ideas, and being concerned with grades rather than achievement may be a real stumbling block to change. Some of this routine can be rather funny (Kaufman, 1964), or it can be quite tragic (Kozol, 1967). There seems to be no doubt that the high school student does build up a resentment to society through his experience in the public schools (Nordstrom, *et al.*, 1967). It may be that if change is going to be made it has to be made by the segment of the high school program that is most flexible and ready to change. Art seems well suited to lead in this respect.

THE ADOLESCENT AND SOCIETY

When one leaves childhood is easy to define, at least from a physical point of view. Puberty is generally recognized as being the end of childhood. Girls usually begin a period of rapid growth at about eleven years, and by menarche at about thirteen they will have developed the usual feminine bodily characteristics. Although girls do not reach their full mature height until about seventeen, growth becomes much slower. Boys start to shoot up about two years later than girls; they do not start slowing down until fifteen or sixteen, and they reach adult height at about nineteen. Their voices may begin to change, the Adam's apple grows, and a trace of fuzz appears on their faces at about fifteen. With both sexes there are skin changes, and it is not unusual for body parts to grow at different rates. All these changes are of concern to these youngsters and obviously have an effect upon how they view themselves in relation to the rest of society.

When adults say they do not know what the younger generation is coming to, they are speaking about the fifteen to seventeen year old. It is rather strange to consider the fact that this is the one member of society who seems to be constantly getting into trouble. He is the one who is caught speeding, he is the one who experiments with drugs, he is

Figure 142. *The high school student is concerned about many problems facing society, and art should provide the opportunity for him to express these feelings. This satirical cartoon is also social comment.*

the one who puts on the protest demonstration, and he is the one who wears absurd clothes. The adolescent is becoming more and more concerned with social problems and cannot accept the values of an older generation without testing them. Parents come in for their share of resentment, and the generation gap may be more a gap in understanding than in age. The sixteen year old has little opportunity for rebelling in a socially acceptable manner, and too often parents are seen as rule makers.

Because there are rather strict laws about child labor which give the older adolescent little opportunity to find a place for himself within the larger society, society itself is responsible for some of this conflict. Some experimentation is now going on within a few school systems whereby youngsters can work part-time and attend school part-time; but, for the most part, society does not provide the means by which a sixteen year old can feel that he has a contribution to make or that this contribution will be accepted by the world of adults.

Art in the high school has tended to reflect society's opinions of the adolescent. To a great extent, school art is too often removed from the real world, and it is concerned with issues that are often removed from controversy, social issues, idealism and the desire for change, and even from the youngster himself. There is no reason why we should not be able to provide an art program that is not only distinct in its nature but that can also provide the necessary basis for helping to satisfy the needs of this age and to unfold possibilities for continued growth.

The Basis for Art in the High School

If a meaningful program is going to be developed for art in the high school, it must be based upon the needs of the youngsters taking these courses. It must provide the opportunity for expression of the thinking, the emotions, and the reactions to the adolescent's environment. It should be basically a program in which the individual can become totally involved, in which the methods and materials are as far removed from the environmental and psychological restraints of the high school as possible, and which involves the student directly in the fundamental process of creating a product with real utilitarian value, not only for him, but for society at large. The high school art program should be based upon young adults who are involved in and concerned about today's world and not a program that is oriented toward making artists.

The still life set-up, the picture made from water colors, the linoleum blockprint, or the small clay sculpture may not be large enough in impact to involve today's youth. There is a sense of urgency, a sense of social involvement, and a desire to make change that cannot be satisfied with typical high school projects. To a great extent, the usual high school project is aimed at self-improvement, while the youth of today is much more concerned with making some impact on society. The usual concept of an artist, painting by himself in a garret, isolated from the world, has little to do with the adolescent. Living is a challenge, and art should provide the opportunity for this challenge.

There is no correct art. Art has traditionally been a reflection of the culture in which it was found. There are no rules to artistic success, for the rules are made by people, and these are constantly changing. For art to be important it must be a reflection of the individual making it. This is as true at the high school level as it is for the professional artist. No art work stands isolated from the culture in which it was formed or from the individual who made it. Art is not done by someone who is unin-

Figure 143. *For the intellectually capable student the school situation usually provides little opportunity for expressing feelings or emotions. Working directly with art materials provides the opportunity for uncensored expression in areas of one's own choosing.*

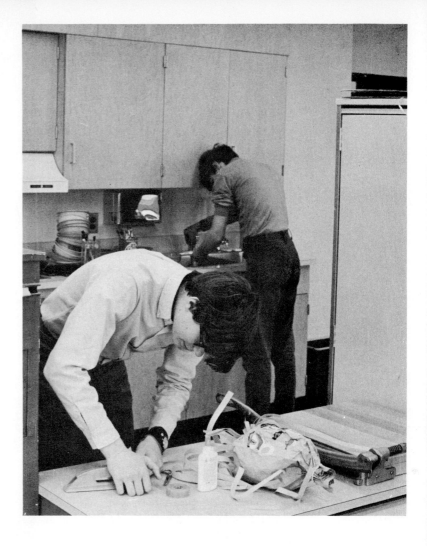

volved. Rather, art is basic to man's emotions and expresses the experience and need of the doer.

Constantly around us are problems concerned with art. Artists and teachers alike lament the fact that we live in a world that ignores the basic qualities of aesthetics. Design seems to play a minor role in society as compared with money, and the arts invariably take a back seat when considerations for change are voiced. The art program at the high school level should be an active one. The subject matter should be based upon more than the teacher's files, more than just the school environment; it should become a vital part of the community.

Working directly with a material provides a tremendous satisfaction and a release from the pressures of intellectualizing that may be only one part of the experience of developing into mature adults. Most of the thinking that goes on within the high school environment is limited to those topics that are prescribed. Little opportunity is provided to think

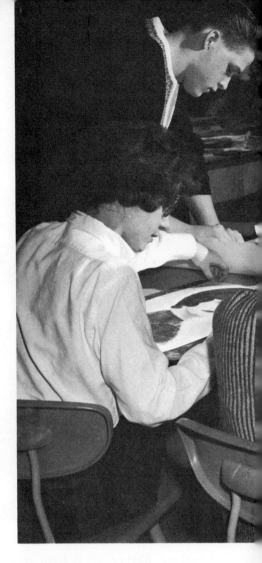

Figure 144. *A typical art class in high school usually includes students who will become business men, laborers, or professional people. Occasionally one student may become an artist.*

as that may be upsetting to the semitranquility of the classroom. Little opportunity is given for the youngster to rebel or to voice his objections to classroom routine. The opportunity to express emotions, feelings, and rebellion in an art form that may have a social function can be of tremendous importance. However, courses in art are not necessarily limited to the expression of resentment; other feelings, such as love, the expression of beauty, and feelings about social issues are equally legitimate concerns of art.

The basis for an art program in the senior high school should therefore be the same as that for the individual in his society. Its purpose should be to involve the student more fully in the culture in which he finds himself, it should provide him with a means of making tangible changes, and it should provide the opportunity for him to face himself and his own needs.

The Structure of an Art Program

Basic to any planning are the students who will be in the art program of a senior high school. We have already discussed some of the general characteristics and problems that the high school student faces. Very few of these students in an art course will actually do anything beyond school with art. Rather, they will become plumbers, scientists, housewives, insurance salesmen, policemen, and so forth. To a great extent, then, we are planning a course of art not for the talented one, but for the youngster who will take his place in society. It is the objective of the art course to

THE PERIOD OF
DECISION

get him involved to such an extent that art becomes a meaningful experience for him, that he discovers that art can be a valuable means of focusing energies into creative problem solving, not only in school but also after graduation.

Probably one of the most important elements is the attitude that prevails. If an art course is looked upon as just another academic course with quizzes, examinations, and projects to be marked, art will lose its significance and impact upon students. Much time and effort can be spent by the students and by the teacher in what is sincerely considered a good art program. Such projects may include embossing metal plaques, designing stained-glass windows, making safety posters, designing monogrammed napkins, carving book ends, copying various lettering styles, or carving a football player out of soap. The list of such school-type projects is unlimited. These tend to parallel the May baskets and sewing cards at the elementary level. This approach to art education tends to make a sham and a frill out of what should be a vital and dynamic part of the school curriculum.

It is possible to deal with art in such a way as to make a meaningful and exciting program. Probably the first element would be to treat the adolescents as adults. The implications of this are great. Nowhere else in the school system can a youngster be looked upon as an important being, one who has a contribution to make, one who is the core of the program. We would not expect a carpenter, or a farmer, or an electrical engineer to stand for some of the nonsense that often passes for art. Nor would we expect adults to be interested in grades or other types of evaluation. Treating the high school student as an adult implies that we respect his opinions and realize he has had experiences that may go beyond ours in certain areas, and that he has turned to art in a free choice.

SUBJECT MATTER

Undoubtedly one of the most important elements of an art class is the opportunity to paint. Painting has long been looked upon as the most expressive form of art. Within painting much can be expressed that is important to the high school student. There is no reason to plan exercises that lead up to painting, exercises that may be important to the teacher, but not to the student. Painting from warm to cool, cutting shapes in order to visualize pictorial design, and exercises dealing with positive and negative space are all important at some point, but not necessarily for all students, and certainly not as an introduction to painting. The painting can be done with a range of materials, and there is no reason to expect that students should be in a lockstep procedure. Some students

Figure 145. *The opportunity to paint is often one reason that students elect an art course at the high school. Students should be encouraged to set their own goals and to feel free to discuss their satisfactions or displeasures with the instructor.*

may enjoy polymers and oils, others tempera, and still others water color. To come face to face with an empty painting surface is a challenge, and the experience should be just as fundamental as that faced by the professional painter. The adolescent is critically aware of the immaturity of his product. He can easily become discouraged by the primitiveness and naïveté of his drawings, and often seems afraid to project his thinking directly upon the paper. The adolescent is disturbed by the discrepancy between what he produces and what he feels is appropriate for an adult to draw or paint.

A very direct approach to this problem would be to enlarge his concept of adult art. Certainly the fresh, and in some cases the blunt painting of some contemporary artists may awaken the adolescent to new possibilities. Even older masters such as Chagall and Klee painted in a very unsophisticated manner. Another fruitful direction is to involve the student with materials and techniques in which the end product is not as readily comparable to adult products. The adolescent has now developed the ability to work with more intricate procedures, and in some cases these can be a challenge. Although we can look at the classroom as a learning environment, the initial drive for this learning experience must come from the individual himself.

A second broad area that should be basic to the art program is the involvement of the student in his own school experiences. Although one sometimes hears of a program in which music, dance, and drama become thoroughly combined with art, these programs are very few. Frequently the art teacher feels that the rest of the school activities are irrelevant to the art program, and for good reason. Such art classes can be used as a cheap substitute for producers of commercial art. However, a real involvement of the student in school activities can work for the total benefit of the school itself. Most high schools have an abundant number of empty halls. These make excellent painting surfaces and there is no reason why art students cannot take advantage of these large blank areas

Figure 146. *One of the purposes of an art program should be to provide the students with some of the abilities and interests that will make art important to them once they leave high school. These girls are learning some of the procedures in weaving.*

to paint murals. It should be pointed out that a mural is quite different from a painting; since the mural will be part of the architectural surface, the shape available becomes a challenge in which the architecture and the mural must be closely interwoven. Exhibits of paintings can also be displayed in the halls, but these must be ever-changing and carefully labeled. Painting flats for the school play or designing the backdrops can be important if the students are used in the planning phases and experimentation is built in. Effects such as the use of film, smoke, flashing lights, and so forth can make this truly an art experience. There is some danger in this type of program, in that it is possible that the administration may consider art a decoration for "true" school activities. If this is the case, it is better to have no involvement in such school activities.

Outside the immediate school is probably the most fruitful area for exploration. If we look upon the field of art in a broad perspective, very few artists are actually painters. Many more people who are considered artists are involved in a wide range of occupations, including architecture, landscape design, interior decoration, and so forth. It is not the intent to provide training in these areas to high school students, but rather to involve them in some of these areas and to provide them with some of these tools, so that art does not stop at the closing of the classroom door. There are many areas outside of the classroom in which the planning and designing functions of students can operate. Landscaping a part of the school grounds, making an abandoned piece of property into a small park, developing a series of benches for a bus stop, all make appropriate art projects. It would be a blow to the high school student if these were left in the planning stage; there is no reason why bricks cannot be laid, trees planted, and benches cast out of concrete. It is this type of involvement in a project that can capitalize upon the youngster's intense desire to make a meaningful impression upon his society.

There is little opportunity in our society for youngsters to get involved in apprenticeship training or to gain an understanding of the type of work that adults are involved in. Often a youngster will graduate from high school without having done any more manual labor than babysitting or shoveling snow from a sidewalk. Part of the art program can be incorporated into the community functions in a way that no other part of the high school can. Such involvement could include the planning and designing of a section of a house, such as the kitchen, garage, or bathroom. Most building today is done by a builder without the benefit of an architect. Builders often offer a variety of services, and sometimes the involvement of high school youngsters in such a program can be considered an advertising asset by the builders. This means that the art classes will actually be criticizing and evaluating different plans, checking the building codes, seeing the structure under way, and making recommendations as to the type of flooring or quality of paint that is put on the walls. Often the art program doodles in house plans, but rarely does the student become committed to a project to the extent that he is able to see changes being made or is able to voice his approval or criticism over an actual structure.

The area of art is almost unlimited in its possibilities. Photography can be important if some culmination, such as a publication, can be the ultimate goal. Working with sculpture, if the sculptural forms become part of the community, can also be a powerful force. Printing can be worthwhile if it is related to actual printing and publication, such as a school paper and the high school yearbook, which are usually removed from the students' hands and put into those of a commercial printing house. Almost any art-oriented project can take on meaning if it is one that combines the needs of the adolescent youngster with opportunities to work on the problems that he is facing.

THE IMPORTANCE OF DESIGN

The art program should also provide the basis for cultural directness and honesty. The negative implications and effects upon our thinking processes of accepting falsehoods and imitation as normal within our own culture should certainly be decried. Pointing out dishonesty and sham when it occurs in architectural planning, in the purchasing of accessories, or in our political life should make for a greater realization of such discrepancies.

The secondary school is an excellent place to begin to re-educate toward a feeling for design as an integral part of the function and use of an object or of a material. Functional design refers to three equally important relationships: the relationship between design and material, the relationship of design to tools or machinery, and the relationship between design and purpose. For example, a piece of pottery made on a potter's wheel should look as if it were indeed made on the potter's wheel. The more we hide the effects of the working methods, the more we move away from the truth of functional design. The purpose of a vase may be purely decorative, in which case it needs to be able to stand, or be hung, or be heavy enough so that it will not be easily knocked over. If the purpose of the pot is to hold flowers, however, its glaze must not compete with the flowers, nor should the pot be too wide or narrow for such a purpose. The natural qualities of the materials should always be utilized and preserved as much as possible. Wood, glass, textile, metal, each should be used in its own right. Simplicity of line is an important prin-

Plate 15. "Waterfall." An example of the subtle and vigorous treatment of space and colors demonstrate a quality. As this illustrates the Nonobjective painting may be visually inspired or it may represent a nonvisual experience.

Figure 147. *"Man Reading." This plaster sculpture shows that it was made from plaster. Every work of art should take advantage of the natural qualities of the material from which it is made.*

ciple of modern functional furniture, with variation introduced by the use of different materials. Fine workmanship is an integral part of the design itself, and joints and braces need not be hidden under a decorative cover.

It is quite apparent that few people would purchase a toothbrush with a Victorian handle or one with an embossed design of flowers. The bristles of a toothbrush are not arranged in little scalloped designs, nor do they attempt to look like something other than bristles. However, we often find tableware with roses on the handle, lamps with scallops on the shade, and chairs with lion's paws for legs. The average American is fairly up to date when it comes to finding a better kind of transportation—the newest car cannot be new enough—or a better kind of range or refrigerator. In his living room, however, he apparently wants to retreat from today's world and is content with the furniture styled for his ancestors, electing flowers for his living room rug and a colonial weather vane for his garage. The question goes deeper than just introducing the best type of modern furniture or contemporary homes to the public. Students must be made aware of the discrepancy between the demand for truth and the quest for scientific knowledge on the one hand and the acceptance of imitation eighteenth-century styles and cute designs of flowers on the other. To a great extent this must be a first-hand learning experience, for there is no formula of "right" answers.

THE ORGANIZATION OF THE ART CLASS

The usual time set aside for art in the curriculum at the high school level is not best suited to art experiences. Sometimes double periods are allowed, but the typical pattern is for the art class to fit in between an English lesson and a gym class. It is obvious that the type of program suggested here cannot fit nicely into a preconceived time schedule, because the involvement of youngsters cannot be automatically switched on and off after forty-five minutes. There may be reason to believe that art classes should not follow the usual academic class pattern. Possibly the usual pattern is not best for academic subjects either, but certainly art might better be offered on a Saturday morning when three hours at a time would be available for pursuing activities. Assuming that such restrictions as may be imposed by the high school administrators are inflexible, it is possible to live within the confines of daily scheduled

Figure 148. *The interests and emotions of high school students need to be captured if an art program is going to be successful. Students can quickly turn their backs on a program that follows the usual pattern of academic subjects.*

periods, but even here other arrangements can often be worked out. The important thing is to remove the art program from the tightly scheduled list of activities, and have it more in tune with the youngster's interests and drives than with the clock.

Although the classroom can be the center of a number of planning and discussion sessions, the real activity of the art class could take place elsewhere. As much as possible, the class should be seen as one which is centered in the community and in the youngster's own life. If some students are involved in architectural planning and building, it does not make sense to put together little models from toothpicks and styrofoam when actual building is going on continually outside school. If some students are involved in landscaping a park, building benches for the area, and ordering trees or discussing planting with the community's building and grounds department, it does not make sense for them to be making sketches or layout designs to be filed in a drawer. If students are involved in painting, the subject matter for these paintings can rarely be found in the art room itself, and there is no reason why pictures or photographs need to substitute for the main street in town. Often sketches can be made elsewhere and the final painting can be completed in the classroom itself, but the involvement in the subject matter should not be vicarious.

For those students who develop an interest in sculptural form, the industrial arts room may be a better place to do some planning; but the hammering together of parts and pieces, or the welding of steel could probably best be done at those commercial establishments that the youngsters will be able to use once they leave school. Even the firing of clay should probably be in the hands of the youngsters themselves so that they develop an understanding of the firing process and the design and operation of the kiln. Essentially, then, the organization of the art activities should be centered in those parts of the community that can give support and facilities to students once they leave the art class. The art room should be looked upon primarily as a central meeting and discussion location, and not as a closed, isolated studio.

Some questions will undoubtedly be raised about the possibility of students running wild with such a type of organization. Art activities are too often planned in a way that insures success. Art is not all sweetness and light, and many failures and frustrations are part of the learning process. The threat of grades or marks is poor motivation; threats are hardly the basis for developing a positive relationship with either art, the art teacher, or oneself. In one year or two, the high-school student will no longer be in a position to be told what to do and when to do it. If the student can be involved in art activities so that he feels that these are truly his, he will be able to turn to the art teacher and others for guidance, but the drive essentially will rest in the youngster himself.

This type of organization is obviously one that will put a great deal of responsibility upon the students. At the same time, it places additional responsibility upon the teacher, for he is no longer able to control the thinking processes of those youngsters who become self-motivated. It is easier to play the role of prison guard, to have students lined up in neat rows in the classroom, to have all students doing the same topic at the same time, to have goals set by the teacher, and to give tests to insure that students are developing those skills that the teacher has decided are important. But this is not art. Art is the quality of being human, a quality that is involved in experiences that provide the opportunity for growth and understanding of oneself and others. The production of some form or shape in which one is not personally involved does not constitute art. The most important task of an art teacher is undoubtedly that of making art important and meaningful to high school students.

Several projects may be going on at the same time within an art class. Youngsters of varying abilities and interests cannot be expected to show equal enthusiasm for all types of projects. The particular projects that these youngsters select are not important. The will to learn, with active involvement in a project, is of prime importance. The art teacher should not feel that he has to be present continually. In fact, his very presence may reduce the amount of self-learning that takes place. He should, however, be available for listening to and broadening the possible avenues of action that students take. It is not just his technical ability that becomes important, for he should be more a model of possible ways to explore and to investigate, not one who provides the answers when called upon. It is probably more useful to say "I don't know, but let's find out" than to always have a ready answer available.

The organization of the classroom takes on real meaning when the emphasis for this organization is placed upon the needs of the students in that class rather than upon the whims of the art teacher. The organization should be flexible, provide opportunities for exchanging thoughts at intervals, and also provide the teacher with the opportunity for group discussion when he feels the need for it. Some basic problems may arise, and an occasional lecture to provide specific information about artistic skill, the problems of architectural design, various methods that have been historically used in printing, or a survey of painting methods may be extremely valuable when the need arises.

Students will develop the need for acquiring certain skills, for these will be necessary to gain satisfaction and a sense of accomplishment and self-confidence. Procedures can be explained. These are the steps in preparing materials, in maintaining their working consistency, and in cleaning and preserving the results. Techniques, on the other hand, are highly individual and develop according to personal needs. Each person has a

Figure 149. *This elaborate doodle is an art form in itself. Each youngster has an unconscious desire for art expression.*

technique which evolves, in part unconsciously, as a result of his experiences in the world that surrounds him. The working through a problem, the development of several possible solutions, the encouragement toward flexibility, and the final achievement of at least partial success will lead to a development of technique. The best technique is therefore developed by each individual and will permit him to express himself more easily and with greater depth.

Since art education in the secondary school does not prepare for a profession but rather serves to develop the mental, aesthetic, and creative growth of the individual, the teaching of skills must be focused upon the problem of finding adequate means of expression for the student. All skills, therefore, must be introduced with the purpose of fostering the individual's free expression.

Art Materials

The material from which an art object is made does not have any artistic quality in its natural form. It is only through expression in art that the form assumes meaning and the material becomes an art material. The more opportunity there is for the high school student to manipulate, change, and build in diverse ways from a material, the better that material is. There are many materials that possess a high degree of structure that can stand in the way of expression. Such materials as colored tissue paper, leather scraps, copper foil, and enameling kits, have limited variability and are usually not suited to high school art programs.

It would probably be best if no art materials at all were available for the high school student to use. This would mean that every material would have to be purchased or obtained through the student's own efforts. The clay would have to be purchased locally or dug from a clay bank. Lumber would have to be obtained from the local building supply house, paper from a stationery store, and sculptural supplies from the local junkyard. The advantage in this type of arrangement is that the student will no longer feel that the art material is the prime responsibility of the art teacher. Also it means that the art student must put forth some effort in obtaining these materials, and therefore he will be able to continue using these sources after graduation. Often the interest in art may die because of the unavailability of materials. Knowing where to get them, how much they cost, and their care and proper handling may be an important element in learning about the production of art. This is not to

Figure 150. *The student is challenged by the possibilities of a fresh approach to using materials, because in this way there is no need to conform to arbitrary standards. Here an interest in light patterns changed by crumpled tissue paper provides the basis for this sculptural form.*

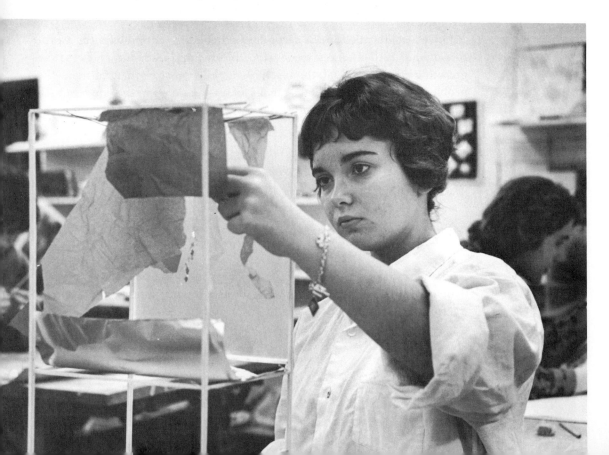

suggest that all students must purchase all their art materials, since this would obviously work to the disadvantage of the poorer youngster. However, the budget for art supplies is customarily an exercise for the art teacher rather than a learning situation for the student. Rather than the art teacher requisitioning the materials and then passing them out when the time arrives, the student should be personally involved in knowing the sources, costs, and availability of the supplies he is using, especially if these are considered part of his education.

The high school student needs to know a good deal about a material before it can be utilized. Just how that material is to be used needs to be considered before an abstract lesson on materials can be presented. A material that is going to be used outside in a structure or art form that takes some strength may be quite different from a material used for an object that is going to be suspended and protected from the weather. A good deal of the student's knowledge can be acquired through experimentation. How permanent is a material? How heavy is it? Can it be colored? Does it burn? Can it be cast or carved? How much weight will it support? Is it waterproof? These are all questions that need to be answered about a material before it can be used appropriately in a given environment. Of course, new materials are constantly available, or new ways of using old materials need investigation. This is one way of involving students in art procedures. Boys particularly can be quickly involved in some problems in art if they need to discover how to join aluminum sheets, and have to decide if the best way is through stapling, riveting, using adhesives, soldering, or by clamping or screwing to a second material.

Materials can play an important role in the design and final shape of an art form. It would be a mistake to consider a material only the means to an end, because thinking with the material itself and developing a feeling for the function and use of materials may well result in changes in design, revisions in original plans, and a greater flexibility of approach.

A word should be said about the use of tools. The usual tools for an art class are often considered brushes, pans for mixing paint, rollers, palette knives, scissors, and staplers. But there may also be need for a range of hand tools such as screw drivers, saws, chisels, hammers, pliers, and a few power tools, including a drill and a sander. These tools should be looked upon as the property of the class, and their main purpose is to be used. Sometimes tools can be made for a special purpose, such as mixing plaster, troweling concrete, or mixing up certain adhesives. These are expendable. Durable and inexpensive cameras should also be considered part of the available tools, as should a tape recorder, record player, slide projector, and some equipment more often considered basic to the study of science, such as scales and a microscope. The materials and tools should be of good quality, and in no way should the expression of the high school student be valued less than the expression of the adult artist. It is probably better to limit the materials and tools available if budget problems are a consideration, than to buy or purchase those which cannot be fully used because they are not substantial enough to withstand the active use that teen-agers will give them.

Summary of Art in the High School

The fifteen to seventeen year old is self-critical, introspective, idealistic, and has a growing concern about his relationship to society. No two teen-agers are alike, but they have concerns that are common. For the most part high school students do not have the opportunity or do not elect to take art courses; the art courses that are offered are often unrelated to the youngsters in these classes. Art should provide the opportunity for the high school student to express his feelings and emotions and feel that his art is important to himself and to others.

The art program is in an enviable position to break away from the usual academic pattern of giving grades and testing for the knowledge that the teacher thinks important. The students and the environment provide excellent sources for art projects that can be meaningful to students and can also have an impact on the school society.

Much of the art that is done by individuals after leaving the secondary schools is of practical value, such as furniture making, rug weaving, photography, pottery making, or even furniture repair and refinishing. However, much misdirected time and effort is presently channeled into nonworthwhile activities by the "easy-to-make, just-follow-the-pattern" type of project. Considerable time within the framework of the curriculum should be set aside to make art meaningful as a continuing activity. People need to have control over, and identify with, a project of their own choosing. From the first conception of the idea, through the problem solving and technical mastery, to the final very personal result—this entire process must be grasped by the individual. Thus, any such creative activity should be an honest representation of its creator and of the material and be designed for its true purpose or function. Art education is ideally suited to maintain this self-identification with the whole span of production, usually unattainable to any one person in our modern, technically oriented age.

RELATED ACTIVITIES

1. Survey the art classes in a local high school to determine who actually takes elective art courses. What major sequence of courses are these students following? How do their academic abilities relate to the total high school population? What are the vocational interests of these youngsters?

2. List the materials presently being used by students in a senior high school. What type of use is made of these? Which of these art materials are used by adults who enjoy and actively engage in art, other than professional artists? On what basis can the use of the rest of the art materials be justified?

3. Observe an adolescent group outside school. Record the way in which these youngsters express themselves, both verbally and socially. Pay close attention to dress, hair styles, cars, verbal expressions. How much of this expression is controlled through pressure to conform to group standards? How do you see this expression relating to the high school art program?

4. List a range of three-dimensional materials suitable for sculpturing. Which of these materials need to be chipped or filed away to make a sculpture? Which need to be built up to make a form? Which materials can be used in both ways?

5. Compile a list of occupations that could be considered as those of practicing artists. What are the specific differences between these occupations? What are some of the skills or training necessary for each of these occupations? What are some of the common backgrounds needed for all fields?

6. Interview several people who are recognized artists in business, in industry, or free-lance. What influenced their choice of career? At what age did they decide to enter the art field? To what extent was the public school art program helpful or influential in their vocational choice?

7. Examine several state syllabuses for art in the high school. To what extent are these programs designed as preparation for an art career? What activities are included that would be valuable for the usual high school student who does not intend to follow an art career?

The Development of   11
Aesthetic Awareness

AESTHETIC DEVELOPMENT cannot be separated from creative development. Both are bound up with the whole process of growing, and are influenced by all of the variables from our environment that make us different personalities. In a broad sense aesthetic education deals with a whole range of experiences in art, including the production of art forms. Some definitions include the observation and understanding not only of art but also of nature, or at least those parts of nature that can be called beautiful. However, in a narrower sense, aesthetics refers only to the perception and appreciation of art. The development of aesthetic awareness is usually seen in a harmonious organization of parts, and this organization changes with age in the same way that other changes can be seen in growth. Aesthetics has little to do with sentimentality on the one hand or the accumulation of factual knowledge on the other. The gushy comment of the overstuffed matron—"I just love modern art, don't you?"—probably shows as little aesthetic awareness as does the art appraiser who may look at the same work of art from the point of view of its value on the market today. Aesthetics is an active perceptual process, it is the interaction between an individual and an object in which the organization of that object provides a stimulating harmonious experience.

In creating a work of art the basis for the form, whatever it might be, comes from the self. Any creative activity originates in a person, and it is through the person that the multitude of cognitive and sensory perceptions take on form. In the process of creating a picture, for example, an artist paints from his conscious awareness and his unconscious or preconscious motivations; he selects the forms and colors which will make up his final painting. In the process, however, the artist may pause and say to himself, "That is not right." Here the interaction between the painting and the artist takes on new meaning, for he has made a judgment about the organization and found it not to his liking. Therefore, it is easy to see that creative expression and aesthetic awareness are closely entwined.

The development of aesthetic awareness is a basic part of art education. Growth is on an ever-changing continuum, and this is very true in the area of aesthetics. The organization of our thinking abilities, the development of our perceptual abilities, and the close relationship to our emotional capabilities can be considered aesthetic growth. There are no rules to aesthetic growth. Aesthetic education does not take place simply by a teacher's criticism or guidance when an individual makes his art product. It is a much larger task and may bear little relationship to making a student aware of the principles or rules for organizing a work of art. Such matters as proportion, balance, and rhythm are often regarded as part of the understanding that a student should develop in relationship to his own work of art and to the art work of others. However, there is no set of rules that can be readily applied to individuals, and aesthetic growth does not happen merely by applying rules that are external to an individual. Developing aesthetic awareness means educating a person's sensitivity toward perceptual, intellectual, and emotional experiences so that these are deepened and integrated into a harmoniously organized whole.

It is possible to get overzealous about the importance of developing aesthetic awareness. We must remember that this is something that cannot be imposed from without. The need for developing an understanding and an appreciation of those things around us must come from the person himself. There is no evidence that aesthetics can be easily measured, or that absorbing the vocabulary of aesthetics will refine one's tastes, make one a better person, or help in the selection of a necktie.

Art Appreciation

Closely related to our discussion is the role that art appreciation plays in the development of aesthetic awareness. Somehow the question of taste enters into the picture, and it may be that taste is something that can be learned. At least the development of the ability to make selections, based upon some criteria that have been established by art authorities, might be looked upon as good taste, and high school students are able with enough encouragement to be selective if they are properly rewarded. This may have very little to do with aesthetic awareness. This does not mean that one's likes and dislikes are purely an individual affair, because obviously we all have different tastes, but that there would be no justification for arranging these on a scale from good to bad. Good taste would probably be defined as what the art critic would select, and the uneducated individual would undoubtedly be thought to have little or no taste. But, of course, this is also tied up with culture, and it is quite obvious that we are not treasuring the same qualities in objects that our grandparents did. Each age has its own peculiarities, and these cultural differences play havoc with establishing rules for good taste. That a thing of beauty is a joy forever is a saying rarely heard today in our rapidly changing culture.

More important than these considerations is the fact that youngsters do not react to the environment in the way that adults do. We have already seen how children's drawings differ considerably from one age to the next, and there is good reason to believe that the objects they appreciate also vary. A ten year old boy will have developed a natural appreciation for stones, frogs, rusty bolts, and other strange assortments of objects that probably mean a lot more to him than the painting that hangs in a museum.

Discussions of art appreciation are often concerned with the principles of design. These are not always given the same names, but are essentially concerned with the surface pattern of a picture; such words as harmony, balance, rhythm, unity, center of interest, and so forth are often mentioned. There is often the notion that learning these particular words bears some relationship to developing an awareness of the good and

Figure 151. *This candelabrum was admired a century ago. "The flesh of the Indians, their costumes, the bark of the canoe are all truthfully rendered. One is also impressed by the classic character of this decoration."* (Nichols, 1877, p. 160)

CREATIVE AND MENTAL
GROWTH

bad qualities to look for in paintings, and that therefore an appreciation of art will result.

Sometimes the history of art is considered an avenue to developing the aesthetic tastes. But there is no genuine history of art; rather, there are historians who have selected art objects from those that have remained within a society, and collected these together in such a way that others look upon these examples as typical of a period in history. Which of these examples are shown depends to a great extent upon the art historian.

Figure 152. *This detail from a Byzantine fresco has a strong linear quality. This was a typical method of representing religious topics in the ninth and tenth centuries.*

For example, the history of the American Revolution can be seen quite differently by an historian who is writing a textbook for the American public schools than by an historian whose purpose is to show the influence of British naval power upon the development of Europe. Hieronymus Bosch is much more popular today than he was fifty years ago. And it is certainly the art historian who has rescued Van Gogh from obscurity. To some extent, then, a study of the history of art can provide the opportunity to follow the development of art styles as seen by an authority, but it does not necessarily provide us with an appreciation of these styles, nor does it automatically develop an aesthetic awareness of objects outside the realm of art history.

Figure 153. "*Madonna, Infant Savior, and St. John,*" *by Bouguereau. This painting, done in the latter part of the nineteenth century, shows great concern for detail and sentimentality. (Collection, Andrew Dickson White Museum of Art, Cornell University)*

Some art educators would no doubt argue that the art appreciation of individuals needs to be cultivated and taught by those who are somehow wise and educated. This goes against the basic assumption of democracy, in which every person, unless previously intimidated, is usually a strong defender of his own views and tastes.

Figure 154. *In this painting by Rouault, there is a marked change in style from nineteenth century painting, and this resembles more closely the Byzantine fresco in the earlier illustration. (Collection, The Museum of Modern Art, New York)*

Culture and Aesthetic Awareness

It might be interesting to contemplate what a future archaeologist would think about our society if he uncovered it a thousand years from now. Art has been thought a good indicator of the values and attitudes

THE DEVELOPMENT OF
AESTHETIC AWARENESS

of the society in which it was made. Today we cherish the remnants of past societies' art forms, and from these we draw conclusions about the particular society in which these forms were found. The Greek temple is very different from the Gothic cathedral, yet each of these forms was expressive of its own culture.

Certainly the Gothic cathedral style would be uncovered a thousand years hence, housing our churches and some of our institutions of higher learning. These Gothic structures would, of course, be false façades, made of steel and covered over to look like Gothic cathedrals. There would be Greek temples too, though somewhat altered, housing what might be government operations. Once again, however, these buildings would not be honest representations but rather duplicates from a past culture that considered these buildings an important part of their society. It may be somewhat symbolic to see governmental functions housed in buildings that are more representative of a bygone age.

The archaeologist a thousand years from now would certainly be confused. He would find homes which were also false façades. Many of them would be built in a style which was popular in the eighteenth century, but for some reason were duplicated like stereotyped patterns for twentieth-century people, complete with big chimneys and small panes of glass. No, not big chimneys, but plywood cubes stuck on these houses to simulate chimneys, and not small panes, but plastic inserts that could be removed easily when the windows were to be washed. Inside, the homes would be even more confusing. The dining room might look surprisingly like a seventeenth century French room, with a chandelier and a table with built-in worm holes. But the chandelier would really be made for electricity and the furniture would have been mass produced. The living room and the bedroom, too, would be from an earlier era, but the kitchen and bathroom would have the most modern of appliances.

Undoubtedly our archaeologist would think that there was something wrong with a society where an individual could walk from one century to another by merely going from one room to the next. Apparently, the occupants of these homes had an unaware acceptance of these stereotyped patterns as symbols of a security that was not present in the culture itself. However, science was evidently an important element, since the range, refrigerator, and dishwasher were of the latest design. The occupants of these homes would seem to have been schizophrenic, escaping into a world of meaningless stereotyped patterns.

There would be some contemporary buildings in existence, and the most forward-thinking architects would have been utilized for building airports, banks, and factories. These, the archaeologist would undoubtedly feel were representative of the civilization. Apparently, he would conclude, this strange culture that he had unearthed had no confidence in their institutions, but a stronger belief in industrial power, transportation, and finance. Evidently, the individual was inclined to hide from the society and felt more comfortable in taking refuge in past periods. Even in the smaller examples of the art forms, the vase and

Figure 155. *"Migration," by Rauschenberg. The artist in today's society has turned away from tradition. Although the artist is making a serious statement, most members of our society look upon such paintings as worthless. (Collection, Andrew Dickson White Museum of Art, Cornell University)*

bottle, the same discrepancy was seen. The most attractive plastic bottles were produced by industry and used for dispensing soap, shampoos, and lotions; whereas the vase selected by the homemaker was a piece of glass pseudo-styled as a sixteenth century hobnailed goblet in which apparently flowers were displayed. Floor coverings, scientifically durable and easy to clean, simulated stone or wood and the "solid" brick wall was made of plastic.

The archaeologist would probably be right in his opinion of our society. This is not just a question of aesthetics, because his uncovering of our art in museums would only make him sure that the artists of our time had turned their backs on the society in which they lived, and were either poking fun at the society from which they had removed themselves, or had become so self-centered and individualistic that they too had lost contact with their own society. The prospect of teaching what is "good taste," in a society which is as confused as ours, seems a little ridiculous.

Aesthetics and Middle Class Values

Not too long ago the prospect of gracious living was an objective to strive for. Just what gracious living meant was apparently a stereotype in itself. Expensive accessories and pseudo-styled furniture were part of the scene; undoubtedly, shutters at the window and an antique knocker at the door were there too. Dinner would be by candlelight with soft music, with modern art looking down from the wall.

Young people today are certainly questioning this as an ideal, but many educators still look upon the gracious-living model as the one they want to impose upon all children as a goal in life. This becomes particularly ridiculous when we realize that many parts of our society may have goals of their own, especially those parts of our society that still retain some of their customs and traditions from Asia, Europe, Africa, or South America. Many children within our society come from environments that are both dirty and depressing, and the image of gracious living is unattainable and bears no relationship to their own existence.

Aesthetics must be removed from the good, the true, and the beautiful. The development of aesthetic awareness must be much more concerned with the individual and not with the imposition of ideas, terms, or certain learnings, regardless of how well intentioned these learnings might be. It becomes very apparent that we cannot teach aesthetic values unless we are aware of the individual and his environment, since this plays an important part in his attitudes toward himself and toward art. Developmental differences will be evident; the five year old will have perceptual experiences and levels of understanding different from those of a ten year old. These facts are basic to any program that attempts to provide growth in aesthetic awareness.

The Development of Aesthetic Awareness

A fifth grade teacher was standing in the front of her room looking through a large stack of paintings, which had just been picked up off the floor where they had been drying. She was saying how much her children enjoyed their art experiences, that is, all but one child, "The one in the back row that needs the haircut," she said, nodding toward one boy who looked as if he could stand a bath. She began thumbing through the paintings. "Aren't some of these lovely?" Most of them looked tightly drawn and carefully colored. Suddenly she came upon one that was full of color, painted very directly, and apparently with a lot of feeling. It was a large head outlined in strong purple with a red background, looking somewhat like one of Rouault's paintings. She looked up and, shrugging her shoulders, said, "See, always this crude scribbling, no talent at all."

It was fairly obvious that this teacher had certain likes and dislikes in art, which she was using to evaluate the children's work. The fact that the boy needed a haircut and a bath may also have influenced her judgment. However, she was imposing her own tastes and aesthetic values upon these youngsters, and in so doing was undoubtedly having an impact upon their own values. Another teacher might not have been as outspoken, or might have selected another picture to decry. There is no doubt that the aesthetic values of our society are transposed to youngsters either directly or indirectly.

Probably our teacher would have been just as much at fault if she had selected the boldly painted head as an outstanding example of art and displayed this for the class to see. Our society has changing values in art; standards of goodness or badness may not be important, but what may be vital is the development of an aesthetic awareness on the part of children, based upon themselves as individuals rather than upon some changing aesthetic standard which may not be appropriate twenty years from now. We should be much more concerned with the fifth grader himself, for he may be the one to direct our society to a new and different form of beauty that may break away from our own narrow definitions.

THE PRESCHOOL CHILD

During the first couple of years of life a child discovers a great deal about his environment. He does this by examining everything that he can touch; he explores it not only by sight, but also handles and tastes everything that he can. He enjoys the opportunity to rattle, move, or put together any object that he can manipulate. He often shows preferences even at this early age for certain toys or dolls. Language is used primarily to communicate his basic needs for food or for attention.

At about the age of three the child can select an object from a series. It is possible for him to select a square from a series of geometric forms although he cannot draw or copy a square until a year later (Brittain, 1969). Apparently there is no evidence to indicate that practice in perceiving shapes is of any value to the preschool child, for he does not improve particularly in ability to select objects or shapes even after being given practice in this task. Even extensive help in showing youngsters how to draw a square does not improve their square-drawing ability.

When the preschool youngster looks at pictures, he is eager to point out those objects that he recognizes, but this may be quite different from getting an understanding of the picture itself. Vernon (1965) states that up to the age of four or five years children can identify familiar objects in pictures but they enumerate them one after another and do not relate them to one another in any way.

The preschool child learns in an active way rather than in a passive way. That is, his actual interaction with his environment, his touching, seeing, manipulating, are all part of his total development, and his cognitive and perceptual growth are closely entwined. The preschool child has little concept of time; to a great extent, the world has little past or future; rather, it is. Often the child will express strong preferences, but these preferences change rapidly and the nursery school teacher will sometimes find that she is hated one moment and loved the next. Pictures on the wall are not art in the usual sense to the preschool youngster. Art is what he himself makes. However, the nursery school child does not remember his own drawings or paintings after a few hours, and it could not be expected that he can develop any learning abilities in terms of aesthetic awareness as adults understand it. It may well be that sensitivity toward living is based on the continual interaction that a child has with his environment. The degree to which this interaction is encouraged and stimulated can be an element in developing the urge and attitude

Figure 156. *The preschool child is at a crucial age in developing aesthetic awareness, for he develops attitudes towards his environment and a sensitivity toward living that will remain with him as he starts his formal schooling. It is important to encourage the youngster's participation and involvement in learning experiences.*

toward exploring and investigating other forms and in voicing preferences or being able to discriminate differences more easily at a later age. The preschool child is probably at the most crucial age for the development of a sensitivity toward living.

THE ELEMENTARY SCHOOL CHILD

There are great changes in physical and mental development from the time the youngster is in kindergarten until he arrives at the sixth grade. We have seen how he changes in his creative art; these changes are also evident in his aesthetic development. Most first grade youngsters can give simple descriptions of pictures, naming the objects that are pointed out to them, if these are recognizable as objects, and can identify colors if they are not too subtle. However, the description is limited to the objects in a painting and does not extend to any interaction between objects. That is, the first grader is able to identify things he recognizes but not the mood or atmosphere, nor is he able to discuss the message that a particular painting might have. It is not until later that a picture can be seen to have a story or interaction within the frame itself. Vernon (1965) indicates from her research that it is not until ten or eleven years of age that children can interpret what is happening in a picture, what the people are doing, and so forth. This inability to see relationships roughly parallels the ability in drawing, for the first grader will draw objects, but these objects are related in his pictures only by being placed one beside the other, and it is not until about ten or eleven that overlapping begins to appear.

There is a difference between aesthetic preference and aesthetic judgment. Most youngsters can tell which picture they like best if given a choice, but the ability to judge one picture as better than another is a different problem. Some youngsters are able to predict quite well what the teacher wants, but this may be quite different from their own likes and dislikes. Child (1964) asked elementary school pupils from grades one through six to choose which of a matched set of pictures they liked and which they thought experts would consider best. Youngsters up through the fourth grade disagreed with the expert choice, and had a strong preference for the "poorer" of the pair of pictures. After fourth grade, the disagreement was not as great. It is rather interesting to note that these youngsters not only picked the poorer picture but thought that the experts would pick the poorer picture too. Child followed this experiment by a training session with fifth and sixth grade youngsters. He found that it was possible to improve their guesses as to what the expert judges would select as the better pictures, but found that the youngsters' own preferences remained unchanged. Although these children had many weekly sessions of seeing slides, including a wide range of landscapes, portraits, still-lifes, sculpture, abstract art, and so forth, the study indicated that this exposure had no effect on children's preferences. In fact, the results were completely negative.

Evidently, it is a lot easier to change what children say than what they think. This might be expected, since children in school are marked on how closely they agree with the textbook or with the teacher, and not on their thinking abilities. An interesting study was done in England by Rump and Southgate (1966) with three groups of children aged seven, aged eleven, and aged fifteen. They found that 77 per cent of the children agreed with their teacher's stated preference for pictures, if the teacher was present. However, 71 per cent disagreed with their teacher's preference when the teacher was not there! Rump and Southgate also found that the children preferred representational pictures, and the younger children preferred simple items or pictures with few elements. The older high school age children had a definite preference for the more complex pictures.

It may be that children evaluate paintings on the same basis that they

Figure 157. *Students can develop a sensitivity to the beauty that occurs in their own surroundings. Commonplace things such as this fishnet may be aesthetically satisfying.*

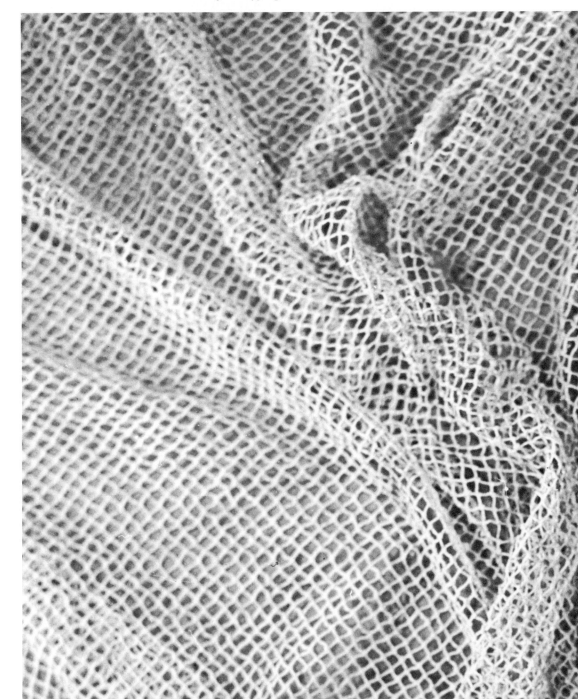

use to determine their behavior in other areas. That is, there is no reason to believe that the development of discrimination in paintings should be different from the discrimination of objects or thoughts in other areas of cognitive processes. We have found that the youngster is striving for what we called realism in his drawings, and that the concern for naturalism does not come until about the age of twelve. That is, the child is satisfied with making representations that are symbolic and definite about his environment, and he does not show concern in his drawings for light and shade, differing atmospheric effects, or variations in color relationships until about the age of twelve. Machotka (1966) did a study analyzing the basis on which children evaluated paintings. This study indicated that children like pictures of increasingly clear and realistic representation until about age eleven. Although younger children would establish an emotional relationship to a painting, it was usually in terms of a personal relationship, such as liking a picture of a person because it reminds him of his father; it was not until the age of twelve that an emotional relationship was established with a picture that was outside the youngster himself, that is, with the atmosphere or character of the picture as a whole. Machotka related this change to a decrease in egocentrism which occurs at about the age of eleven when thought loses its dependence on concrete data.

Many factors within his environment probably will influence the elementary school child in his likes and dislikes, his ability to discriminate, and his development of aesthetic awareness. Schools undoubtedly play an important part in this developing aesthetic awareness, but it may not be as important to guide this development as it is to encourage it.

THE SECONDARY SCHOOL STUDENT

This is a period of developing critical awareness, and although no sudden changes have occurred, the young adolescent has increased in his awareness of himself as a member of society and has left the egocentric stage behind. One would therefore expect that there would be some changes in the ways in which youngsters perceive their environment and possibly an increase in aesthetic growth. However, this does not seem to be the case. Rather, the young adolescent seems to be on a plateau and does not seem particularly committed to art in any form. This does not imply that the young adolescent is not interested in art, but rather that development cannot be easily measured and there seems to be no observable growth or change in art products during these years from twelve to fourteen. In a study of eighth grade students, Frankston (1963) concluded that whether or not the students took an art course had no

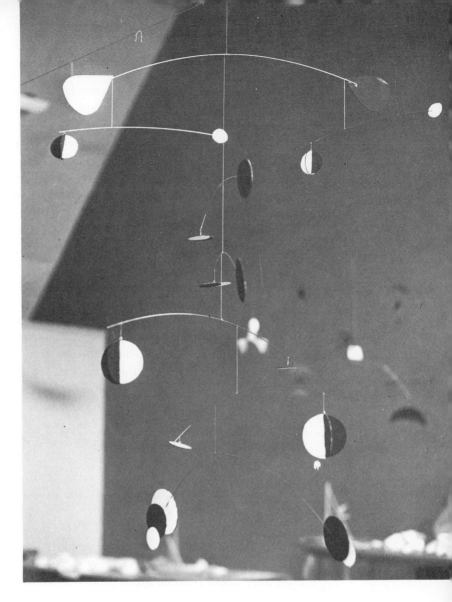

Figure 158. *Often the enjoyment of art can grow from related interests. Obviously a mobile is closely tied to problems of physics, with concern for balance, wind currents, and free movement all playing a part.*

effect on the quality of their art performances. He found no differences from one semester to the next in the quality of the work the students produced, whether they took an art course or not. And he also found the same lack of change in quality in their poetry writing. In a later study, Frankston (1966) tried different methods of teaching with this age and found great inconsistencies in the performances of the youngsters, but again no changes in performance level.

In another study of the same age group, Brittain (1968,a) found that there was general agreement between the adolescents and their teachers as to which drawings were of high quality. Unlike the teachers, these youngsters showed a strong preference for complexity and technical proficiency in drawings. It may be that children at this age are becoming much more aware of their environment generally, though not to the point of being able to sort the variety of experiences into what might be termed acceptable and unacceptable. It is clear that eighth grade youngsters enjoy seeing art that they themselves would like to be able to do. It may be that this is a key to a good deal of aesthetic preference, and that growth in aesthetic preferences is achieved as a youngster grows in his own abilities to portray his environment. Day (1969) found in attempting to teach some art history to eighth graders that those students who had concurrent studio experiences performed better and gained more knowledge of the subject matter in art history than those students who did not have a studio art class. Possibly the introduction of some discussions applicable to the production of art might begin to make sense to this age.

The high school student who takes an art course is in the minority. Although there are occasional classes that are required of all high school students in the humanities, these too are rare. Schools turn their backs upon the importance of aesthetic growth at the time when its development can best be promoted. The high school student enjoys the opportunity to engage in abstract thinking and he is no longer tied to concrete operations. His coordination and drive is such that great gains can be seen in his art products but sometimes these skills are misguided and the student may mimic or duplicate works of art that he considers great. His ability to discriminate is probably at its peak, and although individuals differ considerably, this is probably the best age at which to deal with problems of aesthetics.

Aesthetic awareness is not an isolated variable in human behavior, because it relates to one's total personality. It may be possible to have high school students select the pictures that are judged "better," and even have them become quite proficient at selecting the ones that the teacher himself likes, but changing the patterns of likes and dislikes within the individual student is quite another matter. In a study of male graduate students, Barron (1963) found that there was a definite relationship between the paintings that these students preferred and their acceptance or rejection of tradition, religion, and authority. In general he found that those students who preferred portraits, landscapes, and traditional themes in paintings also preferred simple and predictable sketches; this was closely related to their personality which tended to be conservative, serious, deliberate, responsible, and so forth. Those students who preferred the experimental, sensual, and primitive paintings also preferred sketches that were complex and irregular; the personality of this group of students tended to be more pessimistic, emotional, temperamental, and so forth.

Possibly real changes in aesthetic preference cannot be made unless there is also a change in one's personality. Burgart (1964) found that there was what he termed a creative personality syndrome that was positively related to art experience, and Burkhart (1964) and Hoffa (1964) have also found indications that the creative personality is positively related to art experiences. Attempting to teach taste or standards in art to a senior high school art class may well not produce a sensitive, alert, aware, and discriminating student, unless changes in personality happen at the same time. Obviously this is a difficult task to accomplish, but the objective of providing a more sensitive population—a population that is also willing to make changes—is certainly a goal worth striving for.

Changes in Aesthetic Taste

It is fairly obvious that standards of beauty are constantly changing. A car that is ten years old has no particular value, either for its aesthetic appeal or for its functional use. However, a fifty year old car takes on quite a different appeal and can suddenly be cherished. In the same way, the severity of architectural design that was popular a few years ago is becoming softened, and an interest in patterns and textural qualities is beginning to reappear. The taste and aesthetic standards of our time are undoubtedly influenced by many variables, and trying to put these into a context that can be explained to students in school presents a difficult problem.

It is revealing to look at the textbooks on art education that were published fifty years or more ago. Some of the problems seen at that time are still with us, but the examples of good art and the type of pictures that were supposed to interest children in grade school seem a little ridiculous to us today. However, art education was thought to be a means of elevating the thinking of every person, with the assumption that somehow an understanding of art would make people happier and better. As Nichols (1877, p. 153) put it, "Men are usually selfish because they see so little. Teach them to observe, to compare, and they will discover the good and the beautiful rather than the bad and ugly; for there is nothing evil in itself, but only that which the mind conceives in its ignorance." In a *Manual of Drawing*, Thompson (1895) was quite certain how to produce the good, the true, and the beautiful. Beauty was considered as perfect form, with the principal sensuous elements being regularity, variety, and harmony. Thompson's examples of beauty seem a little

Figure 159. *Educators seem to change in what they feel are appropriate pictures for young children to appreciate. "The Goose Girl," shown here, was typical of the pictures selected for study by children at the turn of the century. (Collection, Andrew Dickson White Museum of Art, Cornell University)*

strange in today's world. Wilson (1899) published a picture series for the elementary schools that attempted to aid teachers in imparting to children a true appreciation of and love for paintings by the world's great masters. In the preface to this series, James Hopkins, who was then director of drawing in the Boston Public Schools, said that picture study should be taken seriously: "The effort is not for amusement, entertainment, or decoration alone; it has an aim and a purpose larger, broader, and more dignified than any of these." The pictures Wilson selected for

CREATIVE AND MENTAL
GROWTH

the children to admire, however, are rarely seen any more, and in some cases even the artist himself has passed into oblivion.

We can be amused at earlier attempts at developing aesthetic awareness in children by trying to establish methods for teaching the good, the true, and the beautiful; however, the uncomfortable thought creeps in that, maybe fifty or sixty years from now, our attempts to impress upon

Figure 160. *In this painting by Picasso we see an example of the type of art to which youngsters are increasingly becoming exposed. (Collection, The Museum of Modern Art, New York. Gift of Simon Guggenheim)*

Figure 161. *"Oeuficiency," painted by Matta, has largely lost contact with a visual representation. It may be more important to include contemporary examples in the scope of art for children than to censor or dilute the art world so as to simplify teaching for the teacher. (Collection, Andrew Dickson White Museum of Art, Cornell University)*

children the beauty of a Picasso, Chagall, or a Klee will also be viewed as mildly amusing.

Changes constantly occur in the art field, and a sudden interest in assemblages gives way to an art that capitalizes on optical illusions. This may be followed by the enlarging or endless duplication of everyday items from the grocery store, which in turn is supplanted by other, newer interests, such as earth sculpture or a self-destroying art form. This is not to say that these art forms are merely styles that change like the seasons, but rather that the teacher of art may be viewing art from the narrow perspective of his own background and training. The excitement he feels about a new art form may not be shared by his students, particularly when yet another direction in art is promoted by the popular magazines and he becomes suddenly old-hat in his ideas.

A development of self-awareness on the part of students, in fact, may be more important in the long run than the appreciation of any particular style of art. Honesty in design and excitement in art are important qualities which can be felt only through the self. Art is a reflection of today's world that can provide a direction for the future; students need to be able to evaluate change and be curious about the new.

A Program for Aesthetic Development

Children have a joy in exploring, investigating, and expressing their feelings about their environment. Possibly the best means of developing aesthetic awareness is through sharpening youngsters' sensibilities and strengthening their power of self-expression. Culture can have a negative influence on this kind of education, even in the form of art. Realizing this, along with the facts that the art of the past is a tradition invariably

Figure 162. *Students should be aware of contemporary developments in art, such as this example of housing and home furnishings. (Furniture and fabric from Herman Miller, Inc.)*

337

Figure 163. *The common recurrence of such surroundings as these reflects our society's lack of concern with aesthetic sensitivity.*

broken whenever new directions in art are taken, and that accepted words chanted over accepted works of art will have little real meaning to children, should make teachers working with elementary children much more aware that aesthetics comes from within a person and is not the sprinkling of culture from the outside.

To a great extent, then, the understanding of art and aesthetic awareness should be combined in a program specifically aimed at the developing child, which becomes part of his natural interaction with the environment. Experiences in buildings, the opportunity to comment on changing colors in foliage, pointing out and enjoying the variety of textures in clothing, the feeling of expansiveness in open areas, all have the primary purpose of expanding the youngster's awareness of himself and those things around him, giving him the chance to develop his ideas and examine them, and to realize that his own opinions about his environment are important.

Every child, as we have noted, treasures certain collections of objects that he or she considers beautiful. These may include pebbles, little toy dogs, broken pieces of hardware, in fact almost anything. The age of the child will to some extent determine his interest in saving and preserving parts of his environment. These collections should be treated in the same way as art forms are treated at the adult level. There is no reason to believe that we should change the child's relationship to things that are important to him; in fact, the opposite may be true. Rejecting these collections as being unrelated to adults, or being disgusting, may turn the child away from his own sensory experiences, rather than making them an essential part of his relationship to his environment. Small children can often bring to school some of the objects that they themselves feel have beauty, or objects with which they have established some relationship. It matters little what these are or whether they are shared by others; the opportunity for a small child to look upon part of his environment as worth saving and examining is more important than the sharing of this experience. A sensitive teacher will provide a place for the child to put his own collection, for it becomes important for the child that this be honored. Sometimes group experiences can be meaningful, such as looking at unusual fossils, branches with interesting bark or leaf development, or pictures and reproductions that some youngsters have found appealing and worthwhile.

Any picture is the result of an expression of an individual. Art expresses the relationship of the artist to himself and to his environment. A painting of a bottle is not the bottle itself, but the expression of the relationship between the artist and the bottle. This is true at all levels of development. The elementary school child, as we have seen, has a relationship to his environment quite different from that of a professional artist, yet both may be painting the same object. The same thing is true for paintings that are nonobjective. It is the artist and his intent that we identify with, not the picture itself; the picture is merely a conglomeration of lines and forms and colors that have little meaning unless we can identify with the artist's purpose. In some modern art expression, the product itself becomes destroyed, or is practically nonexistent, thus placing the focus entirely upon the experience itself.

An art product is meaningless unless the viewer can relate himself to it. Certain pictures selected for youngsters to see and discuss may be unrelated to these youngsters' own interests, and they will probably be unable to identify with the artist who made them. We have discussed the fact that children react differently toward pictures at different developmental levels. The object in showing works of art to children is not to teach them to analyze pictures or to learn to recognize a work of art. There is no reason why students should echo the words of the teacher nor conform to his likes and dislikes.

Simple questions such as "How do you feel about this picture?" or "What part do you like best?" may be enough to get students involved. This comprehension is geared to the individual, and not to an evaluation of a painting itself. Even more important than an understanding of a work of art is the understanding of the artist's drives and motives. "Why do you suppose the artist painted this? Suppose you had painted this picture, what would have been your purpose?" would be one method of focusing upon the process rather than on the product.

The young adolescent finds a vicarious expression in popular music. Possibly there should be popular art for these youngsters too. However, most art teachers are much more concerned about bringing the quality of art up to their own standards, and the likes and dislikes of the youngsters tend to be ignored. It is children of this age who begin to spend money on jewelry, art objects, and interesting trinkets. They need support in their ability to make choices. Exposure to and awareness of some of the variety of forms available and the suggestion of alternate outlets for this interest in collecting artifacts, could well be a starting point in making aesthetics meaningful.

The developing interest in art which can be seen in the junior high school should be encouraged, but not necessarily in the direction of the usual chronological approach to the evolution of modern art. There are many cultures that have expressed themselves in ways which may be closer to the young adolescent than is the sophisticated art of nineteenth and twentieth century Europe and America. Some of the art forms from Africa, early American folk art, and Eskimo sculpture can create great interest, because they express some of the feelings and emotions of these youngsters in a direct naïve manner. Since this age is much more verbal, discussions and examples of a variety of art products can be stimulating, particularly if this is a part of a creative art activity. Care should be taken that these examples are seen as a means of stimulating discussion and a broadening of possible avenues for action rather than as examples to be emulated.

The senior high school student is in an advantageous position for understanding some of the problems facing our society in its ignorance of aesthetic values. However, the temptation should be resisted to cram aesthetics down the throats of the unsuspecting students. Their own knowledge and interests should be the starting point. As much can be learned about aesthetics from seeing alternate methods of organizing pieces of scrap metal into a sculpture or from cropping photographs for enlargement as can be learned from armchair lectures about balance and repetition in a slide of a Mondrian painting.

The senior high school student should feel free to reject or accept the values of the teacher and to develop standards for his own performance and his own discrimination. It is more important to feel that art is relevant than to either ignore it or accept art passively.

Summary of the Development of Aesthetic Awareness

Aesthetic awareness is part of the total growth pattern of children. It is not the imposition of standards or rules from outside the child, but rather the development of his ability to discriminate and make choices. Beauty is something that changes with each culture, and the opportunity for youngsters to express their own feelings and emotions about things around them is more important than the development of taste according to today's standards.

Clive Bell (1914, p. 249) had some rather amusing advice to give about art and children that makes sense even today. "Do not tamper with that direct emotional reaction to things which is the genius of children. Do not destroy their sense of reality by teaching them to manipulate labels. Do not imagine that adults must be the best judges of what is good and what matters. Don't be such an ass as to suppose that what excites uncle is more exciting than what excites Tommy."

Possibly what is necessary in the development of aesthetic awareness is not an appreciation of a particular picture or object nor is it necessarily the teaching of particular adult values or a vocabulary to describe works of art. Aesthetic awareness may be best taught through an increase in a child's awareness of himself and a greater sensitivity to his own environment. There are numerous factors involved in aesthetics, and it is not a simple problem to deal with. Certainly the cognitive behavior of individuals, their affective behavior, and their interaction with themselves and their environment all play a part in the development of personality. The background of a student, his socioeconomic level, the cultural factors of the time, his exposure to mass media, his ability to be flexible in his thinking, and his standing in the classroom all influence the development of aesthetic awareness. It should be understood that aesthetic growth does not necessarily refer only to art; it also refers to a more intense and greater integration of thinking, feeling, and perceiving. It thus may bring about a greater sensitivity toward living, and therefore it becomes a major goal in education.

RELATED ACTIVITIES

1. Ask a seventh grade class which of a series of quite dissimilar pictures they would like to hang on the wall of their houses. Ask them which one their parents would like. Then ask which one their art teacher would like best. Does this give any indication of how they see the adults' taste as different from their own?

2. In a drug or variety store, select a few inexpensive containers that are well designed. Select several poorly designed items. On what basis did you select these?

3. Collect examples of texture and pattern as seen in nature. Design a display of such natural patterns, capturing some of the feeling for pattern in the display itself.

4. Look around your own community and make a note of those buildings that are of the most modern design. Who owns these buildings or what function goes on inside them? Locate some new buildings that are more traditional in design. What are these buildings used for? Can you draw any inferences?

5. Select examples of paintings that are related to a particular period of art. Explain why these are representative of their time, referring to subject matter, technique, and mode of representation.

6. Select one large reproduction that shows some distortion of everyday objects, such as a painting by Modigliani or Chagall. Ask some first, third, and sixth graders to tell you what they think about the picture. Keep track of their comments and their acceptance or rejection of the distortion.

Summary

12

A<small>LMOST</small> <small>EVERY</small> <small>CHILD</small> enjoys the opportunity for creative activity. The preschool youngster, the sixth grader, and the young adult in high school all look upon art as something which is enjoyable. It is rather sad that our educational system is organized in such a way that most students are gradually deprived of the opportunity to paint, draw, or construct the farther they progress in the school system. The need for art is not outgrown.

Children's drawings are always a pleasure to observe. They contain a freshness of outlook that is the essence of childhood. Particularly young children express their ideas, thoughts, and emotions with an honesty that can almost be upsetting to adults. Sometimes professional artists are envious of the youngsters' spontaneous approach to painting; for their

343

directness, frankness, and intuitive feeling for design may be what the artist himself is striving for.

Within itself, the act of drawing or painting is a learning experience. The problem of what to paint, how to paint it, the relationships of form and color, the use of heavy or fine line, the problems of light and dark are all part of the art experience. However, the organization of the elements in the picture or in the construction is only one segment of the experience, because the expression is a concrete configuration of the emotion and perceptual experiences that an individual has had in his interaction with the environment. This is true at all levels of art. It is the expression of the self, the subjective reactions to the environment that make art expressive, not only to the producer but also to the viewer.

Within each work of art a youngster portrays his feelings, his intellectual abilities, his physical development, his perceptual sensitivities, his creative involvement, his social development, and his aesthetic awareness. Although individual children vary considerably, there are general growth characteristics that are typical of any age, and the art products of these youngsters also change in predictable ways.

The very young child enjoys scribbling, but by the time he is four, he is usually making scribbles that begin to look like the typical head-feet representation of a man. Most children when they reach kindergarten can draw a great number of objects, although these are only vaguely naturalistic. Soon a base line appears, and children place the objects they are drawing on this line across the bottom of the page. These early stages of children's development are marked by the direct and bold use of color, and it is at this age that children show a great deal of confidence in their own means of expression.

At about nine years of age or so, overlapping appears in drawings and the youngster draws in much more detail and becomes more critical of his own products. Usually by the age of twelve, youngsters are quite reluctant to show their drawings. For most children the changes in artistic development have come to a halt. Some youngsters may show an interest in portraying the environment naturalistically, and be concerned with the problems of perspective and atmospheric effects; for others, these naturalistic changes are difficult to understand, and they may get more enjoyment from painting nonobjectively.

The changes that take place in the art product are a direct reflection of the changing child; all of the variables that go about making up different individuals with different personalities and different interests are also influencing their art products. It should be obvious that we cannot understand a work of art unless we understand the culture in which it was made, the artist's intentions, and the society and environmental conditions that surrounded its making. The same holds true for children's drawings. The school environment, the intent of the child, the intellectual and emotional factors involved, all must be understood if we are to appreciate the importance of art for children.

Throughout this book we have tried to emphasize the fact that teachers play an extremely important role in the development, not only of art, but of children themselves. Because art is essentially an expression of the self, because there are no answers in the teacher's stack of books, because art cannot be produced by the usual threat of failure or rewards, the teacher of art becomes a crucial person in art production. It is only through a strongly supportive teacher who encourages and interacts with youngsters that an increased sensitivity to the environment can grow. The development of positive attitudes toward the self and toward art is something that does not happen automatically. The creative spirit needs reinforcement, and the teacher is one who can provide the environmental conditions that will make the art experience an exciting and rewarding one. It is through identifying with the child, with his needs and interests, that the teacher can best understand the needs and desires of each child. This is particularly true for the child who may not turn naturally to art as a form of expression, for this may be the child who most needs the art experience.

Too often art programs are planned around materials, with emphasis being placed upon learning how to use each material, in the hope that a breadth of experience will somehow be valuable. It is not unusual to see an elementary classroom using crayons one week, finger paints the next, clay the following, and so forth. This constant changing of materials can be frustrating to a child, who is more interested in expressing his thinking, feeling, and perceiving in a meaningful way than he is in doodling in different materials. Often it may be the teacher himself who thinks that it is important to vary the activities for the mere sake of change. In doing so, he forgets that the opportunity to become thoroughly familiar with a material so that it becomes a natural mode of expression is an essential part of developing competence and confidence in one's own art.

Within the framework of the usual school system, little opportunity is given for youngsters to express feelings and emotions that are anti-school. By the time youngsters are in the junior high school, many have succeeded in developing methods of coping with this system, so that it is not unusual for youngsters to be more concerned with what will appear on a test than with the material to be learned. Art should not fall into the trap of competing with academic subjects, but should have the integrity to remain basically human. It should be the one area in the secondary school that youngsters can turn to without the concern for being evaluated or without the feeling that they must perform according to someone else's standards. Art can be a vital force in the lives of students if it is relevant to their thinking, and becomes the avenue by which they can express the feelings about their society that they are not encouraged to express either in or outside school. For the secondary school student, the potential of art is tremendous, and the energies and enthusiasm of older children can make learning and art exciting and rewarding.

A major emphasis in this book has been that art is entwined with a child's creative and mental growth. There is no pretext that the function of art in the school is to make artists out of children. Rather, the emphasis has been that art can provide the opportunity for growth in ways that other subject matter areas cannot. Growth is not achieved by the development of intellectual capacities alone. The confident, creative child who is eager to express his thoughts, who is sensitive to people and things around him, who is a responsive, productive individual, is much more the concern of an art program. We cannot do this developing for him. Every individual has a potential that is greater than what is realized. Art should provide the impetus for constructive action and the opportunity for each individual to see himself as an acceptable being, searching for new and more harmonious organizations, developing confidence in his own means of expression. The most essential ingredient in an art program is the child, and art education has a vital role to play in his growth.

Bibliography

ALSCHULER, R. H., and HATTWICK, L. W., *Painting and Personality*. Chicago: University of Chicago Press, 1947.

ANASTASIOW, NICHOLAS J., "Success in School and Boys' Sex-Role Patterns." *Child Development*, Vol. 36, No. 4: 1965, p. 1053.

APPLEGATE, MEIDEL, "Relationships of Characteristics of Children's Drawings to Chronological and Mental Age." Unpublished doctoral dissertation, University of California at Berkeley, 1967.

ARNHEIM, RUDOLF, *Art and Visual Perception*. Berkeley, Calif.: University of California Press, 1954.

ASCH, S. E., *Social Psychology*. Englewood Cliffs, N.J.: Prentice-Hall, Inc., 1952.

347

ASCHNER, MARY JANE, and BISH, CHARLES E., eds., *Productive Thinking in Education*. Washington, D.C.: The National Education Asociation, 1965.

BARBE, WALTER B., ed., *Psychology and Education of the Gifted*. New York: Appleton-Century-Crofts, Inc., 1965.

BARKAN, M., *A Foundation for Art Education*. New York: The Ronald Press Company, 1955.

BARRON, FRANK, *Creativity and Psychological Health*. Princeton, N.J.: D. Van Nostrand Company, Inc., 1963.

BEE, HELEN, "The Relationship Between Parent-Child Interaction and Distractibility in Fourth Grade Children." Unpublished doctoral dissertation, Stanford University, 1964.

BEITTEL, KENNETH R., "Selected Psychological Concepts as Applied to the Teaching of Drawing." Unpublished report, Cooperative Research Project No. 3149, Office of Education, U.S. Department of Health, Education, and Welfare, December 1966, 187 pp.

BEITTEL, KENNETH R., "In Reply to Laura Chapman's Critique." *Studies in Art Education*, Vol. 6, No. 1: 1964, p. 30.

BEITTEL, KENNETH R., and BURKHART, ROBERT C., "Strategies of Spontaneous, Divergent, and Academic Art Students." *Studies in Art Education*, Vol. 5, No. 1: 1963, pp. 20–41.

BELL, CLIVE, *Art*. London: Chatto & Windus, 1914 (Republished, London: Arrow Books Ltd., 1961).

BEREITER, C., and ENGLEMANN, S., *Teaching Disadvantaged Children in the Preschool*. Englewood Cliffs, N.J.: Prentice-Hall, Inc., 1966.

BETTELHEIM, BRUNO, *Love Is Not Enough*. New York: The Free Press, 1950.

BIEHLER, R. F., "An Analysis of Free Painting Procedures as Used with Preschool Children." Unpublished doctoral dissertation, University of Minnesota, 1953.

BRADLEY, WILLIAM R., "A Preliminary Study of the Effect of Verbalization and Personality Orientation on Art Quality." *Studies in Art Education*, Vol. 9, No. 2: 1968, p. 31.

BRITTAIN, W. LAMBERT, "Some Exploratory Studies of the Art of Preschool Children." *Studies in Art Education*, Vol. 10, No. 3: Spring, 1969, pp. 14–24.

BRITTAIN, W. LAMBERT, "An Investigation into the Character and Expressive Qualities of Early Adolescent Art." Unpublished report, Cooperative Research Project No. 6-8416, Office of Education, U.S. Department of Health, Education, and Welfare, October, 1968, 55 pp. (a)

BRITTAIN, W. LAMBERT, "An Exploratory Investigation of Early Adolescent Expression in Art." *Studies in Art Education*, Vol. 9, No. 2: 1968, pp. 5–12. (b)

BRITTAIN, W. LAMBERT, ed., *Creativity and Art Education*. Washington, D.C.: The National Art Education Association, 1964.

BRITTAIN, W. LAMBERT, "Creative Art." In L. Fliegler, ed., *Curriculum Planning for the Gifted* (Englewood Cliffs, N.J.: Prentice-Hall, Inc., 1961), Chap. X.

BRONFENBRENNER, U., "Early Deprivation in Mammals and Man." In G. Newton, ed., *Early Experience and Behavior* (Springfield, Ill.: Charles C Thomas, 1968).

BROOKOVER, WILBUR, B., *et al.*, "Self Concept of Ability and School Achievement." In Harry L. Miller, ed., *Education for the Disadvantaged* (New York: The Free Press, 1967) pp. 64–68.

BRUNER, JEROME S., GREENFIELD, PATRICIA M., and OLIVER, ROSE R. *Studies in Cognitive Growth*. New York: John Wiley & Sons, Inc., 1966.

BRUNER, JEROME S., GOODNOW, JACQUELINE J., and AUSTIN, GEORGE A., *A Study of Thinking*. New York: John Wiley & Sons, Inc., 1956.

BURGART, HERBERT J., "The Development of a Visual-Verbal Measure of General Creativity: The Symbol Test of Originality." Unpublished report, Cooperative Research Project No. 7-8168, Office of Education, U.S. Department of Health, Education and Welfare, February, 1968, 71 pp.

BURGART, HERBERT J., "Art in Higher Education: The Relationship of Art Experience to Personality, General Creativity, and Aesthetic Performance." In W. L. Brittain, ed., *Creativity and Art Education* (Washington, D.C.: The National Art Education Association, 1964).

BURKHART, ROBERT C., "The Interrelationship of Separate Criteria for Creativity in Art and Student Teaching to Four Personality Factors." in W. L. Brittain, ed., *Creativity and Art Education* (Washington, D.C.: The National Art Education Association, 1964).

BURKHART, ROBERT C., *Spontaneous and Deliberate Ways of Learning*. Scranton, Pa.: International Textbook Co., 1962.

BURKHART, ROBERT C., "The Relation of Intelligence to Art Ability." In Ross Mooney and Taher Razik, eds., *Explorations in Creativity* (New York: Harper and Row, Publishers, Inc., 1967), pp. 246–258.

CASSIDY, HAROLD GOMES, *The Sciences and the Arts*. New York: Harper and Row, Publishers, Inc., 1962.

CECERE, JAMES GABRIEL, "The Effect of Verbal Stimuli and Artistic Self-Expression on Children's Motivation for Writing." Unpublished doctoral dissertation, The Pennsylvania State University, 1966.

CHAPMAN, LAURA H., "Some Comments on 'Spontaneous, Divergent, and Academic Art Students.'" *Studies in Art Education*, Vol. 6, No. 1: 1964, p. 25.

CHILD, IRVIN L., *Development of Sensitivity to Esthetic Values*. Unpublished report, Cooperative Research Project No. 1748, Office of Education, U.S. Department of Health, Education, and Welfare, 1964.

CHUNG-YUAN, CHANG, *Creativity and Taoism*. New York: The Julian Press, Inc., 1963.

CHURCH, JOSEPH, *Language and the Discovery of Reality*. New York: Vintage Books, 1961.

CHURCH, JOSEPH, ed., *Three Babies: Biographies of Cognitive Development*. New York: Random House, Inc., 1966.

CLEMENTS, ROBERT D., "Art Student-Teacher Questioning." *Studies in Art Education*, Vol. 6, No. 1: 1964, p. 14.

COLE, NATALIE ROBINSON, *Children's Art from Deep Down Inside*. New York: The John Day Company, Inc., 1966.

COLEMAN, JAMES S., *The Adolescent Society*. New York: The Free Press, 1961.

CONRAD, GEORGE, *The Process of Art Education in the Elementary School*. Englewood Cliffs, N.J.: Prentice-Hall, Inc., 1964.

CORAH, NORMAN L., "The Effect of Instruction and Performance Set on Color-Form Perception in Young Children." *The Journal of Genetic Psychology*, No. 108: 1966, pp. 351–356.

CORAH, NORMAN L., and GOSPODINOFF, EVA J., "Color-Form and Whole-Part Perception in Children." *Child Development*, Vol. 37, No. 4: 1966, p. 837.

CORCORAN, A. L., "Color Usage in Nursery School Painting." *Child Development*, Vol. 25, No. 2: 1954, pp. 107 ff.

CORCORAN, A. L., "The Variability of Children's Responses to Color Stimuli." Unpublished doctoral dissertation, The Pennsylvania State University, 1953.

COSTANZO, PHILIP R., and SHAW, MARVIN E., "Conformity as a Function of Age Level." *Child Development*, Vol. 37, No. 4: 1966, p. 967.

COVINGTON, MARTIN V., "Teaching for Creativity: Some Implications for Art Education." *Studies in Art Education*, Vol. 9, No. 1: 1967, p. 18.

CRUTCHFIELD, RICHARD S., "Independent Thought in a Conformist World." In Seymour M. Farber and Roger H. L. Wilson, eds. (*Conflict and Creativity: Part Two of Control of the Mind*, New York: McGraw-Hill, Inc., 1963), pp. 208–228.

CUNNINGHAM, RUTH, et al., *Understanding Group Behavior of Boys and Girls*. New York: Teachers College, Columbia University, 1951.

D'AMICO, V., *Creative Teaching in Art* (rev. ed.). Scranton, Pa.: International Textbook Co., 1953.

DATTA, LOIS-ELLEN, "Draw-A-Person Test as a Measure of Intelligence in Preschool Children from Very Low Income Families." *Journal of Consulting Psychology*, Vol. 31, No. 6: 1967, p. 626.

DAVIS, DONALD JACK, and TORRANCE, E. PAUL, "How Favorable are the Values of Art Educators to the Creative Person?" *Studies in Art Education*, Vol. 6, No. 2: 1965, p. 42.

DAVIS, HAZEL, *Music and Art in the Public School*. Washington, D.C.: National Education Association, 1963.

DAY, MICHAEL D., "The Compatibility of Art History and Studio Art Activity in the Junior High School Art Program." *Studies in Art Education*, Vol. 10, No. 2: Winter, 1969, pp. 57–65.

DENNIS, WAYNE, *Group Values Through Children's Drawings*. New York: John Wiley & Sons, Inc., 1966.

DEWEY, JOHN, *Art as Experience*. New York: Capricorn Books, 1958.

DREWES, HENRY, "An Experimental Study of the Relationship Between Electro-encephalographic Imagery Variables and Perceptual-Cognitive Processes." Unpublished doctoral dissertation, Cornell University, 1958.

DREYER, ALBERT S., and WELLS, MARY BETH, "Parental Values, Parental Control, and Creativity in Young Children." *Journal of Marriage and the Family*, Vol. 28, No. 1: 1966, p. 83.

EFLAND, ARTHUR D., "An Examination of Perception Delineation Theory: Some Proposed Modifications." *Studies in Art Education*, Vol. 8, No. 2: 1967, p. 66.

EISNER, ELLIOT W., *Think with Me About Creativity*. Dansville, N.Y.: F. A. Owen Publishing Company, 1964.

EISNER, ELLIOT W., "The Development of Information and Attitude Toward Art at the Secondary and College Levels." *Studies in Art Education*, Vol. 8, No. 1: 1966, p. 43.

EISNER, ELLIOT W., and ECKER, DAVID W., eds., *Readings in Art Education*. Waltham, Mass.: Blaisdell Publishing Co., 1966.

EL-BASSIOUNY, MAHMOUD Y., ed., *Experiments in Art Education*. Cairo: Dar Al-Ma'aref, 1964.

ENG, HELGA, *The Psychology of Children's Drawings*. London: Routledge and Kegan Paul, 1931.

FLICK, PAUL, "An Intercorrelative Study of Two Creative Types: The Visual Type and the Haptic Type." Unpublished doctoral dissertation, The Pennsylvania State University, 1960.

FOWLER, HARRY, *Curiosity and Exploratory Behavior*. New York: The Macmillan Company, 1965.

FRANK, LAWRENCE K., *On the Importance of Infancy*. New York: Random House, Inc., 1966.

FRANKSTON, LEON, "Effects of Two Programs and Two Methods of Teaching upon the Quality of Art Products of Adolescents." *Studies in Art Education*, Vol. 7, No. 2: 1966, p. 23.

FRANKSTON, LEON, "Some Explorations of the Effect of Creative Visual Art Experiences upon the Poetry Writing Quality of Eighth Grade Students." *Studies in Art Education*, Vol. 5, No. 1: Fall, 1963, pp. 42–59.

FRIEDENBERG, EDGAR Z., *The Vanishing Adolescent*. New York: Dell Publishing Co., Inc., 1962.

GETZELS, JACOB W., and JACKSON, PHILIP W., *Creativity and Intelligence.* New York: John Wiley & Sons, Inc., 1962.

GIBBENS, T. C. N., "Drugs and the Young Law Breaker." *Mental Health,* Vol. 25, No. 3: 1966, pp. 36–37.

GIBSON, JAMES J., *The Senses Considered as Perceptual Systems.* Boston: Houghton Mifflin Company, 1966.

GOERTZ, E. C., "Graphomotor Development in Preschool Children." Unpublished master's thesis, Cornell University, 1966.

GORDON, IRA J., ed., *Human Development, Readings in Research.* Chicago: Scott, Foresman and Company, 1965.

GORDON, WILLIAM J. J., *Synectics: The Development of Creative Capacity.* New York: Harper and Row, Publishers, Inc., 1961.

GRAY, SUSAN W., and KLAUS, RUPERT A., "An Experimental Preschool Program for Culturally Deprived Children." *Child Development,* Vol. 36, No. 4: 1965, p. 887.

GUILFORD, J. P., "Progress in the Discovery of Intellectual Factors." In Calvin W. Taylor, ed., *Widening Horizons in Creativity* (New York: John Wiley & Sons, Inc., 1964).

GUTTON, PH., *Le Rôle du Dessin dans l'Appréciation Clinique du Développement Psychomoteur de l'Enfant.* Laboratoire de Psychologie Clinique de la Faculté des Lettres et Sciences Humaines de l'Université de Paris, 1965.

HAYEK, FRIEDRICH A., *The Sensory Order.* Chicago: University of Chicago Press, 1963.

HARRIS, D. B., *Children's Drawings as Measures of Intellectual Maturity.* New York: Harcourt, Brace & World, Inc., 1963.

HEILMAN, HORACE, "An Experimental Study of the Effects of Workbooks on the Creative Drawing of Second Grade Childen." Unpublished doctoral dissertation, The Pennsylvania State University, 1954.

HESS, ROBERT D., and SHIPMAN, VIRGINIA C., "Early Experience and the Socialization of Cognitive Modes in Children." *Child Development,* Vol. 36, No. 4: 1965, p. 869.

HILDRETH, GERTRUDE, *The Child Mind in Evolution.* New York: King's Crown Press, 1941.

HOFFA, HARLAN E., "The Relationship of Art Experience to Conformity." In W. L. Brittain, ed., *Creativity and Art Education* (Washington, D.C.: The National Art Education Association, 1964).

HOGG, JAMES C., and McWHINNIE, HAROLD J., "A Pilot Research in Aesthetic Education." *Studies in Art Education,* Vol. 9, No. 2: 1968, p. 52.

HOLBROOK, STEWART H., "The Log Cabin Myth." *The American Mercury,* Vol. 61, No. 263: 1945, pp. 614–619.

HOLLADAY, HARLAN H, "An Experimental and Descriptive Study of Children's Pre-representational Drawings." Unpublished doctoral dissertation, Cornell University, 1966.

HUBBARD, GUY, *Art in the High School.* Belmont, Calif.: Wadsworth Publishing Company, Inc., 1967.

HYMAN, RAY, "Creativity and the Prepared Mind: The Role of Information and Induced Attitudes." In Calvin Taylor, ed., *Widening Horizons in Creativity* (New York: John Wiley & Sons, Inc., 1964).

JACKSON, PHILIP W., *Life in Classrooms.* New York: Holt, Rinehart & Winston, Inc., 1968.

JEFFERSON, BLANCHE, *Teaching Art to Children.* Boston: Allyn and Bacon, Inc., 1959.

JOHNSON, LINDA JARSCHAUER, "The Effect of Interpolated Writing on Paired-Associate Learning." Unpublished master's thesis, Cornell University, June, 1963.

JONES, L. H., *Student and Teacher Interaction During Evaluative Dialogues in Art.* Cooperative Research Project No. S-050, Office of Education, U.S. Department of Health, Education, and Welfare, 1964.

KAGAN, JEROME, MOSS, HOWARD A., and SIGEL, IRVING E., "Psychological Significance of Styles of Conceptualization." In John Wright and Jerome Kagan, eds., "Basic Cognitive Processes in Children." *Child Development Monographs*, Vol. 28, No. 2: 1963.

KAUFMAN, BEL, *Up the Down Staircase.* New York: Avon Books, 1964.

KAUFMAN, IRVING, *Art and Education in Contemporary Culture.* New York: The Macmillan Company, 1966.

KELLOGG, RHODA, *The Psychology of Children's Art.* New York: CRM, Inc., 1967.

KENDRICK, DALE, "A Dilemma Concerning the Compatibility Between Creative and Arithmetical Measurements." *Studies in Art Education*, Vol. 8, No. 2: 1967, p. 37.

KENSLER, GORDON L., "Three Responses and Extensions of Efland's P-D Critique: A Critique of Efland's Analysis of Field-Dependence." *Studies in Art Education*, Vol. 9, No. 1: 1967, p. 50.

KINCAID, CLARENCE, "The Determination and Description of Various Creative Attributes of Children." In W. L. Brittain, ed., *Creativity and Art Education* (Washington, D.C.: National Art Education Association, 1964), pp. 108–115.

KOZOL, JONATHAN, *Death at an Early Age.* Boston: Houghton Mifflin Company, 1967.

KUHLEN, RAYMOND G., and HOULIHAN, NANCY BRYANT, "Adolescent Heterosexual Interest in 1942 and 1963." *Child Development*, Vol. 36, No. 4: 1965, p. 1049.

Kuo, You Yuh, "A Comparative Study of Creative Thinking Between Delinquent Boys and Non-Delinquent Boys." Unpublished doctoral dissertation, University of Maryland, 1967.

Lanier, Vincent, *Teaching Secondary Art*. Scranton, Pa.: International Textbook Co., 1964.

Lansing, Kenneth M., *Art, Artists, and Art Education*. New York: McGraw-Hill, Inc., 1969.

Lansing, Kenneth M., "The Research of Jean Piaget and Its Implications for Art Education in the Elementary School." *Studies in Art Education*, Vol. 7, No. 2: 1966, p. 33.

Lansing, Kenneth M., "The Effect of Class Size and Room Size upon the Creative Drawings of Fifth Grade Children." Unpublished doctoral dissertation, The Pennsylvania State University, 1956.

Lark-Horovitz, Betty, Lewis, Hilda Present, and Luca, Mark, *Understanding Children's Art for Better Teaching*. Columbus, Ohio: Charles E. Merrill Books, Inc., 1967.

Lark-Horovitz, Betty, and Norton, James, "Children's Art Abilities: The Interrelations and Factorial Structure of Ten Characteristics." *Child Development*, Vol. 31, No. 3: 1960, pp. 453–462.

Lark-Horovitz, Betty, and Norton, James, "Children's Art Abilities: Developmental Trends of Art Characteristics." *Child Development*, Vol. 30, No. 4: 1959, pp. 433–450.

Lawler, Carol O., and Lawler, Edward E., III, "Color-Mood Associations in Young Children." *The Journal of Genetic Psychology*, No. 107: 1965, p. 29.

Lee, Lee C., "The Concomitant Development of Cognitive and Moral Modes of Thought: A Test of Selected Deductions from Piaget's Theory." Unpublished doctoral dissertation, The Ohio State University, 1968.

Leibowitz, Herschel W., *Visual Perception*. New York: The Macmillan Company, 1965.

Levin, Harry, Hilton, Thomas, and Leiderman, Gloria, "Studies of Teacher Behavior." *Journal of Experimental Education*, Vol. 26: September, 1957, pp. 81–91.

Lewis, Hilda Present, ed., *Child Art, The Beginnings of Self-Affirmation*. Berkeley, Calif.: Diablo Press, 1966.

Lewis, Hilda Present, "Spatial Representation in Drawing as a Correlate of Development and a Basis for Picture Preference." *The Journal of Genetic Psychology*, No. 102: 1963, pp. 95–107.

Lewis, Hilda Present, and Livson, Norman, "Correlates of Developmental Level of Spatial Representation in Children's Drawings." *Studies in Art Education*, Vol. 8, No. 2: 1967, p. 46.

LINDERMAN, EARL W., *Invitation to Vision, Ideas and Imaginations for Art*. Dubuque, Iowa: William C. Brown Company, Publishers, 1967.

LIPPITT, RONALD, and WHITE, RALPH K., "An Experimental Study of Leadership and Group Life." In Haimowitz and Haimowitz, eds., *Human Development* (New York: Thomas Y. Crowell Company, 1960), pp. 312–326.

LOWENFELD, VIKTOR, "Tests for Visual and Haptical Aptitudes." *American Journal of Psychology*, Vol. 58, No. 1: 1945, pp. 100–111 (Reprinted in Eliot Eisner and David Ecker, eds. *Readings in Art Education*. Waltham, Mass.: Blaisdell Publishing Co., 1966, pp. 97–104).

LOWENFELD, VIKTOR, *The Nature of Creative Activity* (rev. ed.). New York: Harcourt, Brace & World, Inc., 1952.

LOWENFELD, VIKTOR, *The Nature of Creative Activity*. London: Kegan Paul, Trench, Trubner & Co. 1939.

McFEE, JUNE KING, *Preparation for Art*. San Francisco: Wadsworth Publishing Company, Inc., 1961.

MacGREGOR, RONALD N., "Imposed Controls in Subject Matter and Art Media Choice." *Alberta Journal of Educational Research*, Vol. 13, No. 2: 1967, p. 103.

MACHOTKA, PAVEL, "Aesthetic Criteria in Childhood: Justifications of Preference." *Child Development*, Vol. 37, No. 4: 1966, p. 877.

MACHOVER, KAREN, *Personality Projection in the Drawing of the Human Figure*. Springfield, Ill.: Charles C Thomas, 1949.

McPHERSON, M. W., POPPLESTONE, J. A., and EVANS, K. A., "Perceptual Carelessness, Drawing Precision, and Oral Activity Among Normal Six Year Olds." *Perceptual and Motor Skills*, No. 22: 1966, pp. 327–330.

McVITTY, LAWRENCE F., "An Experimental Study on Various Methods in Art Motivations at the Fifth Grade Level." Unpublished doctoral dissertation, The Pennsylvania State University, 1954.

MADEJA, STANLEY S., "The Effects of Divergent and Convergent Emphasis in Art Instruction on Students of High and Low Ability." *Studies in Art Education*, Vol. 8, No. 2: 1967, p. 10.

MALONE, CHARLES, "Safety First: Comments on the Influence of External Danger in the Lives of Children of Disorganized Families." In Harry L. Miller, ed., *Education for the Disadvantaged* (New York: The Free Press, 1967), pp. 53–64.

MANZELLA, DAVID, *Educationists and the Evisceration of the Visual Arts*. Scranton, Pa.: International Textbook Co., 1963.

MARGOLIS, JOSEPH, ed., *Philosophy Looks at the Arts*. New York: Charles Scribner's Sons, 1962.

MARSHALL, M. L., "A Comparison of Schizophrenics, Children, and Normal Adults on Their Use of Color." Unpublished doctoral dissertation, Vanderbilt University, 1954.

MATTIL, EDWARD L., *Meaning in Crafts* (2nd ed.). Englewood Cliffs, N.J.: Prentice-Hall, Inc., 1965.

MATTIL, EDWARD L., *et al.*, "The Effect of a 'Depth' vs. a 'Breadth' Method of Art Instruction at the Ninth Grade Level." *Studies in Art Education*, Vol. 3, No. 1: 1961, p. 75.

MENDELOWITZ, DANIEL M., *Children Are Artists* (2nd ed.). Stanford, Calif.: Stanford University Press, 1963.

MERRITT, HELEN, *Guiding Free Expression in Children's Art*. New York: Holt, Rinehart & Winston, Inc., 1964.

MICHAEL, JOHN A., "The Effect of Award, Adult Standard, and Peer Standard upon Creativeness in Art of High School Pupils." *Research in Art Education*, Ninth Yearbook, National Art Education Association, 1959, pp. 98–104.

MICHAEL, JOHN A., "College and University Acceptance of High School Art Credits for Admission." *Art Education*, Vol. 21, No. 7: October, 1968, pp. 30–37.

MICHAEL, JOHN A., ed., *Art Education in the Junior High School*. Washington, D.C.: The National Art Education Association, undated.

MIEL, ALICE, ed., *Creativity in Teaching*. Belmont, Calif.: Wadsworth Publishing Company, Inc., 1961.

MONTGOMERY, CHANDLER, *Art for Teachers of Children*. Columbus, Ohio: Charles E. Merrill Books, Inc., 1968.

MOUSTAKAS, CLARK, *Creativity and Conformity*. Princeton, N.J.: D. Van Nostrand Company, Inc., 1967.

MUNRO, THOMAS, *Art Education*. New York: The Liberal Arts Press, 1956.

NELSON, THOMAS M., and FLANNERY, MERLE E., "Instructions in Drawing Techniques as a Means of Utilizing Drawing Potential of Six and Seven Year Olds." *Studies in Art Education*, Vol. 8, No. 2: 1967, p. 58.

NEPERUD, RONALD W., "An Experimental Study of Visual Elements, Selected Art Instruction Methods, and Drawing Development at the Fifth Grade Level." *Studies in Art Education*, Vol. 7, No. 2: 1966, p. 3.

NICHOLS, GEORGE WARD, *Art Education Applied to Industry*. New York: Harper and Row, Publishers, Inc., 1877.

NORDSTROM, CARL, FRIEDENBERG, EDGAR Z., and GOLD, HILARY, *Society's Children: A Study of Ressentiment in the Secondary School*. New York: Random House, Inc., 1967.

OLDHAM, HILDA WALLEY, *Child Expression in Colour and Form*. London: John Lane, The Bodley Head, Ltd., 1940.

PACKWOOD, MARY M., ed., *Art Education in the Elementary School.* Washington, D.C.: The National Art Education Association, 1967.

PARNES, SIDNEY J., "Research on Developing Creative Behavior." In Calvin Taylor, ed., *Widening Horizons in Creativity* (New York: John Wiley & Sons, Inc., 1964).

PENTZ, MAJEL RICH, "A Study of Kindergarten Children's Concept of Five." Unpublished master's thesis, Cornell University, February, 1965.

PIAGET, J., *Judgment and Reasoning in the Child.* Paterson, N.J.: Littlefield, Adams and Co., 1959.

PIAGET, J., *The Child's Conception of the World.* Trans. by J. Tomlinson and A. Tomlinson. Paterson, N.J.: Littlefield, Adams and Co., 1960.

POMEROY, JANET, *Recreation for the Physically Handicapped.* New York: The Macmillan Company, 1964.

RAY, WILBERT S., *The Experimental Psychology of Original Thinking.* New York: The Macmillan Company, 1967.

READ, HERBERT, *Education Through Art.* New York: Pantheon Books, Inc., 1958.

REICHENBERG-HACKETT, W., "Influence of Nursery Group Experience on Children's Drawings." *Psychological Reports,* No. 14: 1964, pp. 433–434.

ROSENTHAL, ROBERT, and JACOBSON, LENORE, *Pygmalion in the Classroom.* New York: Holt, Rinehart & Winston, Inc., 1968.

ROSS, ALAN O., LACY, HARVEY M., and PARTON, DAVID A., "The Development of a Behavior Checklist for Boys." *Child Development,* Vol. 36, No. 4: 1965, p. 1013.

ROUSE, MARY J., "A New Look at an Old Theory: A Comparison of Lowenfeld's 'Haptic-Visual' Theory with Witkin's Perceptual Theory." *Studies in Art Education,* Vol. 7, No. 1: 1965, p. 42.

RUMP, E. E., and SOUTHGATE, VERA, "Variables Affecting Aesthetic Appreciation, in Relation to Age." *British Journal of Educational Psychology,* Vol. 36–37, 1966–1967, pp. 58–71.

RUSSELL, IRENE, and WAUGAMAN, BLANCHE, "A Study of the Effect of Workbook Copy Experiences on the Creative Concepts of Children." *Research Bulletin,* The Eastern Arts Association, Vol. 3, No. 1: 1952.

SALOME, R. A., "A Comparative Analysis of Kindergarten Children's Drawings in Crayon and Colored Pencil." *Studies in Art Education,* Vol. 8, No. 2: 1967, pp. 21–36.

SALOME, R. A., "The Effects of Perceptual Training upon the Two-Dimensional Drawings of Children." *Studies in Art Education,* Vol. 7, No. 1: 1965, p. 18.

SEGALL, MARSHALL H., CAMPBELL, DONALD T., HERSKOVITS, MELVILLE J., et al., *The Influence of Culture on Visual Perception.* Indianapolis: The Bobbs-Merrill Co., Inc., 1966.

SIBLEY, A. G., "Drawings of Kindergarten Children as a Measure of Reading Readiness." Unpublished master's thesis, Cornell University, 1957.

SIEDLECKI, JEROME T., "Potential Health Hazards of Materials Used by Artists and Sculptors." *Art Education*, Vol. 21, No. 9: December, 1968, pp. 3–6.

SMITH, RALPH A., ed., *Aesthetics and Criticism in Art Education*. Chicago: Rand McNally & Company, 1966.

SNOW, CHARLES PERCY, *The Two Cultures and the Scientific Revolution*. New York: Cambridge University Press, 1961.

STEWART, GEORGE R., *American Ways of Life*. Garden City, N.Y.: Doubleday & Co. Inc., 1964.

STILLER, ALFRED, SCHWARTZ, HAROLD A., and COWEN, EMORY L., "The Social Desirability of Trait-Descriptive Terms Among High School Students." *Child Development*, Vol. 36, No. 4: 1965, p. 981.

STONE, L. J., and CHURCH, J., *Childhood and Adolescence*. New York: Random House, Inc., 1968.

TAYLOR, CALVIN W., "Questioning and Creating: A Model for Curriculum Reform." *The Journal of Creative Behavior*, Vol. 1, No. 1: 1967, p. 22.

TEMPLEMAN, KATHERINE DUDLEY, "A Study of the Relationship Between the Haptic and Visual Creative Types and Reading Achievement in First and Sixth Grade Children." Unpublished master's thesis, Cornell University, 1962.

THOMPSON, COLIN, *Response to Colour*. Second Interim Report, Research Centre in Art Education, Bath Academy of Art, Corsham, England, 1965.

THOMPSON, LANGDON S., *Manual of Drawing for Regents' Schools*. Boston: D. C. Heath & Company, 1895.

TOMAS, VINCENT, ed., *Creativity in the Arts*. Englewood Cliffs, N.J.: Prentice-Hall, Inc., 1964.

TORRANCE, E. PAUL, *Guiding Creative Talent*. Englewood Cliffs, N.J.: Prentice-Hall, Inc., 1962.

TROWBRIDGE, NORMA, "Creativity in Children in the Field of Art: Criterion Development Study." *Studies in Art Education*, Vol. 9, No. 1: 1967, pp. 2–17.

TROWBRIDGE, NORMA, and CHARLES, DON C., "Creativity in Art Students." *The Journal of Genetic Psychology*, No. 109: 1966, p. 281.

VERNON, M. D., "The Development of Perception in Children." In Ira J. Gordon, ed., *Human Development* (Chicago: Scott, Foresman and Company, 1965), pp. 177–184.

WACHOWIAK, FRANK, and RAMSAY, THEODORE, *Emphasis: Art*. Scranton, Pa.: International Textbook Co., 1965.

WALL, JESSIE, "The Base Line in Children's Drawings of Self and Its Relationship to Aspects of Overt Behavior." Unpublished doctoral dissertation, The Florida State University, 1959.

WALLACH, MICHAEL A., and KOGAN, NATHAN, *Modes of Thinking in Young Children*. New York: Holt, Rinehart & Winston, Inc., 1965.

WALTER, W. GREY, *The Living Brain*. New York: W. W. Norton & Company, Inc., 1963.

WEISBERG, PAUL S., and SPRINGER, KAYLA, "Environmental Factors in Creative Function." In Ross Mooney and Taher Razik, eds., *Explorations in Creativity* (New York: Harper and Row, Publishers, Inc., 1967), pp. 120–134.

WHITE, BURTON L., "Informal Education During the First Months of Life." In R. D. Hess and R. M. Bear, eds., *Early Education* (Chicago: Aldine Publishing Company, 1968), pp. 143–169.

WHITE, BURTON L., and CASTLE, PETER W., "Visual Exploratory Behavior Following Postnatal Handling of Human Infants." *Perceptual and Motor Skills*, Vol. 18, 1964, p. 497.

WILSON, BRENT G., "An Experimental Study Designed to Alter Fifth and Sixth Grade Students' Perception of Paintings." *Studies in Art Education*, Vol. 8, No. 1: 1966, p. 33.

WILSON, L. L., *Picture Study in Elementary Schools*. New York: The Macmillan Company, 1899.

WITKIN, H. A., *et al.*, *Psychological Differentiation*. New York: John Wiley & Sons, Inc., 1962.

WODTKE, KENNETH H., and WALLEN, NORMAN E., "The Effects of Teacher Control in the Classroom on Pupils' Creativity-Test Gains." *American Educational Research Journal*, Vol. 2, No. 2: March, 1965, pp. 75–82.

ZAWACKI, ALEXANDER, "An Experimental Study of Analytic Versus Synthetic Modelings and Drawings of Children." Unpublished doctoral dissertation, The Pennsylvania State University, 1956.

Index